Process Management for the Extended Enterprise

Stefano Tonchia · Andrea Tramontano

Process Management for the Extended Enterprise

Organizational and ICT Networks

Foreword by Rosabeth M. Kanter

With 47 Figures and 26 Tables

 Springer

Professor Stefano Tonchia
University of Udine
Department DIEGM
Via delle Scienze no. 208
33100 Udine
Italy
tonchia@uniud.it

Andrea Tramontano
Snaidero R. S.p.A.
Viale Europa Unita no. 9
33030 Majano (Udine)
Italy
atramontano@snaidero.it

ISBN 3-540-21190-X Springer Berlin Heidelberg New York

Cataloging-in-Publication Data
Library of Congress Control Number: 2004107781

Springer is a part of Springer Science+Business Media

springeronline.com

© Springer-Verlag Berlin · Heidelberg 2004
Printed in Germany

Hardcover-Design: Erich Kirchner, Heidelberg

SPIN 10991985   42/3130-5 4 3 2 1 0 – Printed on acid-free paper

Foreword[1]

How to Evolve: Leading Change in the Digital Age

Now that the unrealistic hype about the Internet has died, the promise of the Internet can emerge. Now that the get-rich-quick schemes are gone, the technology can take its proper place as a tool to help enterprises – and people – be more productive, more networked, more connected. The Digital Age is in its infancy, and the Internet is only just becoming a powerful force for change.

As a Harvard Business School professor and expert on leadership and innovation, I know change is hard and can sometimes hurt, so it is all too tempting to avoid it. That would be a mistake. As I write this, the world faces numerous challenges, from economic downturns to terrorism threats; European businesses are conserving resources rather than investing in new opportunities. Uncertainty trumps optimism. But despite a temporary hold on enthusiasm and investment, significant, paradigm-shifting change still lies ahead in the still-unfolding possibilities offered by the Internet.

In today's economy, for example, all organizations need greater reach. They need to be in more places, to be more aware of regional and cultural differences, and to integrate into coherent strategies the work occurring in different markets and communities. The advent of the Internet and the World Wide Web over the past decade has provided the means to achieve greater reach at greater speed, and to work more closely with customers and suppliers in the process. This has created a new idea: that of the boundaryless organization that is known not by its structure of walls but by the processes that move knowledge and information, goods and services, seamlessly across permeable boundaries. The "extended enterprise" is like the extended family – a community of all those with ongoing relationships engaged in tasks toward common ends, regardless of where they live or what their ownership is.

In my recent book *Evolve!: Succeeding in the Digital Culture of Tomorrow (Boston: Harvard Business School Press)*, I noted that mastering this environment requires evolving to a new way of working, a new way of doing business, a new style of human relationships. "The Web rewards organizations that are nimble and innovative, with a freer spirit of creation,"

I observed, "ones that can move quickly because all the right connections are in place. That need for agility has been noted frequently. What has not been examined is the Web's hidden secret: that it provokes a shift toward more collaborative work relationships, ones that resemble open, inclusive communities more than they resemble secretive hierarchical administrative bureaucracies."

The Internet is finally at a point of technological and cultural acceptance that makes effective online collaborative work relationships a growing reality. By moving many tasks to the Web, companies can accrue numerous benefits: speed, influence, innovation, and considerable cost savings. What the authors call B2E, or business to *everything*, is at the core of a new organizational structure. B2E is not a cosmetic change or a program du jour; it represents a fundamental shift in the way organizations interact with employees, customers, suppliers and partners. Companies are moving in this direction because staying in place means falling behind.

But despite the remarkable power and capability of this technology, organizations need more than websites and faster servers to make it work. In a global, high-tech world, organizations need to be more fluid, inclusive, and responsive. They need to manage complex information flows, grasp new ideas quickly, and spread those ideas throughout the enterprise. What counts is not whether everybody uses e-mail but whether people quickly absorb the impact of information and respond to opportunity.

The technology is often the easy part. The harder part is the human side, the challenges of leading change. My years of study and experience show that while bold strokes – courageous decisions by leaders – can trigger change, it takes long marches – independent, discretionary, and ongoing efforts of people throughout the organization – to sustain change long enough to produce tangible results. No matter how the technology advances, these efforts remain at the heart of any organizational transformation. Organizations, after all, are collections of people. Company performance is built on how people interact, how they communicate a message to customers, how they carry forward a corporate agenda and make it profitable and sustainable.

I believe that we are now at the outset of a long march toward a new kind of workplace. In my work with companies struggling with change, I have documented the innovation-stifling, performance-reducing impact of groups defending their turf, clinging to territory, and protecting rather than sharing information. And I have seen the ways in which corporate leaders have addressed the often-daunting issue of bringing these groups together into an effective, cohesive organization.

To guide transformation and create "one enterprise" out of disparate, sometimes warring, tribes, a new kind of leader is required. Obsolete tenets of leadership, steeped in the traditions of hierarchical organizational structure are no longer valid or effective. Corporate chieftains must lead out in the open on an electronic stage that places them in a more visible role than ever before.

I have long argued that open, inclusive communities are a hallmark of corporate culture for high performance, high innovation companies. Creating such communities within large, traditional corporate entities is a scary proposition for many executives. Some leaders are happier as *cheer*leaders, touting the good news, diluting the bad news. Yet the fear factor is likely to be mitigated by the growing realization that the Enron model of closed cultures, communication roadblocks and secretive actions in the executive suite is simply unacceptable in the Digital Age.

If organizations of the twenty-first century are to become effective open communities, their leaders will need role models and lessons, new ways of organizing and managing. And they will need to invest in large-scale organizational change. To get big results, small piecemeal projects won't do the trick. It will take a coherent vision, the desire to innovate, and the courage to keep at it even when the challenges seem overwhelming.

Rosabeth Moss Kanter[2]

Harvard Business School, Boston, Massachusetts (USA)

---

[2] Rosabeth Moss Kanter is the Ernest L. Arbuckle Professor of Business Administration at Harvard Business School, specializing in strategy, and leadership for change. Past editor of *Harvard Business Review*, she advises major corporations and governments worldwide, and is the author or co-author of 15 books. In 2001 she received the Academy of Management's Distinguished Career Award, for her impact on management thought. She also received 21 honorary doctoral degrees from distinguished universities, and has been named to lists of the "most influential business thinkers in the world", the "business gurus to watch", and the "50 most powerful women in the world".

Table of Contents

Part Two: The BPR Project and the Processes

Part Three: From Processes to the Extended Enterprise

Introduction

Nowadays, competition between enterprises is, without doubt, based on value. The concept of value brings to mind a vast, integrated offer of products, services, images and reputation consolidated over time, whose quantitative level is decreed by the customer/consumer who discriminates between the different competitors.

Organisations, whether private or not, must be prepared to face this growing decisional shift towards the customer. This means that they must have a customer-oriented approach to planning and managing *all* business activities. In reality however the situation is quite different: organisations are established so as to be effective and efficient in dividing the work among the employees, creating aggregations of persons – the organisational units (functions, offices, departments, ministries, council offices, etc.) – that in time can lead to uncoordinated actions not in line with the business strategy. Typically, the achievement of certain "local" performances is to the detriment of other organisational units.

Process management, on the other hand, is directly inspired by the business strategy (the key objectives) and permits a natural coordination between the activities (carried out by staff belonging to different organisational units, but involved for reasons of pertinence and competence). The processes cut through the organisation: they preserve the functional organisation (and the efficiency characterising it) and superimpose orientation towards processes (aimed at achieving the target of customer satisfaction). The objectives are thus outside the organisation and embedded in the customers' demands and desires, whether tacit or expressed.

What we are witnessing is a sort of Copernican revolution in business organisation and management: although sometimes the company already implicitly works by processes (in this case they need only clearly express and reinforce them), in other cases a more radical revision is required (and process management is then preceded by a preparatory stage of Business Process Reengineering – BPR).

The remarkable change brought about by process management is due to its two key concepts. The first is that of *internal customer*. Without doubt it is crucially important to satisfy the demands of the external customer, it must be equally clear that this objective has to be shared by all the employees, including those who are not directly in contact with the external customer. This concept must also be translated into practice: everybody inside the company has customers, namely whoever benefits directly from the activities carried out by someone else. Supplier-customer links are thus generated, which must be harmonious and synergic inside the company in order to reach the external environment and the end customer ("value chain"). The other key concept in process management is *process ownership*: as inter-functional barriers crumble, it becomes increasingly important to work less by tasks and more for objectives, taking all the necessary steps to achieve them, regardless of rigid organisational structures and procedures. In other words, methodically and with the operative constraints clearly in mind, the various process owners (i.e. the persons in charge, who are not necessarily part of the top management) act as if they were entrepreneurs. They cultivate relationships, look after their team, plan new initiatives, preside over various activities.

Process management is therefore aimed at orienting the organisation towards objectives of (the external) customer satisfaction, while improving the satisfaction of the employees, who become conscious of their contribution to this aim: they are no longer only suppliers, but also customers, and their way of working improves dramatically. Furthermore, process management preserves the advantages of the more classic organisation in terms of costs and efficiency (indeed, delegation of powers is fully endorsed). A question however arises: with the fall of the barriers between the business units, what *boundaries* will the company have?

In the current world, a company must compete in more extensive arenas and establish numerous relationships: with the market in general, the customers, suppliers, particularly the privileged ones, manufacturing and trading partners, institutions and trade associations; the company may consist of a central office, factories and branches, as well as subsidiaries around the world. Greater interaction and integration is required, which must extend beyond the traditional (space) boundaries of the firm. Thus the concept of *extended enterprise*.

In the extended enterprise the relationships – both internal and external – play a pivotal role, and *networking* assumes vital strategic importance. Just as (intra)business processes are aimed at overcoming the barriers between the company's units, the creation and management of interorganisational processes positions the extended enterprise in more intense networks with other subjects. Many, diverse and complex though they are, the "right networks" are a critical factor for competitive success. Within these networks, partnerships, or relationships ensuring support and exchange of information at different levels can be established; even between similar subjects (co-producers or suppliers/customers) there will be that mix of cooperation/competition commonly known as "co-opetition".

But what is the distinguishing feature of internal and external business processes? Certainly at times the relationships can be translated into the physical exchange of goods, but more often it is information that is shared, i.e. *purposeful information* or *knowledge*.

Process management in an extended enterprise is therefore based on Knowledge Management. The latter is indispensable for creating value, value which – as mentioned previously – is produced through the processes. Knowledge resides in the individual and organisational *competencies* that distinguish a company, enabling it to excel as regards performances.

Competencies may be ascribed to the so-called intangible resources of a company, and can explain why businesses with similar tangible resources can often achieve remarkably different results. The company is, first of all, a reservoir of individual competencies or skills that – thanks to the differences between individuals – allows new knowledge to be absorbed, which is no longer the property of a single persons but is shared by the company, and is manifest in the harmonious and integrated execution of the activities forming the business processes (organisational competencies). Knowledge, unlike other goods, is not consumed but increases as its use intensifies ("learning-by-doing" + "learning-by-interacting").

The "process owners" must be able to create the most favourable environment for adding value to knowledge and govern "communities" of persons striving to meet the aims of the processes: in fact, as mentioned previously, knowledge consists of purposeful, applied information (according to the constructive view of knowledge, which in the enterprise sector prevails over the cognitive one, more typical of science). The customer-supplier links (both internal and external) mobilise and direct knowledge, creating networks. And in effect, in industrialised countries, workers will become "knowledge workers" whilst companies will tend to become extended enterprises where value is measured by the quantity and quality of their relationships.

These wide-ranging *organisational networks,* and the relative flows of information that contribute to the vitality and potential development of the company, even beyond its boundaries, exploit the new Web-based technologies ("Inter-net-working") to translate knowledge management into new or improved ways of doing business. These are *information networks* such as Intranet, Extranet and Internet (to connect to internal units, external business partners and the outside world, respectively). To these must be added knowledge repositories and Decision Supporting Systems (DSS) based on Business Intelligence technology, and the extended management systems (Extended Enterprise Resource Planning – EERP), which are also based on Web protocols. And this will be in the coming years the real, the strongest impact of e-Business: not so much the affirmation of dot.coms (companies quoted on the New Market) as the exploitation of these new technologies by traditional enterprises, with products or services already on the market.

Therefore process management in an extended enterprise finds in new technologies a powerful qualifying factor as well as a catalyst for change and innovation. An innovation that is not so much linked to products or manufacturing technologies, but primarily concerns the organisation and its relationships, that is a distributed, pervasive innovation, which is *based on human resources:* the governance of a professional community and its knowledge, capable of realising a concrete cultural change, at the core of any strategy. The new frontier of competition is *relational advantage* (Figure).

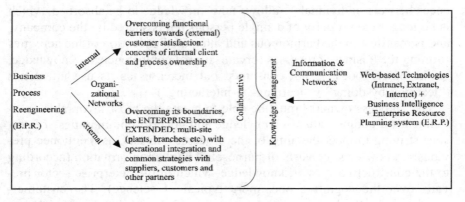

Synthesis of book's contents

This book describes innovative issues depicting the business pathways that will be followed by numerous firms in the near future. It is based on the research and experiments carried out by Prof. Stefano Tonchia in a number of major companies. These are all met with in the vocation for innovation and propensity for experimentation of the Snaidero Group management team. This company is the European leader in the kitchen furnishing sector, with 10 factories, 2000 employees and over 3000 retailers in more than 50 countries round the world. It is moreover at the forefront in the application of e-Business to traditional markets.

The book is aimed at researchers, professionals, managers and chief executives of public and private institutions, agencies and companies supplying products or services, operating in different sectors and firms of all sizes (including small-medium enterprises which often need to clarify and valorise their processes, rather that overcome the inter-functional barriers often present in the larger firms) and is in line with the new standards on quality (Vision 2000) that are focused on process management.

The book is divided into three parts. The first (Principles and Methods) is more general and theoretical-methodological. The second part presents the project of Business Process Reengineering, and outlines the main processes in a company (The BPR Project and the Processes). The third introduces the model of knowledge extended enterprise (From Processes to the Extended Enterprise), and describes a few case studies, assisted by contributions from leading companies in the field of Information & Communication Technologies – ICT, such as SDG, TXT, and Oracle.

In greater detail: Chapter 1 lays out the foundations of process management, the key concepts of internal customer and process ownership, the importance of operating by objectives in order to achieve customer satisfaction, the different degrees of application (from interventions aimed at rationalising and improving, to functional re-designing or even business re-engineering). It furthermore includes process management in the framework of ISO 9000:2000 certification (Vision 2000).

Chapter 2 describes the methodology for designing, implementing and revising process management. This method, articulated into 8 stages and based on the key concepts of internal customer and process ownership, is strongly objective-oriented (and has therefore a powerful impact on the performance measurement system), and the project-portfolio of improvements can be outlined as plans to improve the output of the processes. The main processes of a company are divided into routine and innovation processes (the latter having designed how the routine is carried out). The fundamental techniques and main software products available on the market for collecting data and representing the business processes are described.

Chapter 3 focuses on knowledge management (creation/acquisition, storage, transferring and sharing) which is at the basis of process management that – as seen – deals with information but through human relationships. In this regard, individual and organisational competencies which enable processes are analysed. In the same chapter, the internal relationships, determined by the existence of internal customer-supplier links, is *extended* beyond the boundaries of the company, involving the external networks that the company has established with its suppliers, customers, subsidiaries, institutions and so on. This "extended" management of knowledge may also concern networks in the form of subcontractors with main contractor, supply chains, districts and strategic alliances. The opportunities offered by the new Web-based technologies are described, which transform organisational networks into effective and efficient information networks. By identifying the differences from the purely "virtual enterprises", *the extended enterprise can be considered as an integrated set of processes that carry out activities on organisational and information networks extending inside and beyond the company's boundaries, and is both an operative network (to deliver a product or a service) and a "community of practice" (whose members learn and develop competencies by exchanging knowledge – "knowledge extended enterprise").*

Chapter 4 describes a BPR project, and introduces the Snaidero case study. This is a very practical contribution, and without presuming to exhaust the subject, we present it as a guideline for the reader who intends to set up a similar operation. The chapter starts by describing the basic principles of the project, the methods and supporting instruments, the stages of implementation, and the most common difficulties and immediate benefits arising.

In the following chapters the main business processes are described, both from a theoretical point of view and with reference to some practical applications, particularly regarding Snaidero. Chapter 5 details the change and innovation processes, namely "business development" (marketing strategy, product portfolio definition, product input/output impact evaluation, design and new product development), and the "customer" processes (sales and service); Chapter 6 focuses on the typical processes forming the Supply Chain (logistics, relationships with the suppliers, manufacturing, quality, plants and technology); Chapter 7 describes the directive and support processes (with particular reference to strategic planning, human resource management and management control).

The third and final part of the book describes the transformation from a process-based organisation (mainly internal processes) to an extended enterprise (and its external processes), once again with the Snaidero study case as an example. Since this project has two values – organisational and informational – it is analysed from both points of view. In the former case, the fact could be particularly important that, as described in Chapter 4 regarding BPR, only very few companies have evolved from artisan firms to extended enterprises. In the latter case, it could be very interesting the integration of systems for managing the exchange of goods and services with those for managing information and knowledge, made in a single "open" Web-based technological environment (the Collaboration Platform).

The company and its main project partners both contribute to the analysis, each being specialised in a certain aspect of the varied world of the Web. The brief description given by each to illustrate these "specialties" (from Management Intelligence to the Extended Supply Chain, ending with the more global vision of a "big player" such as Oracle) should give the reader an idea of the possible "passage" leading to a more in-depth analysis.

The last pages of the book list the literature cited in the text, organised chapter by chapter, where greater detail can be found, and also a list of Web-sites on the topics discussed.

Last but not least it is our wish to sincerely thank the author of the Foreword, whose authoritative opinion and vision enrich the subject of this book: a heartfelt thanks to Professor Kanter, world luminary of managerial sciences: her kindness, affability, and constant availability have helped build a rich bond between the Harvard Business School and the University of Udine in the person of Stefano Tonchia.

A sincere thanks also to the Snaidero family for the kindness shown to us, and their active participation in the project.

A heartfelt thanks goes to all those who directly contributed to some chapters of this book, in particular Edi Snaidero (CEO of Snaidero Group) and Samanta Franz (responsible for New Technologies in Snaidero). Many thanks are also due to Fabio Turchini, Stefano Minisini and Michele Valerio (Eupragma Consulting – Udine), and Barbara Cedolini (Snaidero).

A book is always the result of activities and experience developed in collaboration with many other people. We particularly wish to mention Gianni Merlo (HR director – also for the excellent supervision of the training courses), Umberto Moro (head of production – who splendidly translated the theory into practice), Ivano Dri (director of the trade office – a great supporter of trade partnership), and all the management team in Snaidero.

Both authors furthermore wish to thank Michele Riva (director "Management & Divulgazione" of Il Sole 24 ORE – Milan, Italy), and Werner A. Mueller (Publishing Director "Economics and Business" of Springer-Verlag – Heidelberg, Germany) for their trust and collaboration.

Stefano Tonchia particularly wishes to thank Professor Alberto Felice De Toni, mentor and scientific guide. He furthermore thanks Furio Honsell (Rector of the University of Udine, outstanding for capacity and avantgarde), and Guido Nassimbeni (who shared his university career). He dedicates this book to his mother Marisa and his sister Manuela, who have always with their love and devotion sustained him and are a fundamental point of reference.

Andrea Tramontano wishes to thank all the members of the "design team" (in Snaidero and partner companies) for making this book possible; he furthermore thanks all the "Snaidero community" (colleagues, suppliers, agents, retailers and… customers) for their availability and "team spirit" revealed when believing in and adhering to this idea. A special thanks goes also to his "women", Monica, Alice and Giulia, for their patience and loving support.

Stefano Tonchia
Andrea Tramontano

Part One

Principles and Methods

1 Fundamentals of Process Management and Business Process Reengineering

Stefano Tonchia

1.1 Process Management at the Origin of Customer Satisfaction

Process management can be considered by all means a powerful catalyst for programmes aimed at customer satisfaction. It has in fact been designed to overcome problems related to the rigid structure of function-based organisations, where the different units and departments often have discordant performance goals. Consequently, it is easier to co-ordinate all efforts to pursue contemporaneously the variety of performances required by the current competitive world.

The intrinsic nature of process management is such that effectiveness in granting customer satisfaction assumes greater importance than the efficiency of the single functions. Traditionally, each function tries to maximise its result in relation to its goal-parameters, but this may be in contrast with the overall objectives of the enterprise: e.g. quality improvement programmes may be in conflict with productivity aims, or may result in excessive production standards.

Process management – without undermining the functional structure, which preserves its doubtless advantages of an efficient resource management – *overlaps* with it so as to focus more clearly on the customer, who becomes the main driving force for the business, inspiring the co-ordination logics of all the company's activities. The goals of every function must integrate in a synergic manner in order to achieve the objective of customer satisfaction.

The processes, by exploiting the resources of the company's functions, define, co-ordinate and target the activities towards the satisfaction of the external customer, who conversely, in a rigorously functional organization, risks being scarcely "visible" by those functions that are not in direct contact with them (e.g. purchase departments, technical offices, production units, as compared to trade and sales offices).

Figure 1.1 shows the integration between processes and functions (each function rectangle – or functional business silos, so as to stress how, at the lower levels in particular, communication problems may arise with the other functions – covers part of the organizational chart). An example of a process is shown, spanning the organization to reach its targeted external customer: in order to do so, it is necessary to co-ordinate a variety of activities (depicted as oriented polygons) exploiting the resources of the different functions. Human resources can be therefore grouped *according to skills* (with respect to functions) *and goals* (with respect to processes). Consequently, a single human resource necessarily belongs to only one organizational unit (and has therefore a unique position in the company's organizational chart), but may contribute to a multitude of processes.

Already back in the early Sixties, various authors (e.g. Chapple and Sayles, 1961) maintained that organizations should be based on workflow; however, their focus was more on production efficiency than customer response. The concept of process management was first defined by Zeleny (1988), and later developed by Davenport and Short in *Sloan Management Review* (1990), Hammer in *Harvard Business Review* (1990), Kaplan and Murdock in *The McKinsey Quarterly* (1991). These articles, along with the book by Rummler and Brache (1990), can be regarded as turning points in the history of business management, and indeed the titles of two of these contributions (by Hammer, and by Rummler and Brache, respectively) are particularly significant, as, paraphrased, they enclose the philosophy of process management: "don't concentrate too much on automating, reconfigure instead your way of working!" and "improve your business performance by filling in the empty spaces between the elements of the organizational chart!"

An organizational chart simply depicts a vertical hierarchy line, but no horizontal links between its various elements. Yet it is these relations that keep an organization "alive". Indeed, like a living being, a company is born and grows. The company's functions can be compared to the organs of a living organism, which can only survive and carry out "vital processes" (breathing, eating, moving about…) thanks to the harmonious functioning of its various parts. It is therefore important to analyse and subsequently develop these processes, in particular those that are carried out implicitly and are therefore often underestimated (a scuba diver, for example, knows how important it is to learn to breath properly and save air when underwater!). In a company, acquiring customers, covering and managing orders, developing products, innovating technology etc. are vital processes involving, to a different extent, various functions and therefore requiring a transversal approach. The same is also true for Public Administrations, providing services or supervising works where various Ministries or Councils are transversally involved.

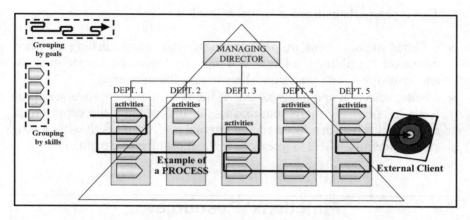

Fig 1.1 Integration between functional organization (by departments) and process management: a process is a set of activities requiring resources which belong to departments

1.2   The Basic Concepts of "Internal Supplier / Customer" and "Process Ownership"

According to the Oxford English Dictionary, a process can be defined as "a continuous and regular succession of actions, taking place or carried on in a definite manner and aimed at achieving some result". A business process consists of a set of activities; each activity is formed by elementary operations, requires specific resources and is aimed at a goal that concurs, with those of all the other activities, to achieve the objective of the process, an objective that integrates all the goals of the different activities. It must be stressed that all these activities have a synergic effect on the process (i.e. the overall result is greater than that sum of the single partial results) and involve a variety of functions/units (which can be considered as reservoirs/incubators of the expertise needed to carry out the process) within the organization. In order to produce outputs destined for downstream, the activities forming a process require upstream inputs, besides the competency of the resources carrying out the activities (resources "loaned" by the functions/units of the company) (Figure 1.2): upstream and downstream can coincide – as described in more detail in the next pages – with other sub-processes within the company or with external suppliers and customers, respectively.

This type of schematization will also result in:

- a better measurement of performances, after distinguishing between output (or "resulting"), internal, and input (or "received") performances, and identifying with precision where to take the measures,
- a better selection and management of the portfolio of improvement projects: by assessing the output and taking into account the cause-effect relationships between received and internal performances, it will be possible to identify where to intervene in the most effective manner.

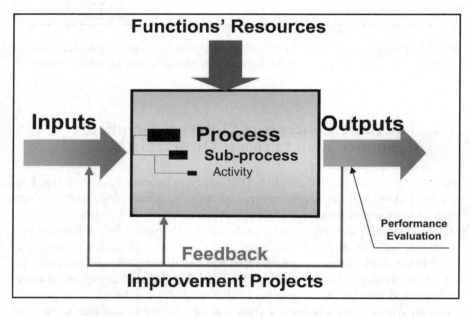

Fig 1.2 A process consists of activities transforming inputs into outputs, thanks to resources loaned by the functions/units of the company

A process can also be viewed as the place where value added is created, or, in other terms, every process generates value added (Keen, 1997). Therefore, process logics combine the typical input/output approach of the system theory, with an economic approach, taking into account that "a process is a combination of activities requiring one or more inputs and creating an output with a value for the customer" (Hammer and Champy, in their "Manifesto" published in 1993) and that "processes constitute a network where the activities of a certain process serve to add value to the inputs deriving from the previous process" (Armistead and Rowland, 1996).

Each process is ultimately targeted at the customers and contributes, with all the others, to their satisfaction. The aim of each process is to *create value added*: this occurs along the entire "value chain" (from design to post-sale assistance), which is therefore entirely focused on the customer.

Table 1.1   The three managerial "hats"

Authority	Skills	Activity / Performances
director of an organizational unit	• Ability to maximise function results in relation to objective-aimed parameters • Technical specialisation	• Preside over technical quality • Comply with function budget • Manage resources efficiently
process owner (process management)	• Ability to act as entrepreneur of one's process • Responsibility for results • Relational skills with up- and downstream • Team leadership skills	• Satisfy downstream customers • Involve / motivate human resources • Manage resources effectively
project manager (project management)	• Ability to manage change • Forecasting talent • Wide knowledge (even if not in depth) • Team leadership skills	• Achieve project objectives • Comply with project budget • Comply with project time schedule

The "visibility" of the final customer is one of the strongest features of process management. Even those employees who are not in direct contact with the final customer (workers, technicians, maintenance staff) share the common goal of customer satisfaction and perceive the importance of their contribution, which is aimed at satisfying those "customers" inside the company who benefit from their job. The value chain is in fact formed by *customer/supplier links* existing within the boundaries of the enterprise, and each work group operating in a process or a sub-process interacts with a customer (another sub-process) and is in turn customer of another upstream sub-process. Thus not only are all the efforts focused on the (final) customer's satisfaction, but also – thanks to the concept of *internal customer* – there are better work conditions, as everybody is also somebody's customer.

The second fundamental concept of process management is that of the *entrepreneurial employee:* it is embodied by the *process owner,* who operates transversally with respect to the company's functions (but may however also be in charge of a specific function). The process owner has a number of tasks: to define the goals of the process (i.e. customer satisfaction, both inside and outside the company), co-ordinate the activity (either full- or part-time) of the functions/units and define the resources in the process, establishing criteria and ways of action, identify the characteristics of the process and the performance indicators, chair all activities aimed at improving the performances of the process. In other terms – within the well-established boundaries of the process – the process owner acts as an *entrepreneur.*

The process owner differs, in expertise and tasks (Table 1.1) from both the organizational unit (function/board/department/office) manager and the project manager, although, at least in theory, it could be the same person playing different roles. It deserves mention that if a project responds to the definition of process given in this paragraph, not all *processes* are *projects*, as the latter are a combination of activities with a beginning and an end.

1.3   Importance of Objectives and Consequences on Performance Measurement

As mentioned previously, process management, by identifying precisely the supplier/customer links and the ownership of each activity, sheds light on the genesis of output performances, which emerge from the analysis of received input performances and those of the activities forming the process. By mapping the processes, it is possible to improve performance measurements, knowing *what* (inputs, internal activities, outputs) and *where* (at the upstream or downstream interface, or within the process) to measure, and clarifying the cause-effect relationships at the basis of the managerial action ("When executives observe their companies, they don't see structure, they see processes" – Ghoshal and Bartlett, 1995; "Reengineering has allowed managers to look beneath the 'surface structure' of their organization, and focus on its fundamental objective: to serve value" – Hammer and Stanton, 1999).

In this sense, if it is legitimate to state that "one can manage what one measures" and therefore, without underestimating experience, intuition, good luck (factors that, however important, only play a marginal role in "scientific" management), process management doubtlessly represents a key to business success.

A process approach extends the concept of "working by objectives" from the top management to the entire organisation. Originally deriving from "Management By Objectives" (MBO), a theory formulated by Peter Drucker in 1954, process management revises it completely, overcoming its two main limits:

- MBO focuses on the objectives and goals of an activity rather then the activity *in se* (i.e. responsibilities regard more the results than the activities),
- MBO is a managerial technique involving only the highest levels of the organisation.

MBO emphasizes the manager's ability to define the objectives, be motivated and endorse performance-oriented plans thanks to his/her authority, the knowledge of the motivations within his/her group and personnel, the cycles of top-down analysis and bottom-up synthesis, and possible "trade-offs", as instruments to divulge and clarify the birth and development of the performances.

An "objective" is a clear and formal description of an "end result" which one intends to achieve through well-defined intermediate "goals"; particular care must be given to indicate "what" must be achieved, why, for whom and within what time limit (there will be relative freedom concerning "how"). The objective must be: clear, comprehensible, motivating (it must be seen as a challenge) and inherent to the specific competency. Moreover, it must be achievable with the available resources and expertise, measurable and assessable (for an example, see Odiorne, 1965).

Process management is aimed at introducing and spreading throughout the *entire* company the idea of operating by objectives, following the new strategic trends that have shifted the focus of companies from mass production to "mass customization": this way, the enterprises can exploit the traditional cheapness of wide-scale production to meet the specific and pressing demands of the customer.

Briefly, process management postulates an organization (thus, the involvement of the *entire* company) oriented towards objectives/results rather than on one based on tasks, and makes a leap from "control-order-prescription" to "acknowledge-create-empowerment" (Evered and Selman, 1989). Functional and hierarchic structures are thus superseded: a task-based aggregation leaves space for objective/competency aggregation; responsibility is empowered by role and not necessarily by authority.

The consequences for all the workers are remarkable: there is an *empowerment* that leads all the employees to take on greater responsibilities and understand the effects of their actions on the global performance of the company; there is a continuous quest for improvement, expertise (in the sense of technical knowledge, reliability and personal character) which may service various processes is highly regarded, careers become transversal and linked to role rather than level. Work within the process is firmly organized in teams, into which flow different, specialized competencies, and the sense of belonging to a work group is enhanced, since teams are encouraged by the management to make decisions regarding the process. Moreover, the objectives of the work groups act as integrating mechanisms: *team working* creates a fertile ground for learning and adapting continuously to external stimuli. The group is headed by the process owner, who must possess leadership qualities and an enterprising spirit (Youkl, 1981).

From a performance viewpoint, the attention is placed on the *interfunctional effectiveness* of the process (e.g. customer satisfaction in terms of perceived product & service quality), on the *global efficiency* of the process (e.g. reducing the overall costs relative to nonconformities rather than the productivity of the single departments), on the *system flexibility* (defined as a quality, rapid and low-cost adaptation to the changes in the environment – De Toni and Tonchia, 1998). As regards *costs,* process logics provides a better understanding and identification of the genesis of costs in the various areas of the company and during the different stages of design, engineering, production and sales/distribution.

In general, process management requires the company to revise its Performance Measurement System (PMS) and arrange for a widespread use of Information Technology (Davenport and Short, 1990; Davenport, 1993), including web-based technologies such as Intranet/Extranet and Business Intelligence (Part Three of this book).

The main consequences of process management on the characteristics and indicators of the Performance Measurement System can be summarized as follows (De Toni and Tonchia, 1996):

- there must be overall process indicators, transversal to the organization, that can measure the effectiveness of the process in achieving its primary objective; the latter is the result of the harmonic, converging and synergic sum of the goals pertaining to specific sub-processes of the above process,

- the performances concurring in determining the primary objective and those pertaining to the single functions and units/departments (e.g. efficiency performances), which supply the necessary resources to carry out the activities of the process, must be considered together,
- in the framework of the customer-supplier chain, the system must be able to identify the performances that can be ascribed to a process and which, although deriving from activities of the same process, depend to a great extent on the performances of upstream processes (suppliers),
- the performances concurring in achieving the primary objective will not only be assessed in absolute terms, but also in relative ones, i.e. between the functions/boards, in order to assure the best combination with the available (limited) resources: an excellent performance of one function/unit must not be obtained to the detriment of others.

The comparison between aim and result must occur at all levels of the company's organizational pyramid, from strategic performances (critical success factors) to functional and operational ones, but in particular – from a process management viewpoint – it must support the "revolution" that took place with the introduction of the customer-supplier "internal links".

For example, according to the Accenture's model (Hronec, 1993), a distinction must be made between *process measures* and *result measures:* one or more critical processes correspond to each goal, and one or more result (or output) measures correspond to each critical process. Result measures are determined by the key activities of each single process, and these activities are assessed through process measures (thus, within the process).

Table 1.2   Performance Measurement System and Process Management

from	to
Financial results	Value creation
Standard achievement	Customer satisfaction
Control	Learning & improvement
Individual measures	Team measures
Task/function measures	Transversal measures
Hierarchical synthesis	Synthesis by customer-supplier links
Performance trade-off	Performance synergy

Table 1.2 reports the most significant differences in the evolution of company's PMS following the decision to adopt process management.

1.4 From Process Management to Business Process Reengineering

Process management can be applied at different levels of intensity, from a simple rationalisation of the work process (Process Management in a stricter sense) to its deep reengineering (Process Reengineering). Business strategies may also be revolutionised (Business Reengineering): in the latter two cases we witness what is commonly known as *Business Process Reengineering (BPR)*, a term coined at the MIT in Boston in the late Eighties. In greater detail:

- *Process Management* consists in the rationalisation of processes, the quest for efficiency / effectiveness, a sort of simplification/clarification brought about by "common-sense engineering",
- *Process Reengineering* consists in re-designing processes, always aiming at efficiency / effectiveness,
- *Business Reengineering* consists in restructuring the business from a strategic viewpoint (e.g. repositioning the company in a different market etc.). Some authors simply prefer to distinguish between gradual improvement ("Business Process Improvement" – BPI) and radical change ("Business Process Reengineering" – BPR); in other words, "the aim of *reengineering* is to build a correct process, and that of *improvement* is to have a better process" (Johansson et al., 1993). Childe et al. (1994) suggest a solution involving continuous interventions that from individual and group improvements can lead to process and business reengineering; risks can however increase during this path, and the scope passes from operational to strategic.

Some features are common to BPI and BPR (Harrington, 1991):

- change is focused on and driven by the customer,
- the object of the change are the processes (or their composing parts),
- there is a real sponsorship by the management (top management in the case of BPR),
- interventions focus on organizational-managerial variables rather than technological ones,

- there is a precise identification of process ownership,
- there is a precise measurement of the process performances (before and after),
- both can start up as pilot projects.

On the other hand, there are also remarkable differences, as reported in Table 1.3.

Table 1.3   Improvement or reengineering of business processes

Business Process Improvement	Business Process Reengineering
Gradual approach to change	Radical approach to change
Absence of an emergency situation	Strong urge to change
Limited/indirect dependence on business strategy	Direct involvement of business strategy
Ability to grasp even the slightest opportunity	Aptitude to take risks in the presence of big opportunities
Involvement of circumscribed processes	Involvement of larger, more transversal processes
Marginal involvement of several processes	Involvement of fewer, but more critical processes
Identification (also empirical) of the opportunities	Complex project reengineering management
Bottom-up contribution	Top-down organisational review
Lower costs and implementation times	Higher costs and longer implementation times
STAGES	STAGES
1) Identification of the processes to improve	1) Strategy reformulation
2) Definition of an intervention team	2) Assessment of the inadequacy of current key processes
3) Analysis of current processes and improvement methods	3) Reengineering of the key processes
4) Implementation of improvement interventions	4) Tuning of the new key processes
5) Assessment of the results	5) Evaluation of the results

In practice, however, it is often impossible to define beforehand whether it is more profitable to improve a process (BPI) or carry out a more radical intervention (BPR). In the latter case, the delicate nature of this type of intervention must be kept in mind: BPR has a strong impact on the human resources and on their way of working, fears and problems of adaptation could make it ill accepted or even opposed (a company turned inside-out like a glove could have more problems than benefits!). The solution often lies in a gradual change, having the features of a BPR rather than a BPI in the case of critical or priority processes. In Chapter 2 change will assume the features of BPR or BPI without discontinuity, according to the gap between actual and expected situation. For this reason, from now on we will only refer to *process management,* without distinguishing between BPI and BPR (Figure 1.3).

Hammer and Champy (1993) consider it useful to identify precisely the "actors" in the reengineering process:

- a leader (a high-level manager who authorizes and endorses the changes),
- a managerial committee (formed by the top management and the different area managers, and chaired by the above leader, whose task is to define and develop the reengineering strategies),
- a process owner for each main process hypothesized (in charge of the process and its reengineering),
- a reengineering team (i.e. a group of persons committed to the integrated reengineering/revision of the processes, with delegates from the various macro-processes identified (Rohleder and Silver, 1997),
- a person in charge of improvement/reengineering (who must develop and implement it, by co-ordinating the different, related actions).

Dutta and Manzoni (1998) have presented an interesting series of "pedagogical" case studies on the implementation of BPR, revealing on one hand the indispensable need for these interventions ("there had to be a better way to carry out things"), and on the other the risk of frustration, mainly resulting from two causes: 1) a limited emphasis and integration of the human factor in the interventions ("the human side of BPR"); 2) the need to consider BPR as an effort with a greater strategic outcome than is usually believed. Moreover, it should be kept clearly in mind that BPR is only a *pathway* towards improvement, "a race without a finish line".

It is also important to consider beforehand a possible reluctance of the organization to accept change (Hall et al., 1993; King and Sethi, 1998). The reasons can be ascribed to:

- fear of novelty (uncertainties),
- worries of an economical nature,
- fear of losing power and influence,

- difficulty to change habits and consolidated ways of thinking,
- problems at a personal level (anxieties),
- previous negative experiences concerning changes,
- legitimate doubts regarding the proposed changes.

Cagliano et al. (1998) also observe that the BPR methodology has been mostly developed with an eye to large businesses, and its application to smaller ones is more difficult and requires adequate support instruments. These can be offered by service centres, science parks and associations of industrialists (in terms of "best practice" transfer, knowledge-sharing between small enterprises, assistance in the creation of competency networks).

Process management, both in terms of BPI and BPR, does not impair the classic, function-based organizational structure (and its doubtless advantages in terms of work specialization) displayed by its organizational chart. Process management mainly consists in orienting the human resources of the organisational chart towards the respective process goals, and requiring an additional contribution so that the processes run smoothly (and thus having a positive impact on work conditions, as provided by the concept of inside customer).

For this reason, we prefer not to refer to *process organization,* a deceptive definition, as it seems to point to abandoning the pre-existing organizational system for a new one. This does not imply that no change will be made to the organizational chart after an intervention of process management: there will be new "role actors" by appointing tasks of process ownership. So process management is not an organizational model *in se,* but a managerial model requiring an end-to-end vision that, as a result, compels a restructuring of the organization.

Moreover, process management does not imply a matrix organizational structure, as in the case, for example, of project management (where there is a co-ordinator/manager for each project, "intersected" with a number of functions), with the relative problems connected to hierarchic authority ("strong" and "weak" matrixes and "competition" between the different projects). In process management, the objectives do not coincide with those of functional management and, if processes have been mapped correctly, there should be a balance of resources for all the various activities of the various processes.

Besides the difficulties that may arise in the implementation of process management, there may also be others related to the situations in the different businesses. Ostroff (1999) supports the validity of vertical organizations lacking process orientation when business objectives have not yet been clearly identified or are still anchored to efficiency-oriented perform-ances (cost leadership strategies). Moreover, whenever human resources are particularly critical, because asked to contribute to too many processes, new resources (either within the company or from outside) must be found to act as sub-process owners, and answer to a process owner of a higher level. In other terms it can be necessary to introduce one (or more) hierar-chic levels of process ownership. Compared to the more traditional enter-prises, actors in their new roles could be better rewarded and advance in their career.

It mustn't be forgotten that, formally, nothing forbids a function man-ager to be also a process manager, and indeed, this is often a way to intro-duce process management more gradually.

Other authors – such as Biazzo (1998) – maintain a more critical ap-proach to BPR, observing on one hand that process analysis/design coin-cides with comprehending/changing a "socio-technical system", and on the other there is the concrete risk of using an over-scientific (simplistic) ap-proach to the complexity of an organization and its internal network of re-lationships. Grover and Malhotra (1997), after stressing a few false truths about BPR (underlining such aspects as incrementality, intra-functional improvement, the objectives of cost reduction together with empowerment and team working, the difficulty in standardizing and managing interven-tions from the top) observe that a more contingent approach to BPR would be required, depending on the single business situations.

Process Management	Business Process Improvement (BPI)	Process Management
Process Reengineering	Business Process Reen-gineering (BPR)	
Business Reengineering		

Fig 1.3 Process Management ranges from the improvement to the reengineering of the organization's way of working

Finally, connected to process management from a terminological view-point, two other practices are often cited: Activity-Based Management (ABM) and Process Value Analysis (PVA). These are however applied in a more circumscribed field than process management, which is instead more pervasive and inherent to the performances of the entire business.

ABM developed from Activity-Based Costing (ABC) and is formally aimed at managing the activities so as to reduce costs (See Paragraph 7.3). Likewise, PVA is aimed at reducing the overall costs within the company by focusing on the activities. Already in 1990 Johnson had presented a case study on General Electric, and had distinguished between value-adding activities (VA), those that added no value (NVA) – such as set-ups, queues, maintenance and quality controls – and "grey activities" (unclassifiable, or with both VA and NVA features). Turney (1992), one of the world experts of ABC, suggests – as well as the ABC technique – revising the use of the resources, eliminating NVA activities, reducing times of VA activities, and that more products may share the same VA activities.

1.5   Process Management and ISO 9000:2000 Quality Standards

The *process approach* is also strongly promoted by the new family of ISO standards published in December 2000 which regard "Quality Management Systems"; these standards are the result of the project "Vision 2000", aimed at revising the previous regulations dating back to 1994.

The new quality standards included in the "2000" family are to date: ISO 9000:2000 ("Quality Management Systems – Fundamentals and vocabulary"), ISO 9001:2000 ("Quality Management Systems – Requirements") and ISO 9004:2000 ("Quality Management Systems – Guidelines for performance improvements").

The new standards aim at overcoming what were the limits of the previous series, namely: the lack of consideration for continuous improvement and preventive actions, the scarce attention devoted to costs, efficiency and resource management, the limited importance given to measurable goals, the lack of integration with other interested parties (suppliers, customers, etc.), the scarce co-ordination between 9001 and 9004, the lack of connections with the ISO 14000 environmental standards, the limited role of top management; moreover, the new standards fully endorse in an explicit way a process approach.

According to ISO 9000 (clause 2.4), a process is defined as a "set of interrelated or interacting activities which transforms inputs into outputs. In order to run effectively, a company must identify and manage different processes which are interrelated and interdependent. The output of a process is often an input to another one, thus the systematic identification and management of the processes within an organization, and the interaction of these processes, can be summarized in the expression 'process approach'. The aim of this international regulation is to promote process approach in the management of a company".

In particular, ISO 9001, which certifies quality systems, promotes the continuous improvement of the above systems, in accordance with the PDCA or Deming cycle (ISO 9001 – clause 0.2 "Process approach"):

- *"Plan:* establish the objectives and processes necessary to deliver results in accordance with customer requirements and the organization's policies,
- *Do:* implement the processes,
- *Check:* monitor and measure processes and product against policies, objectives and requirements for the product, and report the results,
- *Act:* take actions to continually improve process performance."

There is no explicit request to select specific processes, as "the managers should identify the processes needed to manufacture products that satisfy the requirements of customers and other interested parties" (ISO 9004 – clause 7.1.3.1). Some indications of the types of processes may be inferred from clause 7 of the ISO 9001 standard. The requirements of the quality management system, object of the certification, pass from the former twenty elements described in Section 4 of the past ISO 9001 to the current four: i) "Management responsibility" (clause 5); ii) "Resource management" (clause 6); iii) "Product realization" (clause 7); iv) "Measurement, analysis and improvement" (clause 8).

Clause 7 ("Product realization") is articulated in what could be interpreted as macro-processes:

- *planning for product realisation,*
- *processes related to customers and other interested parties,*
- *design & development,*
- *purchasing,*
- *production & service provision,*
- *control of measuring and monitoring devices.*

Moreover, support processes should be taken into account, such as "managing information, training of people, finance-related activities ..." (ISO 9004 – clause 7.1.3.1).

Finally, for all the processes, ISO 9004 (clause 7.1.3.2) encourages acting in such a way that "the inputs are defined and recorded in order to provide a basis for formulation of requirements to be used for verification and validation of outputs. Inputs can be internal or external to the organization... The outputs should be recorded and evaluated against input requirements and acceptance criteria. This evaluation should identify necessary corrective actions, preventive actions or potential improvements in the effectiveness and efficiency of the process".

Process management can also be used for a preliminary assessment of the state of the quality system: in order to avert the risk of ritualism and identify the real distance from the requirements provided by ISO 9000:2000 standards, and avoid that current practices may be manipulated or adapted so as to only respond to the above requirements, it is advisable to adopt a model of process management and not the norm itself, which should therefore rely on a solid model of process functioning. The processes should *first* be re-organized, and *subsequently* conform to quality system requirements.

Processes also play an important role within *quality awards*. For example, they are one of the nine evaluation elements provided for the European Quality Award (EQA), forming the link between the four "factor" elements

- leadership,
- policy and strategy,
- human resource management,
- partnerships and resources.

and the four "result" elements

- employee satisfaction,
- customer satisfaction,
- impact on the society,
- company's key performance results.

2. Methodology for Process Management Design & Implementation

Stefano Tonchia

2.1 Content and Deployment of the Methodology

When introducing process management into a company, it is important to keep in mind the organization's pre-existing mission/vision and strategy (see top part of Figure 2.3). At times, however, it can be necessary to revise/reconfigure the business strategy (in terms of competitive priorities and action levers), while taking into account the strengths and weaknesses of the company and the opportunities or threats in the market (S.W.O.T. analysis) (Paragraph 7.1).

In particular, the macro-objectives of the company must emerge during this phase: these are considered Key Successful Factors (KSF), and all the processes to be defined or developed have to be aimed at their achievement (the targets in Figure 1.1).

We will now describe the main features of this method, which has been implemented in several, important companies. The method consists of eight steps, as shown in Figure 2.1. Steps 1 to 4 are closely related to the *concept of "internal customer"*, whereas steps 5 to 8 mostly regard *"process ownership"* (or "entrepreneurial employee"); both concepts are fundamental features of process management, as described previously in Paragraph 1.2.

Although many processes are implicitly operative, this methodology aims at their *explicit* management. Some processes in fact need only be studied to be improved: breathing, for example, is an instinctive process that occurs thanks to various organs – the body's "organizational units" – but scuba divers know that in order to save air, they must "learn how to breathe".

The sequence listed in Figure 2.1 need not necessarily be carried out in this order, but it is important to control each step and check on improvement. For instance, if problems arise in the identification of the customers or suppliers, it could be useful to anticipate the definition of activity, thus asking oneself which not yet available inputs are needed to carry out the activities, and what are the outputs of the activities; only later will it be possible to connect inputs to possible suppliers and the outputs to the customers who receive them.

1. PROCESS identification
2. Definition of BOUNDARIES (Start = supplier processes; End = customer processes)
3. Formalization of INPUTS and OUTPUTS exchanged (with suppliers and customers, respectively)
4. Formalization of ACTIVITIES and their procedures, including value-added analysis
5. Analysis of TIME (events triggering activities + activities' durations)
6. PERFORMANCE evaluation (outcoming perf. resulting from the combination of internal perf. and received or incoming perf.)
7. Definition of RESPONSIBILITY ("process ownership")
8. RESOURCES assignment (loaned by organizational units)

Fig 2.1   The eight steps of the proposed methodology

Internal customers and suppliers (intended as processes, and *not* business functions or individual persons) must be clearly distinguished from inputs and outputs (the exchanged "goods" - materials, but often information – that are the object of performance measurement/assessment).

A process consists of a pool of activities, which are carried out under well-defined circumstances (point 5). Thus the activities may be: in a sequence, complementary or alternative. Moreover, the details of these activities should be defined to a degree appropriate for their management (and not that required, for instance, by an ISO 9000 quality certification): an over-detailed description does not give rise to sub-activities, but only to the operational "procedures" of the above activity (an activity is universally recognized as the elementary level forming a process, which in turn consists of a number of activities; it might be useful to define these procedures in order to carry out/define/improve the activity).

The first step of the methodology is particularly critical, and it may be difficult to identify the process and a level of detail useful for process management. A combination of "top-down" and "bottom-up" approaches are often employed for this purpose. Save for those processes that have already been well defined to an operational level, it is convenient to start by hypothesising a process, and making a list of all the activities involved ("top-down" stage); subsequently, if the list proves excessively long, and problems arise in the management of the process, the activities are grouped into two or more different sub-processes ("bottom-up" stage). *The eight steps of the methodology are then repeated for each sub-process thus defined.*

The processes will be managed at sub-process level, as it would not help to resolve them any further, as they are the "leaves" in a hierarchic, tree-like representation of the processes. Each "leaf-process" consists of an integrated and coherent pool of activities, and although operativeness is defined at this level, it is worthwhile keeping the resolution process in mind so at to identify processes of a higher level (in order to attribute, for instance, an ownership to a set of processes). The leaf-processes thus form a *network of relationships* represented by arrows.

Figure 2.2 depicts three different detail levels relative to processes (i.e. "mega", "major" and "sub" processes): the nodes of each process must connect with those of other processes of identical level. The links can also be bi-directional, since a process can at the same time be supplier and customer of another one (for instance: it supplies specifications for a report and then receives the report filled in). This process network superimposes the traditional organizational chart, where there are no operative relations except for hierarchic line.

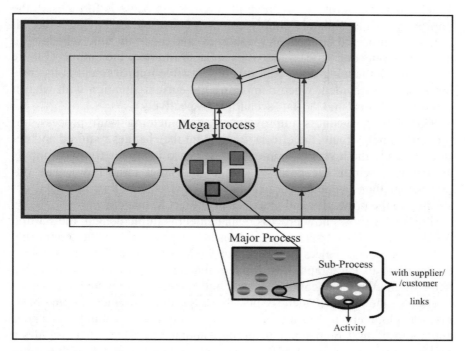

Fig 2.2 An example of process network hierarchy

This type of representation summarises the fundamental contribution made by process management: an organizational chart is essential for the definition of hierarchy, but a company operates through links, or processes, so it can aim the activities towards result-oriented performances. These are targeted at specific customers who will receive well-defined outputs produced with inputs supplied by specific suppliers.

The output performances of each process (result performances) derive from the combination of internal performances (relative to how the activities are carried out) and received performances (validity of the inputs received from the suppliers). The process hierarchy makes it possible to consider the result performances of mega-processes as the competitive priorities of the business strategy, which will be subsequently analysed to a greater detail taking into account the result performances of the processes of a lower hierarchic level (major and sub processes). Process mapping therefore sheds light on the *essence of management:* the interpretation of (transversal) cause-effect links, while at the same time defining the (vertical) organizational structure for synthesis. Thus, process mapping can be interpreted as a "rational reconfiguration" of the business system.

This is not a purely speculative plus. Once a process is formalised, the improvement plans should simply consist of feed-backs, having - like all projects – allocated budgets and resources, and a certain time schedule, to act upon inputs and process activities so as to improve the outputs (Figure 1.2). Process mapping often conceals the possible improvement at its core, but it becomes evident when comparing the current situation with what it should be ("as-is" and "to-be" scenarios, respectively).

Considering business improvement as coinciding with process improvement helps focus the efforts, implement the changes required and define precisely the levers to employ and where to intervene (on what inputs or activities within the process, and, in the latter case, how). The improvement thus becomes "project-based", and is therefore managed according to the principles and practices of Project Management.

Figure 2.3 shows how process management is implemented: the starting point is the analysis of strategy, and further steps consist in the monitoring of business performances (the Performance Measurement System – PMS – is described in Paragraph 7.3). Process management by process mapping helps define the technical, managerial and relational competencies needed to endorse the changes, identify possible gaps and consequently plan business development by means of education, training, coaching, assistance and counselling. Competency mapping, endorsed by PMS, also provides a tool to assess the potential of the organisation, and better define the strategic objectives.

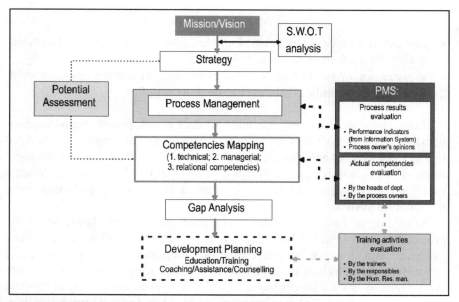

Fig 2.3 Implementation of Process Management

2.2 The Main Processes in a Company

The processes of a company must have:

- a primary objective, resulting from the harmonious composition of all the sub-goals, even when the latter are different or discordant,
- a synergic effect on the overall performance (the result of the single performances are greater than their sum),
- a transversal involvement of a multitude of functions or organisational units.

Various authors have expressed their views on how processes should be classified. Rummler and Brache (1990) distinguish between three types of processes: 1) *primary processes* (production, logistics, order management, product development, marketing, sales, etc.); 2) *managerial processes* (such as strategic planning or total quality programmes); 3) *support processes* (such as human resources management, information management, technology management).

This type of classification derives from Porter's (1985), who identifies nine value-adding "activities" (although it would be better to define them "processes"). These are:

- *primary activities*: 1) in-bound logistics, 2) operations, 3) out-bound logistics, 4) marketing & sales, 5) service,
- *support activities*: 1) business infrastructure, 2) human resource management, 3) technological development, 4) supplies.

Bartezzaghi et al. (1994) consider product development, logistics, production and administration as operative processes; these are characterised by: a) organisation and management of the human resources; b) management systems, involving Just-in-time, Total Quality Management, Concurrent Engineering techniques, etc.; c) process technologies and supporting information systems.

According to Earl and Khan (1994), processes can be classified on the grounds of their structurability and impact on business performances: core (internal) and network (external relations with suppliers and customers) processes, characterised by high and low structurability, respectively, are considered to have a *direct impact* on the performances, whereas support and management processes, characterised by high and low structurability, respectively, have an *indirect impact* on the business performances.

Gilbreath (1986) simply distinguishes between *flow processes* (such as production processes characterised by repetitiveness in execution and standardisation of the output) and *impulse processes* (such as the processes of product innovation).

We refer to this type of classification to make an initial rough distinction between processes of a higher level: as shown in Figure 2.4, in any one company it is immediately possible to identify routine mega-processes and those of innovation/change. The term "routine" used in this context has a positive meaning: these are the processes that generate income, as they have the purchasing external customer as their final target. These processes start from the external suppliers and end with the external customers, after covering the entire "operative value chain": operative, as it consists of routine operations, value, since it is along this chain that value is added to the product (in fiscal terms, the value is measured by VAT – Value Added Tax), and chain, as it is formed by internal customer/supplier links. The innovation and change processes on the other hand are aimed at defining reference/operative standards for the routine processes: these standards are not only those relative to the product (product specifications, etc.) and production process (cycle specifications, etc.), but also to all the working methods of the company and its relations with external subjects, such as suppliers and customers.

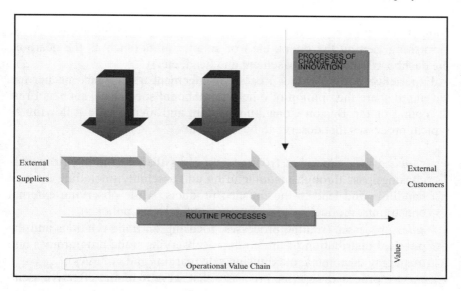

Fig 2.4   Mega-processes of change/innovation and routine

Given the length of the routine process chain, it may sometimes be helpful to divide the processes into two groups: *supply chain* processes, aimed at warehousing the correct amounts and types of finished product when they are required, and *sales/service* processes, aimed at building a relationship with the customers, and delivering the finished product in the most appropriate and customised manner (Figure 5.1).

Three groups of mega-processes exist, two that are routine, and an innovation/change one. This type of classification is used by the "customer durables" area in Electrolux Home Products (the world leader producing powered domestic appliances), where three types of processes have been identified: 1) "Supply Flow Management", relative to all the industrial and logistics activities (purchasing, production, distribution and quality control); 2) "Customer Relations Management", in charge of sales and relations with distribution channels and retailers; 3) "Product Category Management", supervising the categories of products so as to respond to the needs of the customers. Electrolux was one of the first companies to adopt process management, in the framework of the Total Quality Programme in the late Eighties and with the introduction, in 1992, of the so-called I.M.A. (Integrated Management Areas).

Likewise Fiat in the early Nineties, when launching the Fiat Punto on the market and improving the "Fire" engine of the Uno, passed from a High-Automation to an Integrated Factory structure, featuring the so-called Elementary Technological Units or E.T.U.s, multi-functional and multicompetence units regarding technological cycles (assembling the chassis, varnishing, setting the doors, etc.) or smaller units (such as the gearbox, the dashboard, the engine basement and head, etc.).

Experience in the field as process management trainer and coacher has led me to share the opinion of other international specialists, such as Ernst & Young or the Boston Consulting Group, and identify the following as typical processes that deserve to be analysed:

- *supply chain* processes (routine processes that, beginning from purchasing, pass through manufacturing and assembly, including internal handling, and lead to the finished products, while observing external constraints, production requirements and delivery policies),
- *sales* processes (routine processes, focusing on trade relations and the physical distribution of the products, observing trade programmes and managing customers, maximising sale margins and volumes),
- *service* processes (routine processes that serve to assure effective assistance to the customer before the purchase, during delivery and after the purchase),
- *business development* processes (change and innovation processes from a "company-wide" point of view, aimed at giving new, improved working standards to routine processes),
- *control/support* processes (aimed at supporting all the processes and verifying their objectives),
- *management* processes (addressing and co-ordinating the various processes).

Table 2.1 shows the typical, possible sub-processes ("major" processes) forming the above ("mega") processes.

It is clear that – following the current trend towards an integrated supply chain (Supply Chain Management, SCM) – the traditional purchasing activities can be classified as in-bound logistics, in the sub-sub-process "materials and stock management" (suppliers, from an integrated logistics viewpoint, are considered at the same level as internal departments); on the other hand, the selection, management (contracts, competitiveness mechanisms, development and partnership) and assessment of the suppliers – namely, procurement – are considered processes of "business development" (although they may be carried out by the same persons). Logistics therefore concerns all those activities aimed at rendering available materials, components and products where and when they are needed (space-time availability).

Table 2.1   Typical firm's processes and sub-processes

Supply Chain	Production	Stage A
		Stage B
		Stage …
	Logistics (In-bound and Internal)	Production Scheduling
		Materials Management
		Capacity Management
		Shop Floor Control
	Quality Management	
	Maintenance	
Sales/Service ("Customer")	Negotiation	
	Order-, Contract Management	
	Distribution	
	Forecasting / Demand Management	
	Service & Assistance	
	Spare parts Management	
Business Development	Product Innovation	Research & Development
		Design/Product Development
		Engineering/Industrialization
		Product Launch
	Technology Management / Plant Management / Safety	
	Suppliers Management (from selection to evaluation)	
	Marketing	Product-Portfolio Definition
		Price Policies
		Retailers' Network Organization
		Promotion / Communication
		Customer Satisfaction Analysis
Control/ Support	Accounting (Balance-Sheet)	
	Cost Management	
	Budgeting	
	Finance	
	Information Systems	
Managerial	Strategic Planning	
	Human Resources Management	

Likewise, trade dealings and customers' order management – being "routine" processes – can be classified as sales/service processes (also known as Customer Relationship Management, CRM), whereas the organisation of the sales network, the planning and management of the relationship with the agents over a medium-long term or, if existing, the trade-partnership with the retailers are considered processes of "business development", together with the definition of the product portfolio, price policies, promotion and communication strategies, and the analysis of customer satisfaction (activities that can be typically ascribed to marketing and its famous "4Ps": Products, Prices, Placement – where and how the products are sold, and Promotion).

2.3   Process Management and Information & Communication Technologies (ICT)

Process Management in its more radical sense, that is Business Process Reengineering (B.P.R.) was first formulated during a research programme carried out by the Massachusetts Institute of Technology (MIT) in Boston, over a five-year period beginning in 1984 (Scott-Morton, 1991). It consisted however in a "business reconfiguration brought about by Information Technology – I.T." and in fact was the third stage out of five. After the first two levels, where there is a local/functional exploitation, followed by inter-functional integration, I.T. can induce the reconfiguration of the business processes so as to fully exploit its potential (as maintained by several manuals and guides, such as that issued by IBM in 1975). The fourth level concerns the use of I.T. to re-design the exchanges that take place between companies belonging to a network, whereas the fifth level focuses on the opportunities offered by I.T. to reengineer the entire mission of the company.

Though the research at the MIT is acknowledged to be the precursor of a subject still considered topical, a Copernican revolution has taken place in the approach, i.e. passing from process management as a consequence of the implementation of Information & Communication Technologies (I.C.T.) to process management fostered by and exploiting the opportunities offered by I.C.T. In other words, passing from technology inducing/guiding the organisational-managerial reconfiguration to that enabling, endorsing and catalysing change of an organizational-managerial nature and a strategic origin. This also explains why any type of intervention regarding information technology (introduction of Enterprise Resource Planning – E.R.P., use of an Intranet, etc.) *should be preceded* by an organisational-managerial analysis/revision by processes.

Process reengineering in a company is therefore a prerequisite for the introduction of advanced information systems; for instance, the implementation of E.R.P. systems without adequate analysis and revision of the business processes can result in a longer and more expensive process of implementation and less benefits: "It is impossible to get the full benefits of an ERP system without having integrated processes" (Hammer and Stanton, 1999).

The role of I.C.T. as the "natural partner of processes is linked to the fact that process logics, by concentrating on the transversal interdependencies between activities, focuses on information flows and information elaboration procedures, thus supplying two fundamental elements to create an effective information system" (Davenport and Short, 1990, and Davenport, 1993, two works that have become classics). The support given by I.C.T. to B.P.R. initiatives mostly occurs through access and sharing of databases, and thanks to communication by information networks (Bhatt, 2000). Companies must however endorse and instil principles and values into their employees that will lead to an effective and efficient use of I.C.T.s, considered as instruments to improve business performances in a process management framework (Marchand et al., 2000).

2.4   Techniques and Software Packages for Process Data Management & Representation

Standard instruments to collect data and represent processes are important for two fundamental reasons:

- the processes can be better understood and therefore improvements made,
- they create a common language for discussion (often the first result is "let's talk it over!").

Representation techniques exist that define both syntax (a set of rules and symbols that combined, define a process model) and semantics (the meaning of the above symbols); the symbols commonly used are those standardised by the American National Standards Institute (A.N.S.I. – www.ansi.org). Listed below are some of the main techniques:

1) *flowcharts*. The sequences of activities forming a process are represented through a flowchart. The activities are identified by geometrical figures, different for each type of activity, and are connected to each other by arrows. A considerable drawback is that it is impossible to mark out the inputs and outputs of the activities, unless they are specified beside each arrow,

2) *functional flowcharts*. The flowcharts pass through a series of columns, each referring to a specific business function: it is therefore possible to mark out the actors and resources involved in the process,

3) *IDEF-0*. One of the most popular techniques. Acronym of Integrated Computer-Aided Manufacturing DEFinition Method, developed in the late Seventies in the framework of the U.S. Air Force project "Integrated Computer-Aided Manufacturing (ICAM)", it draws its origins from the graphic language known as SADT (Structured Analysis and Design Technique – Ross, 1977) used in the framework of information systems.

According to the IDEF-0 technique, a process is regarded as a set of activities transforming inputs into outputs, consuming resources and subjected to constraints and controls (Figure 2.5). Moreover, it is possible to analyse the process at various levels of hierarchy: each explosion ("zoom") preserves the input/output connections with the exterior of the level immediately above (Figure 2.6). All the activity boxes are identified by a number (placed inside the lower right-hand corner of the box), which refers to the sequence of activities represented, and by a number outside (preceded by the letter "A" and positioned outside, below the previous one) that "explodes" the box onto another page, where the activity is exploded in sub-activities (the level of detail increases by adding numbers on the right hand side) (Figure 2.5).

IDEF-0 gave rise to similar approaches: *IDEF-1*, concerning information instead of activities, evolved into *IDEF-1X* (=eXtended), specifying the "objects" or entities (data + attributes) and their logical relations (entity-relationship model); *IDEF-2*, producing a dynamic model of the relations between activities,

4) *IDEF-3*: an autonomous technique that unites flowcharts representing the sequence of activities within a process, and OSTN – Object State Transition Network diagrams, which instead focus on the objects (both physical and informational) transformed by the activities,

5) *Data Flow Diagram (DFD)*. Mostly used when planning to re-design the information system, it illustrates the relations between internal data-stores, the data-supplying external entities, the internal processes transforming them and the flows of information,

6)   *Role Activity Diagram (RAD)*. It marks out the activities within an organisational role in terms of "what to do and when to do it", and the interaction between roles, necessary to achieve the process objective (Ould, 1995). If on one hand it is true that RADs fail to mark out inputs and outputs, on the other they are ideal for identifying overlapping or parallel activities, a feature that other techniques, based on sequence logics, do not possess,

7)   *action workflow*. Once again of a relational type, it focuses on the customer-supplier interaction, which is split into four stages: preparation, negotiation, action, acceptance, represented as the four portions of an ellipse.

In order to be considered complete, a technique should permit both a hierarchic subdivision (a macro-process would be divided into processes, each process into phases, then into activities and finally into elementary operations) and identify all the key elements of process management: activities (type, duration, and interdependence with other activities), events (triggering the activities), inputs and outputs (their type and the information support required), actors and resources.

During the second half of the Nineties, the Centre for Coordination Science of the Massachusetts Institute of Technology (MIT) in Boston completed the mapping of the main business processes in different sectors, producing a "Manual of Organizational Processes" and an "Electronic Repository" of over 5000 processes and activities, with maps, procedures, images, and navigation & data elaboration softwares (http://ccs.mit.edu/ph). The type of representation used is based on a "specialisation hierarchy" of the processes and on the management of the resources deriving from the "coordination theory" (which distinguishes between "fit", "flow", and "sharing" activities – Malone et al., 1999). The results of the research can be purchased, on MIT license, from Phios Corp. (http://www.phios.com).

The implementation of these techniques through specific software programmes for process management also refers to the "holonic" approach theorised by Arthur Koestler in 1967 in his book "The Ghost in the Machine". The term "holonic" can be used to describe any entity that contemporaneously "encloses all and is part of a greater whole" (a process, but also a sub-process). A similar concept is that of "fractal" ("worlds within worlds" – from the seminal book by Mandelbrot, 1982), a geometrical figure that, when enlarged, always reveals new details (indefinite resolution) while preserving a similarity at all levels of enlargement (self-similarity). A brief description follows of the main Process Management-supporting software packages (the list does not include exclusively graphic programmes, such as "Microsoft Visio"), listed according to their diffusion, completeness, innovativeness, adaptability and simplicity.

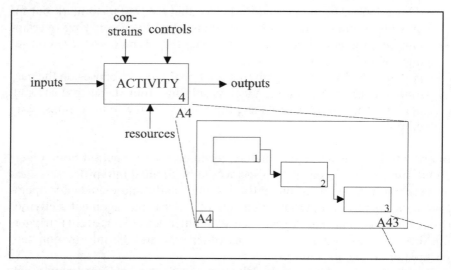

Fig 2.5 Syntax and semantics of process representation according to technique IDEF-0

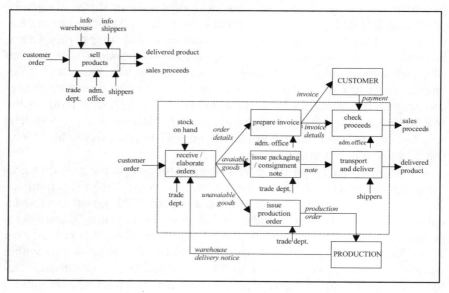

Fig 2.6 An example of IDEF-0 representation, with explosion ("zoom")

ARIS – IDS Scheer (www.ids-scheer.com)

ARIS (Architecture of Integrated Information System) is the world's market leader in the field of Business Process Management or Business Process Reengineering (source: Gartner Group, data 2001).

It consists of an integrated package of tools ("ARIS 6.1 Collaborative Suite") developed by IDS Scheer, a German company established by Professor August-Wilhelm Scheer in 1984. With over 1500 employees and branches in many countries around the world, IDS Scheer counts many leading companies and corporations among its customers (Scheer et al., 2003).

The fundamental tool is "ARIS Toolset": the over 30000 licences released make it the best seller in the world for designing, analysing, implementing and optimising/reengineering business processes. ARIS supplies a large number of methods to represent processes, including IDEF. It operates on Windows and integrates with "SAP-R/3" E.R.P. system.

The suite also includes: "ARIS Simulation" (to simulate process executability), "ARIS ABC" (for cost analysis, according to the logics of Activity-Based Costing – See Paragraph 7.3), "ABC BSC" (to create a Performance Measurement System such as Balanced Scorecard – See Paragraph 7.3), and "ARIS Web Publisher" (a software supporting both HTML and Java languages, designed to publish the processes on the Intranet or the Internet).

Sciforma Process – Sciforma Corp. (www.sciforma.com)

Another world-wide selling software: produced by Sciforma (independent of Scitor Corp. since 2002), it has won many awards and is used by numerous, important companies operating in a wide range of fields (including that of services).

Launched on the market in 1995, it has now reached its fourth version, which provides for the mapping, simulation and web-publishing of all the processes of a company. It operates in Windows and supports Object Linking and Embedding (OLE). The main tool consists of the "Diagram View", where the user inserts figures, lines and texts selected from a "Style Palette" that provides all the typical process symbols.

Activities have fixed and variable costs, associated with resource exploitation; the latter resources have in turn work-loads defined as "efforts". By inserting these data, together with the calendar of the activity, it is possible to obtain different simulation scenarios and the respective statistics. So-called "Swim Lanes" show the allocation of activities against their respective functions or departments.

ProcessGuide – QPR Software Plc (www.qpr.com)

The "ProcessGuide 6.0" suite, distributed in over forty counties, is produced by the Finnish company QPR. It is compatible with Windows, requires a data-base server supporting Oracle, SQL or MS Access, and allows web-publishing through Java Script and the most widespread browsers (Explorer or Netscape).

"ProcessGuide" depicts the processes, their relationships and hierarchies though flowcharts, that can be enriched with the resources used, the inputs and outputs. The language used can be customised or refer to such standards as IDEF.

The software provides a useful tool for process simulation, thus optimising the use of resources, testing different scenarios, illustrating process dynamics through animation. The results are shown graphically.

iGrafx – Micrografx, Corel Corp. (www.igrafx.com)

Recently acquired by the Canadian multinational company Corel, Micrografx has deservedly earned a reputation for the quality and innovativeness of its software products. It provides four products for process management.

The simplest and cheapest is "iGrafx FlowCharter 2003", which represents processes as flowcharts. "iGrafx Process 2003" on the other hand is more complete, providing an effective tool for managing costs and resources, analysing "what-if" scenarios, and accessing the most widespread data-bases (ODBC, SQL, etc.). It can interact with SAP and the user can also intervene in Visual Basic for Applications (VBA).

"iGrafx IDEF0 2003" provides a step-by-step procedure for modelling processes according to the IDEF-0 standard and includes a number or ready-made templates that can be easily adapted. Finally, "iGrafx Process Central 2003" provides a collaborative environment for workgroups dealing with process management, and is complementary to "iGrafx Process 2003".

Workbench – Holosofx Inc., IBM (www-3.ibm.com)

The American company Holosofx, acquired by IBM in 2002, supplies business process management solutions for process modelling and management. It boasts over 5000 licenses world-wide.

There are two fundamental tools in the package: "Holosofx Workbench", designed for process modelling by means of flowcharts, which provides over fifty different types of analysis, as well as simulation facilities, and "Holosofx Monitor" (Java web-based), which enables the user to retrieve historical data regarding the processes, see the activities involved or in progress, and identify possible bottlenecks.

Pro Vision – Proforma Corp. (www.proformacorp.com)

Located in Michigan (USA), Proforma produces "Pro Vision Modelling Suite", a software package devised to manage processes, and is integrated with a "central data repository". On request, it can be furnished with the E.R.P. developed by J.D. Edwards.

The main tool is "Business*Pro*", compatible with Microsoft products (Word, Excel, PowerPoint, Project, Visio), which consists of over ten "modellers": the models thus generated can also be published on the web.

The user finds a "command centre model inventory", articulated in the principal dimensions of a business: 1) "Strategy modellers – *why*" (to define the objectives and link them to the processes); 2) "Organization modellers – *who*" (to describe the organization structure, the roles and competencies, the customers, suppliers and competitors involved in the processes); 3) "Communication modellers – *where*" (to define the functional specifications of the information system supporting the processes); 4) "Process modellers – *how*" (to define processes and activities); 5) "Workflow modellers – *when*" (to control the scheduling and correctness of the processes); 6) "Data/class modellers – *what*" (to insert the data relative to the processes).

WizdomWorks! – Wizdom System Inc. (www.wizdom.com)

Wizdom System Inc., with headquarters in Illinois (U.S.A.), produces "WizdomWorks!", a B.P.R. software kit, the main tool of which is "ProcessWorks!". Based on the standard IDEF-0 representation at different hierarchic levels, it enables the user to analyse the impact of any change before implementing it ("what-if analysis").

The package also includes separate tools for managing data, standard electronic documents and the Windows interface, as well as "CostWIZard", "TimeWIZard", "QualWIZard", for process performance management in terms of cost, times and quality, respectively.

TurboBPR 2.5 – OSD C3I (www.c3i.osd.mil/bpr/bprcd)

TurboBPR, developed by the "Command, Control, Communication, & Intelligence (C3I)" Office of the United States Department of Defence (DoD) – is a Windows-based tool consisting of five modules: 1) "Strategic Planning" (where mission is developed by defining, in sequence, objectives and performance indicators, linked to strategies); 2) "Operations Analysis" (depicting the hierarchic tree of activities and relative costs); 3) "Initiatives" (improvement plans to connect the two previous fields, i.e. the operative and the strategic ones); 4) "Alternatives" (where costs and performances of different scenarios are compared); 5) "Actuals" (to monitor the actual performances).

3. Knowledge Management in Enterprise Networks

Stefano Tonchia

3.1 Foundations of Knowledge Management

In recent years, the pivotal role of knowledge and, more in general, intangible resources in creating value and competitiveness has been the object of much research (Conner and Prahalad, 1996; Hitt et al., 2001), which can be ascribed to the strategic issues of business "Core Competencies" and "Resource-Based View" (see Paragraph 7.1 for details).

"It is the firm's knowledge, and its ability to generate knowledge, that lies at the core of a more epistemologically sound theory of the firm... knowledge is today the most strategically important of the firm's resources" (Spender, 1996).

The activities involved in the creation and management of *knowledge* are fundamental for the generation and preservation of *competencies* (Leonard-Barton, 1995), and derive from the combination of business "knowledge assets" and "knowledge processes" (Teece, 2000; Schiuma and Marr, 2001). The company should therefore be considered as "a 'repository of knowledge' stored in organizational routines", the latter term being synonymous with competencies, or the ability to manage resources (Edith Penrose, creator of the Resource-Based View, 1959). Business *processes* are the result of these competencies (Teece et al., 1997); some processes are common to the best companies in the field – the so-called "best practices" –, whereas others are distinctive for each firm (Eisenhardt and Martin, 2000).

Knowledge management can thus be associated with the process of transforming "knowledge into value" (a concept echoing the words of the Seventeenth century philosopher Sir Francis Bacon, 1605: "Knowledge itself is power"). Figure 3.1 illustrates its deployment (it is worth specifying that this is an organizational-relational and psycho-social perspective, which should not be confused with the *lever-performance* management approach described in Figure 7.1 or the *input-output* information approach in Figure 1.2).

According to the knowledge-based approach, an enterprise is the environment where specialised knowledge is integrated, knowledge that is possessed by individuals and "dispersed" in them, but which can only be applied *within* an organization (Grant, 1996). Knowledge is "embedded in the 'Ba'" ("Ba", Japanese term originally meaning "place" – Nonaka and Konno, 1998): "the 'Ba' can be considered as a common environment where relationships emerge". This place may be either physical or virtual, but knowledge without a 'Ba' reverts back to being simple pieces of information (which instead can be communicated independently of the 'Ba').

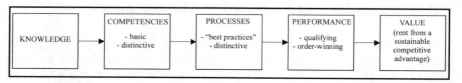

Fig 3.1 From knowledge to value

It must be noted how, "unlike property, labour and capital – which are *private goods* – knowledge is a *common good,* infinitely extensible, the use of which does not depress its use by others" (Spender, 1996).

There exists an ontological problem concerning knowledge: knowing about knowledge implies knowing, and therefore it is impossible to know without possessing knowledge. The problem moves from "know-what" and "know-how" to "know-whom", i.e. who possesses the knowledge, thus creating and developing systems promoting the circulation and diffusion of knowledge (Nahapiet and Ghoshal, 1998).

The solution becomes the interconnection of "distributed knowledge", which spreads beyond the boundaries of the company, extending to the socio-economic and cultural network (Tsoukas, 1996), in an attempt to "reconstruct" knowledge (Becker, 2001).

On the other hand, although necessary, the creation of even the best channels is an insufficient condition to integrate knowledge: what is really needed is the consciousness, motivation and ability to use it: in other terms, an "absorptive capacity" (Cohen and Levinthal, 1990).

Research on Knowledge Management (K.M.) follows two streams:

- The first stream focuses on the research of knowledge itself: *knowledge* is defined as a *purposeful set of information through which an individual selects the most appropriate actions in response to certain external stimuli,* basing the choice on personal principles and beliefs (Davenport and Prusak, 1998). It is fundamental to characterise knowledge as being purposeful: the definition of "actionable or workable information", i.e. information that makes it possible to carry out an action or make a decision (Tiwana, 2000), overcomes the traditional tautology that defines knowledge as "what is known" (O'Dell and Grayson, 1998). Although knowledge is partly based on data and information received from the outside world *(cognitive vision)*, it is the individual who translates these data and information into useful knowledge *(constructive vision)* (Grover and Davenport, 2001). Setting aside the conceptualisation of knowledge – a subject that has fascinated philosophers from Plato to Popper – a classification (taxonomy) of knowledge from an epistemological point of view can be based upon:

- *content*, distinguishing between *declarative knowledge* ("know-what"), *procedural knowledge* ("know-how"), and *causal knowledge* ("know-why") (Zack, 1999),
- *typology*, distinguishing between *explicit* and *tacit knowledge* (the former being more easily codified, whereas the latter is more difficult to formalise and communicate) (Polanyi, 1967),
- *level*, distinguishing between *individual, group, organizational* and *network knowledge,* the latter two referring to the entire company or the business network, respectively (Nonaka, 1991; Nonaka and Takeuchi, 1995).

- The second research field is that focusing on the flow of knowledge, which has defined models and rules for the process of knowledge management (which is also a business process!), and has stressed its dynamic features throughout time, intended as the historical memory of both the individual and the organization (Prahalad and Hamel, 1990; Stalk et al., 1992). Consequently the research in this field concerns:

  - the identification of the different *stages* of knowledge flow. The various steps, not necessarily in this order, are:
    1) *creating/acquiring* knowledge, i.e. the development or the acquisition of new facts and truths gained from the outside world, which replace or update previously possessed beliefs (Makadok, 2001),
    2) *storing/retrieving* knowledge,
    3) *transferring/spreading/sharing* knowledge,
    4) *applying* knowledge, in other words, exploiting it to create value. The source of competitiveness does not reside in the knowledge possessed, but rather in the ability to use it effectively in relation to market dynamics and thus forestall competitors (Eisenhardt and Martin, 2000),

- the identification of the *conditions* within the organization providing a better flow of knowledge. Human relationships, strictly within the boundaries of the enterprise, and "care" for persons are strongly contributing factors (Von Krogh, 1998). Using the term "fair process", Kim and Mauborgne (1997) underline the voluntary nature of co-operation when creating and sharing knowledge: the people involved in the process therefore expect respect for their ideas and understanding for their behaviour.

Some of the most critical factors for knowledge-based strategies are: the definition of flexible learning objectives, the commitment of the top management, the existence of a trustworthy environment, a tolerance to redundance, the presence of a "creative chaos", short-sightedness for performances granting a more immediate profit.

The transfer of knowledge alone is insufficient, and at least two other conditions are necessary for its flow (Grant, 1996): 1) an *appropriate* recipient (giving value to what is received); and 2) an *integration* of knowledge (it is less efficient for two individuals, possessing different knowledge, to "learn" everything from each other than to establish a "way of interacting" by which to integrate each other's knowledge for the benefit of the established purpose). Thus the importance of establishing a *common language*, sharing patterns and benefiting from redundancies to "invade" territories belonging to others (Nonaka and Takeuchi, 1995).

K.M. can therefore be defined as the complex of organizational, managerial, information and communication systems through which an organization takes possession of individual and group knowledge, assimilates it and provides a fertile environment to create new knowledge, transfer and spread it, capitalise on it and incorporate it into products and services, thus making a profit and gaining a competitive advantage throughout time.

Some of the features of K.M. are listed below:

- the consciousness that knowledge resides in persons or at the very most in small groups (Cross and Baird, 2000),
- knowledge is a set of purposeful information,
- knowledge accumulates throughout time,
- knowledge circulates at an organizational level, and can be endorsed and coordinated through "communication",
- digital technologies can play a fundamental role in retrieving, storing, transferring and spreading explicit knowledge (Hansen et al., 1999;

Alavi and Leidner, 2001), as proved by the fact that although intellectual assets were fundamental for the industrial revolution, it was only in the Nineties – with the advent of I.C.T. (Information & Communication Technologies) – that companies have gained consciousness of K.M. ("the revolution in I.C.T. makes knowledge the new competitive resource" – Webber in "Harvard Business Review", 1993),

- the differentiating competitive value embedded in tacit knowledge makes information systems an important but not exhaustive component (McDermott, 1999),
- in most cases, new knowledge is created on the "borderline" of old knowledge (Wenger and Snyder, 2000) and thus in an incremental manner (it is the output of a learning process). New knowledge derives from combining, comparing and synthesising previously possessed knowledge, both in an explicit or tacit manner (embedded in the person's experience and ability).

One of the more stringent problems concerning K.M. is the *measurement of knowledge,* or the assessment of intellectual capital. A variety of "knowledge assets maps" have been proposed, the most famous of which is probably Edvinsson's (1997 – Figure 3.2). The market value of a company is given by its "shareholders' equity financial value" and its "intellectual capital", which includes both the "human capital" (which is not property of the company, but is "rented") and the "structural capital"; the latter comprises both "environmental knowledge (relative to customers, suppliers, competitors, institutions, etc.) and "organizational knowledge" regarding the organization, its technology and way of operating (both routine and innovation processes). With our type of elaboration, intellectual property (such as patents, trademarks, etc.) is included in the balance assets together with tangible assets (infrastructure) and financial ones (monetary investments).

Given these dichotomies, certain authors prefer to distinguish between *Intellectual Capital Management (I.C.M.),* having a more strategic and managerial perspective, and *Knowledge Management (K.M.),* more operational and instrumental, aimed at planning, executing and monitoring initiatives inherent to knowledge management.

The measurement of knowledge and, in general, knowledge management, can be ascribed to one of the four dimensions of Kaplan and Norton's "balance scorecard" (1992), i.e. that relative to learning/growth. On the other hand, the other dimensions – financial, customer satisfaction, and internal processes – would be related to the practices of Budgeting/Cost Management, Customer Relationship Management, and Business Process Reengineering, respectively (www.balancescorecard.org). The definition of Business Process Reengineering given in this book is vaster, including both Supply Chain Management (for internal processes) and Customer Relationship Management.

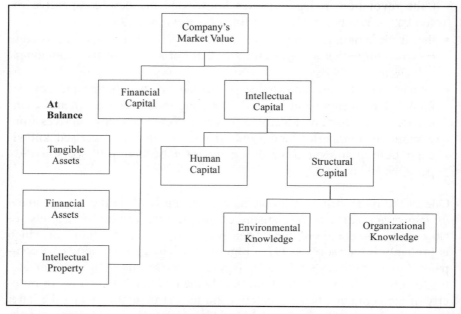

Fig 3.2 A "knowledge assets map" (modified from: Edvinsson, 1997)

3.2   Knowledge, Competencies and Process Management

From the position of the processes depicted in Figure 3.1, it is clear that *process management* is fundamental for the exploitation of business competencies. From an organizational-relational perspective, competencies become part of the process (which instead, from a material & information perspective, transforms inputs into outputs, by using resources). Setting aside the technological-infrastructural factors, the output of a process therefore depends on competencies, which can be distinguished as *individual* or *organizational* (Figure 3.3).

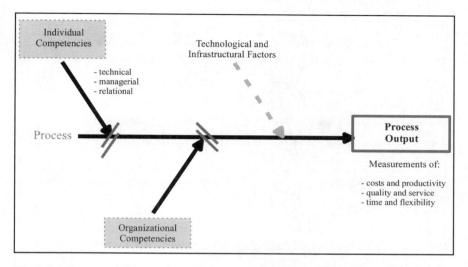

Fig 3.3 The organizational-relational approach to Process Management

What clearly emerges is the importance to *"map" competencies* when implementing process management (Figure 2.3). The changes derived concern the entire management of the human resources, to the extent of describing it as a "competency-based model" (competencies associated with jobs or tasks aimed at determined objectives – Spencer and Spencer, 1993). Mapping is mostly relative to individual competencies or *skills*, since – as mentioned previously – in general, organizational competencies can be mainly ascribed to strategic planning rather than human resource management.

Many attempts have been made to translate this concept into concrete measurement instruments, which would then be followed by interventions aimed at coaching and teaching the human resources. The company Eupragma (www.eupragma.com) has developed a specific software, called "competension" ("tension" towards "competence" + "competition"), an example of which is shown in Figure 3.4.

Name and position: XXXXXXX YYYYYYY (ZZZZ ZZ ZZZZZZZZZZ)	Wei-ght	Competence Evaluation	Actual Point	Target Point	Actual Weighted Evaluation	Target Weighted Evaluation	Target-Actual Gap	Notes on Development Objectives
TECHNICAL Competencies	30				15,0	23,2	35,3%	
Product competence	5	1 2 3 4 5	2	4	2,0	4,0	50,0%	
Production process competence	8	1 2 3 4 5	3	4	4,8	6,4	25,0%	
Control criteria knowledge	7	1 2 3 4 5	3	4	4,2	5,6	25,0%	
Stock mngt criteria knowledge	4	1 2 3 4 5	2	3	1,6	2,4	33,3%	
Information system knowledge	6	1 2 3 4 5	2	4	2,4	4,8	50,0%	
MANAGERIAL Competencies	40				20,6	30,8	33,1%	
Entreprenuership	7	1 2 3 4 5	4	4	5,6	5,6	0,0%	
Management-by-objectives	8	1 2 3 4 5	3	4	4,8	6,4	25,0%	
Planning ability	10	1 2 3 4 5	3	4	6,0	8,0	25,0%	
Problem solving ability	6	1 2 3 4 5	2	3	2,4	3,6	33,3%	
Change proactiveness	9	1 2 3 4 5	1	4	1,8	7,2	75,0%	
RELATIONAL Competencies	40				13,4	23,2	42,2%	
Leadership	5	1 2 3 4 5	2	4	2,0	4,0	50,0%	
Team working	8	1 2 3 4 5	2	4	3,2	6,4	50,0%	
Communication	7	1 2 3 4 5	3	4	4,2	5,6	25,0%	
Negotiation	4	1 2 3 4 5	2	3	1,6	2,4	33,3%	
Emotional control	6	1 2 3 4 5	2	4	2,4	4,8	50,0%	
				tot.	49,0	77,2	36,5%	

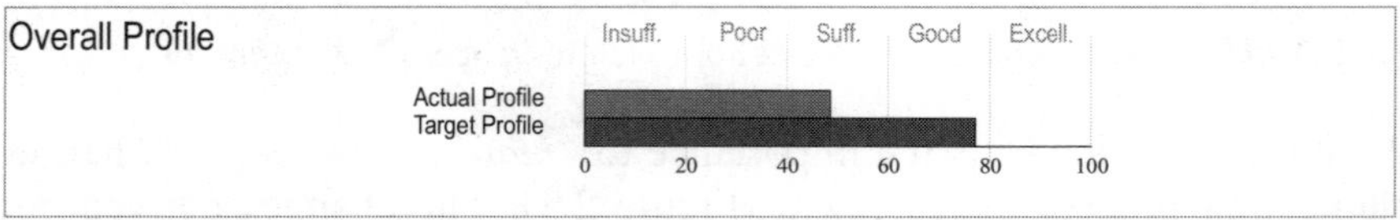

Overall Profile

Insuff.   Poor   Suff.   Good   Excell.

Actual Profile
Target Profile

0   20   40   60   80   100

Fig 3.4 An example of "Map of Competencies"

As mentioned previously, process management is based on two critical concepts: that of *internal customer* and that of *process ownership* (embodied by the entrepreneurial employee).

The latter concept can be extended to knowledge management: "knowledge-based economy" requires a new type of manager, who is capable of sharing ideas and experience throughout the entire company ("process owner") while remaining in charge of the organizational units or functions. These sort of managers have been termed "T-shaped managers" by Hansen and von Oetinger (2001), as they play both a transversal role (symbolised by the horizontal bar of the letter "T") and a hierarchic or vertical one (the upright bar of the letter "T"). The critical role of the "process owner" emerges clearly in "knowledge enterprises" (den Hertog and Huizenga, 2000), where hierarchy or authority cannot fully direct inputs to obtain the desired outputs, as these processes are substantially based upon knowledge.

In the new economy, the top managers must be able to evolve from "directors analytically guided by strategy to contextualizers of person-oriented strategies", not only by directing the activities of the persons towards strategic objectives, but also by "injecting motivation into their efforts and creating a community to which they are proud to belong" (Bartlett and Ghoshal, 2002). This considerable change derives from the fact that knowledge cannot only be accumulated at the top, and then distributed downwards, but resides at all levels and is embedded in all intra-enterprise relationships. Strategy also evolves, passing from the Porter-type, characterized by "zero sum" competition (favourable product/market positions with respect to competitors) to a resource-based strategy (where, by means of competencies, value creation prevails over value appropriation), to a knowledge-based one (where zero sum disappears, as knowledge increases by use). According to Bartlett and Ghoshal, this new type of competition can be seen as that of *talents and dreams* (Table 3.1).

This change however does not only concern top managers and their "art of managing the talent of people" (one of the definitions of "leadership"), but all the employees, through their ability to build up a team and cooperate ("team working").

The other key concept of process management, namely that of internal customer (besides that of external customer) must also be organised in the sphere of knowledge-based strategies. Process mangement thus focuses on the transformation of virtual inputs (information) into outputs, and is strongly oriented towards the goal or target of customer satisfaction: knowledge can be defined – as mentioned previously – as purposeful information.

The customer-supplier links, i.e. links of purposeful information, are such that knowledge management occurs in a context of *knowledge network, internal* when occurring along the internal customer-supplier links, and *external* by means of inter-firm networks.

Table 3.1 Knowledge Management and strategies (Bartlett and Ghoshal, 2002)

	Competition for products and markets	Competition for resources / competencies	Competition for "talent and dreams"
Strategic Objective	Defensible product-market positions	Sustainable competitive advantage	Continuous self-renewal
Major Tools	Industry analysis, Market segmentation, Strategic planning	Core competencies, Resource-based strategy	Vision and values, Front-line entrepreneurship, Network
Key Strategic Resource	Financial capital	Organizational capability	Human and intellectual capital
Employees viewed as	Factors of production	Valuable resources	"Talent investors"
HR's Role in Strategy	Implementation and support	Contributory	Central
Key HR Activity	Recruitment and training	Aligning resources / competencies to achieve strategic intent	Building human capital

3.3   Process Management and Enterprise Networks: The Extended Management of Knowledge

Enterprise or inter-firm networks are one of the topical issues of economy and organization (Aoki, 1984; Nohria and Eccles, 1992; Grandori, 2001 and 2003). The terms "enterprise/inter-firm network", and "network governance", are preferable to "network organization", as many, either implicitly or explicitly, define "organization" as a single entity (Jones et al., 1997).

The traditional perspective held by Organizational Economics (Williamson, 1975), supports cooperation between enterprises (even when differing in the objectives, behaviors and information possessed) when profits, with respect to mere market transactions, increase for all the companies involved (profits deriving from reductions in transaction costs, greater efficiency, synergies or scope economies, reduced costs of flexibility, complementary tangible assets, risk sharing, etc.). Enterprise networks would therefore be a compromise between "governance" choices that place the enterprise and its hierarchy at one end, and the market and its rules at the other: in the "inter-firm network" – or "enterprise network" – there is reduced autonomy and greater coordination than in companies operating in a context of pure market that is in full competition; the network can be informal (as in industrial districts, with "flexible specialisation" – Piore and Sabel, 1984) or formal.

Coordination is one of the most salient and variable aspects of networks (Kogut and Zander, 1996; Nassimbeni, 1998): it can be implicit, intentionally distributed, headed by the leading enterprise, or have the features of a "near-enterprise". The network itself is not static, but can evolve from a series of mainly social relationships to a more consciously and intentionally-managed form, once the costs and benefits have been formalised (Hite and Hesterly, 2001).

The bonds between the members of the network thus become stable and strategically important ("strategic networks" – Dyer 1997; Dyer and Singh, 1998; Gulati et al., 2000).

Among the various types of enterprise network, the following deserve mention:

- *supply networks*, where relationships are determined – as the name suggests – by flows of materials. Among the various supply networks, it is possible to distinguish between those where a "main contractor" (generally a large enterprise), oriented towards outsourcing, governs a large number of suppliers and sub-contractors, and "supply chain" networks (where one dimension prevails, along which there is a specialisation by stage),

- *agreements, alliances, temporary aggregations* between enterprises, where the integration mostly revolves around common strategies and functional synergies (e.g. commercial ones) or risk sharing and financial commitment ("joint-ventures"), rather than operational features,
- *industrial districts*, industrial systems located in a circumscribed territory, generally providing a certain category of goods (with companies specialising in the production of components or process phases); one or a few companies ("hub firms") may be pivotal for all the others and the district can operate on the global market like a corporation,
- *extended and virtual enterprises* (explained in detail in the following Paragraph).

In the framework of competition increasingly based on knowledge, a further step forward could consist in cooperation aimed at integrating competencies, which is not necessarily supported in the short term by economic reasons (Inkpen, 1996; Combs and Ketchen, 1999).

Such an integration of competencies, aimed at *creating a system*, should not be seen as an "addendum" of competencies, but rather as "learning-by-interacting", with a synergic effect on performances (i.e. the overall result is greater than the sum of the single results). This can be defined as a "relational ability", a distinctive organizational competency that confirms how enterprise networks can be deliberately devised and conformed (Lorenzoni and Lipparini, 1999) and become part of global competition starting from local scenarios (Kanter, 1997).

K.M., originally developed in an intra-firm perspective, has evolved in recent years, and now mostly consists in the *extended* management of knowledge, involving systems or networks of enterprises (inter-organizational perspective). A company alone is in fact unlikely to possess all the necessary knowledge to face the current competitive market, as the risks and costs are often too high (Quintas et al., 1997).

To be more precise, process management and relative K.M. should be considered from an *extended enterprise* viewpoint. In this case, however, K.M. would not only reflect on the company's internal processes, but also on others, such as: 1) partnership with suppliers and customers 2) outsourcing of supporting processes, 3) agreements and strategic alliances, 4) supply-chain integrations. According to Lee et al. (2001) the intensity of the *external networks* can be measured on the: *partnership networks* (strategic alliances with other enterprises, collaboration with universities and research centres in general, joint ventures and venture capital initiatives) and *sponsorship networks* (financial and services support by banks, trade associations and public boards).

In this connection, it is interesting to note the analogy existing nowadays between an entrepreneur or manager, endowed with all the relationship skill needed for his job, and a company: "The new large successful enterprise can be better conceived as a manager able to create new ventures within a network" (in the words of management guru Tom Peters).

The subtitle of one of the most visionary books on management published in recent years – "5th Generation Management" by Charles Savage – summarises effectively all these considerations: "Co-Creating through Virtual Enterprising, Dynamic Teaming and Knowledge Networking". Thanks to the new technologies, the enterprise can extend beyond its actual boundaries ("extended/virtual enterprise" – see following Paragraph); the traditional value chain becomes an extremely dynamic environment where interpersonal team relationships emerge, and extend outwards in knowledge networks: "Knowledge networking is the process of combining and recombining one another's knowledge, experiences, talents, skills, capabilities, and aspirations in ever-changing, profitable patterns" (Savage, 1996).

These theses are also supported in the framework of the *complexity theory* applied to management and enterprises (Stacey, 1995; Senge, 1990), according to which "the strategic success is a function of a firm's talent for thriving in dynamic nonlinear or chaotic systems, that rely on network feedback and emergent relationships... a blend of competition and cooperation ... a dynamic tension embedded between various actors and processes, as well as between a firm and its context" (Lengnick-Hall and Wolff, 1999).

Consequently any attempt to measure the value of a company beyond mere financial aspects must take the role of *communities* and *location* into account, and in general what is known as the "social capital": "social capital was originally used in community studies to describe relational resources embedded in personal ties in the community" (Yli-Renko et al., 2001).

If on one hand it is true that knowledge resides in single persons as a "sticky residue of insight about using information and experience to think", it is equally true that "it flows through professional communities ... the core of knowledge is a community in discourse, sharing ideas ... to leverage knowledge we need to focus on the community that owns it and the people who use it ... finding, nurturing and supporting the communities that already share knowledge about key topics ... it is the communities that spread cultural change" (McDermott, 1999).

Consequently, a revolution in innovation science is taking place, the first real "leap forward" since the classic theory of innovation (Schumpeter, 1934) linked to products and production or service processes developed within a circumscribed "locus": communities arise which "distribute innovation", thus the importance of integrating analysis with a sociological approach (Sawhney and Prandelli, 2000). The management of "distributed intelligence systems", where learning and training play a fundamental role, represents a new challenge for the world of business management.

3.4   Organizational and ICT Networks: The Extended Enterprise

The advent and continuous evolution of Information and Communication Technologies (I.C.T.), together with changes in inter-firm competition/cooperation (defined as *"co-opetition"* by Afuah, 2000), have given rise to an increasingly resourceful field of scientific research: *digital economy*. Indeed, according to Boisot (1999), the neoclassical production function "Capital versus Labour" would be replaced in the New Economy by the evolutionary "Information versus Material" production function.

Innovation follows new rules: relational networks, supported by new technologies, have created an *e-culture* that will play an increasingly predominant role in our work- and life-style, and will also influence creativity, laying the foundations for an "intellectual revolution" that will change the face of organizations (Kanter, 2001).

Indeed, e-Business models have a strong impact on strategic planning (see special issue of IJBPM – editor Tonchia, 2002): the customers and channels precede and draw the definition/reengineering of internal processes (Kalakota and Robinson, 1999) affecting, to different extents, both New Economy enterprises (also termed "dotcoms" or "pure players") quoted on the Nasdaq stock exchange, and traditional enterprises (Porter, 2001) that consider the web technology a unique strategic tool for interacting and integrating with other manufacturers on the market (Armstrong and Hagel, 1996). Proof of the revolutionary potential of new web technologies is that both entrepreneurship and strategy research flow into e-Business studies (Amit and Zott, 2001).

Be it B2B (Business-to-Business) or B2C (Business-to-Consumer), the traditional value chain changes dramatically, and the most remarkable consequence is the reduced number of intermediaries. At the same time, a reconstruction of the value network takes place, with new environments / actors such as the "cybermall" (or "e-marketplace"), i.e. horizontal (general) or vertical (sectorial) virtual markets (Benjamin and Wigand, 1995), or enterprises that through the web, take on the role of "network coordinator" (as described in the following pages, when explaining the concept of "extended enterprise").

At present, the strongest impact of web technology is on B2B, i.e. interfirm relationships, and on management processes inside the enterprise (B2E – Business-to-Employees). Web technology affects business efficiency, providing lower transaction and control costs, which in the past only occurred in long-established and consolidated relationships of partnership, but are now available independently of these (Bartezzaghi and Ronchi, 2002, when referring to the market outlets, maintain that the low switching costs assured by the Internet now provide the opportunity to build short-term relationships with the trading partners).

Web-based information technology provides on one hand more efficient communication and transactions, and on the other a tool to codify and formalise at least part of the relational and cognitive heritage of network enterprise. Therefore, in the short term, new technologies represent an operative opportunity, while in the long term they provide a strategic opportunity, since the distinctive capacities of these companies rely on specific competencies and knowledge acquired over time.

In order to fully exploit a web-based organizational system, it is necessary to implement processes for the management and circulation of information and knowledge; the new web-communication digital technologies can apply this model, implementing shared knowledge systems and providing an optimal tool for data, information and knowledge management (Bolisani and Scarso, 1999).

Digital economy expands and re-articulates the cognitive system of the industrial society, generating economic value though the extensive use of new knowledge and competencies, nurturing the cognitive potential, and giving rise to a cumulative evolution. Meanwhile, however, the average level of complexity increases, meaning by *complexity* (of a problem, a situation, an action) the sum of variance, uncertainty and entropic disorder: complexity, from a cognitive point of view, is the opposite of knowledge. New technologies can be used to limit the variance (by an effective and efficient transferral of knowledge), uncertainty (by codifying the range of possible events) and entropy (generating order from disorder while allowing ample space for creativity). These technologies, when used in the framework of organizational networks, give rise to relationship systems or cognitive networks that can be exploited to replicate efficient solutions ("replication economies", by sharing cognitive work, more extended geographically and more intense instrumentally), select and manage different actors ("flexibility and differentiation economies"), and produce value through creative actions ("exploration economies") (Rullani, 1997). The web is both a neat world of information and a system "out of control", the latter feature being the main key to its potential.

Unlike a computerised factory (endowed with E.D.I. – Electronic Data Interchange, "groupware" such as Lotus Notes, and dedicated networks), the web-based virtual factory is both easily and safely accessible to partners. Moreover, its members can: 1) establish different stages of partnership; 2) possess different computer-based information systems; 3) share information at different levels (Upton and McAfee, 1996). Such languages as XML can produce hypertext interfaces independently of the connected computer systems.

I.C.T.s provide a formidable tool for implementing process management, and its internal and external "organizational networks" (Fisher, 2000); particularly useful in this sense are the following information networks (Watson et al., 2000):

- *Internet*, the public net par excellence, "a reservoir of customers",
- *Extranet*, connecting computers of different organizations (suppliers, customers, other partners),
- *Intranet*, connecting computers of the different organizational units within the same company (spread out in different branches and locations).

The list should also include *knowledge warehouses* or *repositories* and the *Decision Support Systems (D.S.S.)* exploiting them. In particular, data can be extracted by using OLAP and Data-Mining D.S.S.s (intersecting them in n-dimensions – "hypercube" – and exploding them on various levels – "drilling down"), which also show relationships and predictive models (through dynamic simulations and statistical techniques).

The term *Business Intelligence (B.I.)* was coined to describe the integration of these systems with web-based technologies, the most distinctive feature of which is accessibility through "web portals" (unlike traditional D.S.S.s, which are desktop-, or at the very most enterprise-accessible, although only on dedicated networks with non web-based protocols, i.e. non TCP/IP). The term refers to all the "knowledge workers" in the company, and is not only limited to the managers as in the case of D.S.S. (www.cherrytreeco.com). B.I. can be therefore defined as "business knowledge acquired through the use of various hardware/software technologies enabling the organizations to turn data into information... the value of information integrated *throughout* the entire enterprise" (www.dmreview.com). This decisive *transversal* characterisation makes

B.I. an essential instrument for implementing process management: there is a single business data-base, accessible to all although filtered, and information is readily spread and so turns into knowledge. It is thus possible to "analyse and manage every aspect of business across the entire value chain (the processes!), including external relationships with partners and customers" (www.sap.com/solutions/bi).

B.I. also supports the evolution of tactical and operational planning and control systems (E.R.P. – Enterprise Resource Planning – Paragraph 6.2) from a strategic and decision-making viewpoint, leading towards an integrated management of different organizational units, even when juridically distinct. These *evolved, extended* or *second-generation E.R.P.s.* (also known as N.E.R.P. – Networked Enterprise Resource Planning or E.E.R.P. – Extended Enterprise Resource Planning: see list of websites in the References) combine E.R.P. logics with web technologies. The result is inter-firm effectiveness in managing flows of materials following orders or forecasts, the productive and distributive capacity of the various units, and that of integrated services. They must concretise operative models that are *flexible*, so as to adapt them to different network configurations, in terms of roles and relationships between the nodes, *scalable*, as they must integrate nodes of different types, and *decentralised*, so as to respect the autonomy and viewpoint of each node.

Remote or collaborative planning and control ensured by N.E.R.P. (or E.E.R.P.) systems require an analytical sharing of business, an overall strategic planning (business plan and budget), a balanced scorecard for performance measurement, simulation of predictive and proactive hypotheses, and in general mechanisms which are more oriented towards dialogue than transactions, all typical features of B.I. instruments.

As mentioned previously, process management and relative K.M. should be considered in a framework of *Extended Enterprise (E.E.)*. This is now possible thanks to the new web-based technologies (TCP/IP): Intranet, Extranet and Internet aid and multiply the organizational networks established inside the traditional boundaries of the company, including departments, factories, branches and subsidiaries (as provided by the concept of "internal customer"), and the external organizational networks (deriving from: 1. "co-opetition" with other subjects, such as suppliers, subcontractors, shipping companies, agents, retailers, other manufacturers and business partners; 2. information and support networks set up by trade associations, consulting companies, public boards; 3. closer relationships with the final customer).

An extended enterprise is therefore a company that *extends its boundaries outwards,* by setting up a collaborative network with others: the new technologies thus provide an environment where transactions occur and, more important, knowledge (information aimed at creating value for the final customer) is shared and increased.

Figure 3.5 develops the concept of extended enterprise, showing who is typically involved and the information networks used.

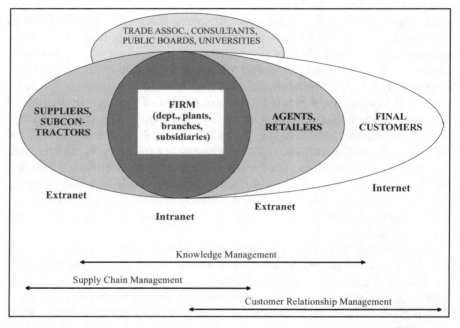

Fig 3.5 The Extended Enterprise

The term *"Extended Enterprise"* was probably coined in Chrysler ("suppliers, producers and distributors acting in tune…"). During the IFIP (International Federation of Informational Processing) Conference held in Ascona, Switzerland, in 1997 (Buchel and Schonsleben, 1998), it was observed that production management is no longer confined to individual production facilities, and extended enterprise can be seen as a combination of cooperation between enterprises and supply chain management. Two factors have led to the concept of extended enterprise: 1) increasingly specialised enterprises focus on their core competencies, outsourcing all other activities, and 2) globalisation, brought about by new technologies, has intensified the range of choice among collaborating enterprises.

The *collaborative advantage*, consequence of the extended enterprise, is the new frontier of business competitive advantage, for too long considered and investigated within the boundaries of the company or too generally ascribed to global business networks (Dyer, 2000).

The extended enterprise is both the protagonist and stimulator of market *globalisation*. Global economy does not merely coincide with a flow of goods (international trade has existed for centuries), but rather as a flow of capital, persons and information; the computer world-wide web has pulled down the space-time barriers, allowing instantaneous transactions and access to a planetary market (Kanter, 2000). Boyson et al. (1999) underline the aspect of a global supply chain.

Connectiveness (fastness and reduction in distances) and *open system* are the typical features of e-Business technology: when combined with extended enterprise strategies, namely network and process knowledge management, they become the tools providing greater value to the customer at lower costs, thanks to the enterprises' timeliness, flexibility and quality (Tonchia, 2002).

Following the creation of extended enterprises, the traditional value chain (typically streamline, extending from suppliers to customers – Porter, 1985) undergoes a radical change: the extended enterprise becomes the "network coordinator" for all the activities required. It is important to underline how the extended enterprise can hold a predominant position with respect to the others (interpreting the famous *principal-agent* theory, according to which the "principal" is the owner of the transaction and employs "agents" for specific operations), although this is not always the case: the various members of the network may in fact all act as extended enterprises.

The most remarkable aspect is therefore the *reconfiguration* of roles and relationships among the various actors (internal ones, as well as suppliers, customers, partners in general, etc.), and the presence of new supporting subjects ("providers", "infomediaries", "e-content consultants", etc. – Hagel and Rayport, 1997). The result is an evolution *from a value chain to a value constellation* (Normann and Ramirez, 1993).

At times, in particular in B2B, the relationship between supplier and customer becomes so strong, personal and interactive, that the latter is often termed "prosumer" (a combination of "producer" and "consumer"), to underline the strong influence exercised on the production of goods (Tapscott, 2000).

The concept of Extended Enterprise (E.E.) must not be confused with that of *Virtual Enterprise (V.E.)*, although the two terms are often used indifferently both in literature and in practice. The virtual enterprise can be defined as a temporary venture of enterprises, usually small or medium-sized and geographically far apart (Presley and Liles, 2001): a virtual enterprise has a virtual organization that *does not belong to any of the member enterprises,* but acts as a broker, namely allowing businesses to meet and establish relationships and possibly offering supporting services (Camarinha-Matos and Asarmanesh, 1999; Burn et al., 2001).

Conversely, in the extended enterprise, the organization remains within the boundaries of the enterprise, and in the absence of a leading enterprise, each firm acts as an extended enterprise.

Because of the dynamics and transitoriness of the bonds, it is possible to classify a virtual enterprise in the framework of "agile manufacturing" (Duguay et al., 1997; Goranson, 1999) and/or "hyper-competition" (D'Aveni, 1994). The lack of a proper owner organization makes it a "hollow company", which is mostly trade-oriented (managing at one end the demand and at the other the supply of competencies and production facilities required).

A virtual enterprise is therefore similar to an e-marketplace – that is a subject of e-Commerce – which can also be shared by the network enterprises. Alternatively, there is a "federate model" but always with a leading member who solves the problems of authority and decisional autonomy of the different nodes. In other terms, if the virtual enterprise is like a multi-centred nervous system ("heterarchy" or "virtual cluster" – Hedlund, 1986), where is the "brain" and how can it be "decentralised"?

Virtual enterprises can also be considered from a different viewpoint, taking into account the goods exchanged. In alternative to the Porter's material value-chain, there is a "virtual value chain" based on information (Rayport and Sviokla, 1995); the strategic and managerial principles of enterprises belonging to the "information-based" sectors (i.e. show-business, publishing, software, and financial companies) are based on this type of value chain (Shapiro and Varian, 1998).

According to Venkatraman and Henderson (1998), the virtual organization is at an evolutionary stage characterised by having the inter-organization as "locus", a virtual encounter with the customers, virtual sourcing (as regards the assets) and virtual expertise (leverage on knowledge). These factors determine: 1) customer communities, 2) coalitions of resources, 3) expertise communities. Moreover, the global performance objective moves from ROI (Return On Investment) to EVA (Economic Value Added) and MVA (Market Value Added) (www.sternstewart.com).

In short, the e-Business revolution has led on one hand to the creation of "New Market" enterprises (occupying increasingly larger spaces, although it is still unclear how and when) and on the other hand to the evolution of traditional firms into Extended Enterprises (a potential scenario, that will however follow definite and to some extent compulsory pathways – as described in Part Three of this book).

Finally, the Extended Enterprise consists of an information and organization network, extending inside and outside the company's boundaries, and is at the same time an operative network (delivering products or services) and a "community of practices" (whose members learn and develop skills by exchanging knowledge – Knowledge-Extended Enterprise). This viewpoint introduces the management paradox of the near future: a learning community is informal, self-disciplined and cannot be forced in its ways and times, but like a garden, it needs supervision in order to blossom (Wenger and Snyder, 2000)

Part Two

The BPR Project and the Processes

4   The Business Process Reengineering Project: A Successful Case Study

Edi Snaidero[1] and Andrea Tramontano

4.1   A Product-Oriented Company Opts to Become Customer-Oriented

It is rather difficult to relate a successful case study after months spent in the fore front, initially nurturing an idea then a project and eventually developing a new way of *doing and being in business*. One of the risks here is to boast or, even worse, to give a detailed account of what should have been achieved and yet remained in paper.

Well aware of this danger, we will try to analyse the context, guidelines, methodologies and phases of this transition project just like an outsider visiting the company would try to convey this information, in a straightforward and practical way, to someone currently implementing or about to embark on a similar project.

It is not unusual for outsiders, consultants, and managers of other companies, etc. visiting our company to ask us how we succeeded in achieving what in most cases remains confined to theory.

Usually there is not just one answer, but rather several hypotheses, which may later become elements of a successful BPR project, such as:

- the absolute need to implement change due to the company's actual development phase,
- the liberal interpretation of theoretical models, as applied and adapted to a business entity and not the other way around,
- an *enlightened* entrepreneur who is himself in the forefront promoting change,
- a team of people who are by nature self-responsible and co-operative,
- a company which is neither too big nor too small,
- a company which is innovative and endowed with a strong will to be in the lead.

Some of the above points are strictly related to the context within which the project developed therefore, introducing Snaidero and its Group is un-

---

[1] CEO of Snaidero Group

doubtedly the best way to start explaining how theory merged with the *hard business reality* in their specific case.

First of all, we would like to highlight some features common to Snaidero (Table 4.1) and many other Italian companies, which make the company representative of a wider industrial fabric. This is undoubtedly of interest to those attempting to make a comparison with their own businesses.

Some of the reasons which led the company to implement change and therefore to get reorganised are to be found in the evolution of both Snaidero and the markets in which it operates.

Modular kitchens, along with many other durable and semi-durable goods, became part of the life of Italians in the '60s, at the beginning of the economic boom. This period witnessed the development of the Italian furniture industry and marked the transition from traditionally handcrafted to manufactured furniture. Rino Snaidero recognised the potential scope of this new business sector and in a few years became, just like other well-known entrepreneurs heading companies such as Salvarani, Scic, Patriarca, Cumini etc., a point a reference and a guide in the field.

In that period, companies paid attention to product quality (manufactured items were meant to replace the traditional *sturdy* handcrafted furniture) but their efforts were mostly directed to producing on a large scale in order to satisfy a strong domestic demand for goods which, at the time, were looked upon as status symbols.

Clearly, Snaidero and other companies operating in the same business sector changed their production strategies and became more product-oriented, by designing and producing kitchens suitable for mass production.

Time passes, things change and so do the needs of the Italians. Once the first wave of modular kitchens was over and many of the Italian homes had been fitted with this new type of kitchens, with the onset of the '80s a new consumption pattern emerged. Customers became more selective and started asking for more geometric products and a wider range of materials and colours. Thus, even if a company was able to manufacture kitchens it might have been unable to sell them unless it offered a large assortment of products in many versions or, where required, even customised off-catalogue products. In other words, kitchens too were not immune to *mass customisation*. Whereas some new manufacturers (especially companies in the Pesaro area, such as Scavolini and Berloni) perceived this market change as an extraordinary opportunity, for many others already operating on the market it represented a threat. As a result, old hierarchies were overthrown and almost all former market leaders disappeared from the scene, except Snaidero which, in the meantime, had wisely carried out a diversi-

Table 4.1   Snaidero's key features

GENERAL FEATURES	PECULIARITIES OF SNAIDERO R. S.P.A.
Medium sized, both in terms of turnover and employees	Approximately € 310 million turnover and 2,000 employees as at 31 December 2003
Industry-niche leader	The company produces for the medium-high market segment and often cooperates with internationally acclaimed architects and designers such as Gae Aulenti and Pininfarina
Manufacturing distinctive and high-quality products according to the *"made in Italy" design*	Established in 1946, it became first a manufacturing concern in just over a decade (late '50s) then an international company (early '70s) and finally a European group ('90s) with sales offices and production sites in Italy, Germany and France
A long-established company dating back to the end of the Second World War	Established in 1946, it became first a manufacturing concern in just over a decade (late '50s) then an international company(early '70s) and finally a European group ('90s) with sales offices and production sites in Italy, Germany and France
Initially just a work-shop, it then developed into a manufacturing concern thanks to the drive of the entrepreneur-founder	Rino Snaidero is certainly one of those entrepreneurs who have linked their businesses and names with growing entities which have later grown into industrial groups, especially in the North-East of Italy
Second generation management, but with an entrepreneur and a family still behind	Edi Snaidero is the Managing Director and ownership is still in the hands of a family-owned holding company, though the plan is for the company to be listed on the Stock Exchange in the near future
Well-known brand as Snaidero is a long-established company	Approximately 67% of Italians know Snaidero brand
Natural propensity to export	It started exporting in the late'70s and has done so ever since. In the '90s it started expanding internationally (Germany, France and Austria) by pursuing a strategy of acquiring brands and plants designed to enhance local market penetration

fication of its distribution channels becoming the forerunner of the Italian furniture export.

In the years which followed, the above trends became more and more accentuated, and customer-oriented marketing strategies became an absolute *must*. Leading furniture companies became extremely sensitive to the taste and lifestyle of consumers, and where possible, attempted to anticipate them by offering new products and customisations and, in particular, new ancillary services related to the purchase and use of modular kitchens.

The change from the product-oriented to the customer-oriented marketing strategy, which affected nearly every line of product at different points in time, did not spare Snaidero's business sector. Nevertheless some questions are likely to be raised:

- Can a company respond to a much different competitive environment and be effective without changing or questioning its fundamentals, that is its management?
- Can it meet its customers' requirements by maintaining the same organisational structure?
- Is company personnel ready and prepared to face this new competition?

The answer is always no. Or at least we believe that being really *customer-oriented* (as long as this remains simply a slogan) would be very difficult without changing the company's organisation and mentality.

That is the reason why we opted for a complete and radical change. This was implemented through a BPR which involved restating our company mission, clarifying our strategy and, in the immediate period, introducing a new type of organisation.

4.2   Basic Principles of the Reorganisation Carried out in Snaidero R. S.p.A.[2]

As we shall illustrate later on, the reorganisation developed, from a *technical* point of view, through project phases during which new methods and tools were introduced, both at strategic and operational level.

However, at this point it is worth noting that, regardless of the project's *technical* success, an even more important one was obtained in terms of a

---

[2] S.p.A. is the acronym for Società per Azioni and stands for Ltd company

new company's mentality. The latter, which embodies some basic principles, which we shall highlight in this paragraph (see also Figure 4.1 – where each box lists the sub-paragraphs which follow) is also the best response to the opportunities/threats of the present business context. Acquiring and accepting this new company's mentality and making use of it while expediting daily activities is in itself a significant competitive advantage and becomes the utmost objective of the reorganisation project.

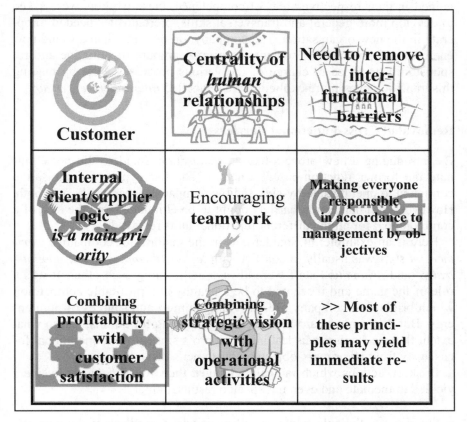

Fig 4.1 Process basic principles in Snaidero

The Centrality of the Human Factor

It is not by chance that our starting point will be the centrality of the human factor. Snaidero has long since realised that any company comprises of several *assets*, most of which (warehouses, machinery, computers etc.)

can be acquired at a set price. However, there is something very special which cannot be bought and that is know-how, i.e. knowledge, skills and experience gained by the people working in the company. The safeguarding, development and improvement of this *asset* becomes one of the keystones of company success. To Snaidero, the introduction of a process-based organisation represented a fantastic opportunity to confirm and reinforce the pivotal role played by its *knowledge workers* relative to all the company's development strategies. In addition to the consolidated skills gained in their respective areas of competence, these workers were asked to develop more general and transversal skills, prerequisites needed to operate in the new organisation. The company, on the other hand, found new energies and potentials by delegating a great amount of initiative and responsibility to those in charge of the various processes who, by making this transition even more explicit, were relabelled *internal entrepreneurs*.

Removal of Cross-Functional Barriers

By introducing a new process-based organisation Snaidero did not eliminate the former function-based structure. The two types of organisation continued to operate side-by-side and the company reaped the best of both. However, communication barriers ought to be eliminated and the lack of a common goal for all the different functional units resolved.

Here is an example: in Snaidero, as in the majority of companies, *commercial* staff was usually in conflict with *technical employees*, or *administrative* and *production* staff were always confronting each other. It was a rule of the game and it seemed to be a healthy and profitable competition which brightened company life, providing stimuli and sources of pure energy. But it was not clear who was actually paying for all this, and to what extent this mechanism was leading Snaidero's strategic and operational focus away from its primary objective: customer satisfaction.

In short, actions which radically changed the way of *being in business* yielded immediate and even unexpected results, namely:

- the client is the sole arbiter of all decisions, regardless of the persons' *political influence*,
- functions are real service areas, both internally and externally, and not just empty power centres,
- communication should flow freely and continuously and should not be hindered by a set of narrow and rigid rules maintained only to protect a strict functional hierarchy.

The Internal Customer/Supplier Logic

This is another basic principle which is very effective as soon as it is applied and which changes the way of being in business. A process-based organisation is by definition one which provides to all company staff a complete scenario of its end customers and their requirements so that personnel can act accordingly. The same kind of approach could then be applied to any internal processes; as a result, each member of staff, in relation to the activity they are in charge of, should be *served and satisfied* as if they were external customers, thus giving rise to the so-called "client / supplier" logic. As a result, staff members will change the way they behave towards each other or the way they offer their services to colleagues whose requests have been tolerated and badly served up until then. Thus, since everyone within the company is at the same time someone else's customer and supplier, a virtuous circle soon begins to yield benefits in terms of cooperation, assistance, willingness to communicate, quality of internally supplied services (information flows, documents, etc.). This way of being in business, which some may consider trivial, brought advantages not only to Snaidero's employees, who ended up working in a supportive and confidence inducing atmosphere, but also to the end-customer who is the last link of a long chain made of several clients and suppliers.

Working as a Team

Working as a team may seem easy and obvious but it is not always so.

In a function-based organisation, decisions within each relevant area are usually taken hierarchically and the rare and often badly tolerated cross-functional meetings are occasions for conflict rather than real constructive confrontations, the solution of every disagreement being left to the next hierarchical level.

As in Snaidero the project was at the initial stage, company training courses were used to deliver *heavy injections* of *Team working* and *Team building* to most of company's employees, ranging from managers to factory personnel.

Organising cross-functional and cross-process working teams, learning how to manage and guide them, how to exploit them to provide solutions to everyday problems or to work on improvement projects have become our daily task and a really new way of being in business.

Giving Staff more Responsibility and Working by Targets

Earlier on we hinted at the role of the process owner, the *internal entre-preneur* of this new type of organisation, the person who is supposed to manage, in a completely autonomous way, large areas of activities and who has the task to carry out initiatives aimed at the continuous improvement of the company's business.

The introduction of this new role led Snaidero to a *flatter and more streamlined* organisational model in which responsibility was gradually delegated to an ever-increasing number of staff (even though at different levels).

In this way, *process owners* are given clear objectives to pursue which are in line with the strategic lines of actions which have been identified. They will be later evaluated on the achievement of these set objectives both in terms of quality and quantity relative to a number of previously assigned *performance indicators*.

Combining Efficiency with Effectiveness

The main objective of a function-based organisation is to carry out its activities in an efficient manner, where efficiency is measured by the extent to which results are in line with budget, although this is no proof that these activities have been effectively performed.

It is therefore of fundamental importance that efficiency and effectiveness go hand in hand, and that targets assigned to process owners aim at both of them.

This is the reason why Snaidero asked its process owners to pay attention to both and probably made their objectives *twice as hard* to achieve, but at the same time it gave clear directions as to the activities required to ensure that customers are *really* satisfied. Effectiveness targets were also set to make sure that some of the activities currently being developed, became the firm ground on which to build the company's future.

These new type of objectives, focused on the effectiveness of operations, required responsible officials to develop ad hoc activities. This was an exercise which involved the allocation of part of company's resources, but also the identification of solid reference points, from both a strategic and operational point of view.

Strategies and Operational Activities in a Single Integrated Context

This is the last basic principle of Snaidero's re-engineering project.

Some companies struggle to find an effective way to combine their strategies with operational activities. A clear vision of *what to do* (strategic area) does not always imply an ability to define and attain, in a coherent and coordinated way, *how to do it* (action plans). Others, instead, are highly focused on everyday ordinary activities and less active in planning their future.

On the other hand, Snaidero believed that finding the right balance was crucial for the success of the project and therefore introduced tools and methodologies capable of satisfying both requirements. In addition, a suitable environment (see the following paragraph) was created for process owners who were thus continuously stimulated to operate in both terms.

The principles of this project which, so far, have been described in a totally theoretical way, will be constantly applied in the following paragraphs which will examine the methods and tools introduced by the company and the main phases of the BPR project.

4.3 New Methods and Tools Supporting the Customer-Oriented Company

As stated earlier, the company transition from being product-oriented to being strongly customer-oriented, inevitably calls for the introduction of a new mentality based on the abovementioned principles, but also of new tools and methods in order to support the various areas of the company's operations. In other words, taking up change, questioning oneself and innovation, require strong support otherwise change will not be sustainable or feasible. This should apply for individual processes but also for the entire company structure, and by that we mean the most transversal and general areas which are particularly affected by the processes.

Thus, this paragraph intends to illustrate the main methods and tools introduced by the company in order to build a solid and general *framework* which is supposed to be an integral part but also a major enabler of all Business Process Reengineering activities. (Table 4.2).

Strategic Area: Three-Year Business Plan and Inter-Process Brainstorming

Having a clear strategic picture is crucial if the company's BPR activities are to lead off with the right foot. The company, in fact, should endeavour to create the best possible organisation in order to be able to define targets and then work towards their achievement.

Table 4.2 Main methods and tools supporting the customer-oriented company

Company Areas	New Methods and Tools
Strategic	Three-year Business Plan Inter-process brainstorming
Organisational	Process structure Process Owners Committee Management of improvement projects
Communication	Process Intranet
DSS (*Decision Support System*)	*Business Intelligence* software

But are targets always clearly identified? Does the company have a complete picture of the competitive environment in which it operates and can it meet its challenges? Is it capable of making the right decision by knowing exactly *what to do* in each situation?

Snaidero found out the answer to those questions when a new procedure (three-year *Business Plan*) was introduced with the aim of supporting strategic clarification activities.

Business Plan activities are developed, once a year, between September and December and consist of several phases which are summarised in Table 4.3.

In line with the general reorganisation principles mentioned above, this procedure as well is based on information sharing and team working. In fact, 'adjustment' sessions are envisaged to deal with the information prepared by the single process owners. These meetings take the form of cross-process brainstorming sessions where everybody is expected to provide effective support through ideas and proposals.

The result of these activities which are by nature, both creative and unstructured, is indeed an extremely structured *SWOT Analysis* (where SWOT stands for Strengths, Weaknesses, Opportunities, Threats), used by the company to plan its strategies for the next three-year period. These, in turn, are developed into action plans and improvement projects, and represent as a whole, the policy defined by the company to face the challenge of external competition, analysed in terms of existing threats and opportunities, and to guide internal growth based, in turn, on the twofold perspective of company's strengths and weaknesses.

Finally, the Business Plan, in addition to its intrinsic strategic purpose, can also be considered as an *operational planning* tool. In the final stages, *process owners* use it to develop medium and long-term policies in actual plans to support the daily activities.

Table 4.3 Business Plan deadline/activity chart

by September	Initial strategic analysis of the competitive environment	• Analysis of web-based information sources and carrying out of market researches / benchmarking • Comparison and summary with the previous year's B.P.
by mid-October	Meeting with Process Owners	• Joint analysis of external sources • Processing of internal information • First strategic hypotheses
from the end of October	Meeting with General Management	• Market analysis • Comparison of overall strategies with the previous year's B.P.
Brainstorming for strategies' definition and updating Definition SWOT analysis draft and discussion with POs		
at the end of November	Processing of the data relating to the three-year period: • Profit & Loss Account • Balance Sheet • Cash Flow • Target KPIs	• On the basis of a careful analysis of the effect of action plans developed within the strategic context
by the end of December	Final discussion and presentation of the three-year forecast	• Focusing on the following year's budget

Thus the Business Plan is no longer a mere intellectual exercise and three-year economic-financial projections are a natural consequence of a process whose main objectives include the development of a strong link between strategy and effectiveness.

Organisational Area: Process Structure ("Mapping")

This is clearly one of the basic elements of the project general framework and, as a consequence, its fine tuning or "mapping" phase, is one of the most important and delicate steps of the project.

The structure shown in Figure 4.2 highlights the two main categories of processes identified in Snaidero which apply to any type of activity, namely *Mega Processes* and *Major Processes*. The former ones play a mere coordinating role, whilst the latter ones relate to activities actually performed. Major Processes can then be further subdivided into Sub-processes and even in Sub-sub-processes which nevertheless are co-ordinated by the Major processes.

This is an important issue and deserves a brief comment. A process-based company is naturally prone to become somewhat *anarchical*. Assigning wide delegation powers to process owners, giving less importance to *old* hierarchies and fostering cross-process activities are all factors which may cause the company to fall into the trap. One of the new organisation's first concerns is therefore to sustain the required co-ordination activities, by resorting to the structure described above (Mega Processes in particular) and to other tools, such as Committees and new communication flows. These, however, will be dealt with in later paragraphs.

With regard to *process mapping*, it may be worthwhile highlighting some of its features, which, if on the one hand make it a very practical and effective tool, on the other hand facilitated its smooth introduction in the company. At this point, it should not be forgotten that, if BPR projects fail, it is generally due to the company's inability to manage change, starting from the inevitable loss of *power* by the former "function-based organisation". The latter, however, is not altogether eliminated, on the contrary, it is supported by the new "process-based organisation". In order to achieve this objective *efficiently*, the map has been devised so that many of the activities carried out by the *old* functions could be assigned to processes managing similar activities. Even the supervision of these processes was entrusted to process owners previously in charge of the same function but only on the condition that they were fit for the task (an assessment would be made of their potential aptitude to operate according to the previously illustrated basic reorganisation principles).

At first sight, the resulting map may appear to be just like the old functional structure except that it would be rotated by 90°, from an original vertical structure to a new horizontal one. This is not the case, however, as its contents, objectives and the way of *being and doing business* are so different as to radically change the company organisation, in particular personnel mentality. All this was achieved through a sort of "bridge" which, we believe was instrumental to overcome the inevitable friction arising when two organisations start running parallel or the new organisation is superimposed on top of the previous one.

Returning to the map, we would like to point out yet another important aspect considered by Snaidero at the process mapping stage. More than once, reference has been made to the fact that strategies and effectiveness should always go hand in hand. One of the most effective ways to achieve this synergy is by giving first priority to strategically significant areas of activity and by safeguarding these using a process-based structure and converting them into Mega or Major Processes. Here are some tangible examples: in Snaidero's map, the "Customer Service" process was given the title of Mega process due to the importance and focus for company's strategies; the "Show room" organisation activities (Exhibitions & Fairs), instead, fell under the Major processes category as they are one of the pivotal points of the company's commercial policies.

In brief, the first draft of the company's process map could be obtained through the following outline plan:

Top-Down Phase (with the support of General Management):

- Analysis of the function-based structure,
- Analysis of the company's main strategies,
- Mapping processes of activities carried out by existing functions,
- Mapping strategic activities to be safeguarded or developed from scratch,
- Assignment of strategic targets to each process (as per Business Plan) and initial identification of main activities and possible KPIs,
- Appointment of process owners.

Bottom-Up Phase (with the involvement of Process Owners):

- Acceptance of task by process owners,
- Final discussion on strategic targets, activities and KPIs (with relevant target).

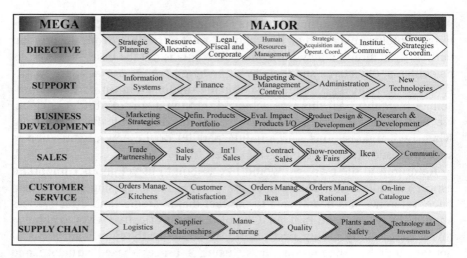

Fig 4.2 "Process Map" at Snaidero R. S.p.A

Organisational Area: Process Owners Committee

The various activities autonomously carried out within each process need to be co-ordinated in the most effective manner and we have seen that there are additional tools and procedures to achieve this goal (Business Plan, Mega Processes, etc.). The most important one of these, both from a strategic and operational point of view, is probably the *Process Owners Committee*.

The scope of the Committee is twofold. First, there are the so-called *Pre-committee Meetings* which are organised by Organisation Responsible Officials and where all process owners participate in separate sessions. These are a sort of informal meetings where, by taking the Business Plan as a benchmark, committee members examine process performance indicators (KPIs) both in terms of predefined targets and trend but also any important improvement projects still running and pertaining to the same business area. If any difficulties or problems arise with regard to the above, suitable procedures are recommended so that appropriate steps are taken to redress the issue.

Second, there are the *Process Owners Committee*. Meetings are held once a month and all process owners participate. Thanks to the preparation work done at the Pre-committee stage, in a meeting of less than three hours, the Committee will be able to take stock of the company situation, analyse the critical areas of the various processes and any related improvement projects (see the following sub-paragraph) and finally approve the resulting corrective action plans. The Committee's meeting starts with the examination of the current economic and financial situation which is compared with planned budgets (the former functional structure is still in place!). Afterwards, the Committee analyses the table of the main KPIs (about twenty). These have been selected out of more than 120 KPIs, depending on whether they are strategic or on their overall ability to safeguard the four perspectives on value creation (according to Kaplan: financial, customer, internal business process and learning and growth), thus developing a sort of company *Balanced Scorecard*. Exceptionally, the Committee will examine any additional KPIs which during Pre-committee meetings have been found to be critical and in respect of which improvement initiatives have been planned. At the end of the meeting the Committee will draft a concise report on the topics discussed but most importantly on any decisions taken. The follow-up on those decisions will be examined at the start of the next meeting.

Organisational Area: Management of Improvement Projects

In a process-based company, where personnel is generally invested with responsibility and objective performance measurements are in place, for well defined and agreed targets, *continuous improvement* is fostered and, as a result, all new projects thrive.

However, the company may lack the ability to manage these projects due to organisational problems which, if not properly tackled, risk to defeat this boost towards *change*, or even create internal pressures which are incompatible with normal company's operations and its economic / financial stability.

This is the reason why Snaidero decided to introduce a new procedure to manage improvement projects, namely:

- individual skills,
- management of the project program ("portfolio").

As regards the first area, training sessions on *Project Management* were planned and organised for all process owners with the aim of providing the latter with new ad hoc skills.

In the second area we addressed *Program Management* in order to:

- optimise the timing of interventions,
- remove interferences between the various projects,
- promote synergies between human, technological and organisational resources invested in the various initiatives,

- ensure adherence to the company's strategic policy.

An action plan was defined and structured with the support of a major consulting company (see Table 4.4).

Also in this case, increasing the value of human resources, investing them with responsibility and ensuring their professional growth marked the introduction of a methodology suitable to manage each improvement project.

On the other hand, due to the need to manage the whole portfolio, the company preferred staking on the development of a new organisational structure which, in accordance to the criteria of sharing and transparency, could ensure the achievement of a set of objectives, including:

- formal approval of projects to be launched (following indications given in the Business Plan or by the Process Owners Committee),
- appointment of Project Leaders (usually the process owners in charge of those processes more closely involved in the project);
- definition of priorities,
- verification of Work Advancement System,
- final evaluation of achieved results.

For this reason, an *Improvement Projects Committee* was set up comprising of members of the Management Committee (this in turn is made up of process owners of Mega Processes only), the person in charge of the Information Systems (critical area and potential "bottleneck") and with the participation, upon request, of those in charge of most important projects still running.

From an organisational point of view, it is worthwhile noting how the abovementioned activities, aimed at safeguarding the implementation of organisational change, added to those aimed at controlling that the company is operating properly. Thus, if it is good practice to set budgets to ensure that actual results are in line, or else to identify a number of KPIs to monitor their behaviour against established targets, it is just as important for a company to take steps to see that improvement projects are correctly structured and regularly monitored.

Communication Area: The Process Intranet

The improvement of the company's internal communications is one of the most important elements of a successful BPR project, but it is also one of the basic requirements for the proper running of the new organisation.

Table 4.4 Operation plan for the management of improvement projects

---

Analysis

- Acceptance of the company's Business Plan
- Evaluation of macro-processes and of organizational structure

Implementation

1) Interventions on the present status

- Mapping of projects under way and of initiatives
- Collecting significant information from all members of staff
- Verifying strategic alignment
- Defining a list of priorities
- Developing a "multi-project" integrated transition plan

2) Designing of a model for Project Management

- Project Management methodology
- Identification of the portfolio manager
- Methodology for identifying improvement opportunities
- Methodology for evaluating received suggestions
- Implementation of a company dedicated Intranet

Output

- Map of projects
- Files of projects
- Reports on the state of advancement (work-in-progress)
- Matrix of strategic alignment
- Projects' priority plan
- Intranet site

Training

- Training of Project Leaders

The main features of the latter, which have been pointed out earlier on, require a strong co-ordination of the activities carried out within each process. More generally, what is under construction is a more streamlined company made of responsible, autonomous members whose operation and knowledge are all-embracing and where decisions flow horizontally just as much as relationships. All this obviously implied the introduction of new communication flows, innovative as far as usage is concerned and characterised by selected contents.

Therefore the company opted for a *web-based* environment, an Intranet, in which Snaidero's personnel could find new, ever growing information areas and *knowledge repositories* (first embryo of a larger project on *Knowledge Management,* currently under review) which are expected to grow as *knowledge workers' involvement* in other business areas increases.

On the other hand, this means that information, activities and performances are more transparent, but also willingness and ability to work 'in the spotlight': all factors which often prove to be a remarkable stimulus to effectiveness. Just to quote an example, it is not by chance that meetings become more frequent or projects reach completion as the publishing date of the Work Advancement Stages becomes closer.

Thus, Intranet was conceived as a *free zone* and was initially used to share the main contents and supports of the re-engineering project under way. The company's general activities, the development plan, outputs of activities carried out and training material are only few of the issues which are managed by the Intranet.

In the following operational phase of the new organisation, new areas were added and dedicated to company news (in order to strengthen "corporate identity"), to the support of more transversal processes (which as a consequence have greater need to communicate), to the co-ordination of activities (Intranet areas of the Process Owners Committee and Improvement Projects Committee) and, last but not least, to the measurement of performances (see the following sub-paragraph).

DSS (Decision Support System) Area: Business Intelligence Software

Based on what has been said so far, besides the technical terminology, it should be easy to guess what topic will be discussed here. It is the acid test of the process-based system, the performance measurement area, the real drive of this change and the perfect boost towards continuous improvement.

The best way to ensure the completion of this part of the project is to provide the company with an ad hoc software (Business Intelligence) to be integrated with the company's Intranet. In this way, the company can significantly increase its ability to transform data into information which is a necessary requirement for the decision-making process, hence for company management.

This topic will be addressed again later on in a specific chapter edited by SDG Consulting, one of our project partners.

4.4   BPR Project Phases in Snaidero R. S.p.A.

The project, aimed at introducing a process-based organisation, was subdivided in a number of phases which commenced in February 1999 and were completed in the first months of the following year, as illustrated in Figure 4.3.

Period: February - July 1999

1) *Preliminary study*. From the beginning of February to the end of March, meetings were held by function managers to identify organisational needs, establish the advancement stage of improvement projects under way and to find out what was the "state of the art" of business processes.
2) *Training on processes*. From about mid-March to mid-July, the Head of Personnel organised a preliminary training session for managers and other responsible officials. This initiative succeeded in laying a firm foundation for the theory on which the new organisation is based, by clearly setting out all the procedures for coexistence and transition by taking into account the previous functional structure.
3) *Mapping of processes*. From the end of March to mid-May, with the aid of an external consultant, the mapping of company processes was completed. The logic of the mapping, which was subdivided in Mega Processes and Major Processes, was co-ordinated with the immediately preceding activities involving the definition of the company's mission and the drafting of the 1999-2001 Business Plan. The next step was the identification of Process owners, that is the entrepreneurs of the activities of the single processes.
4) *Definition and sharing of KPIs*. From mid-May to mid-June, each process owner identified the performance indicators considered as most appropriate to measure the achievement of process objectives. At the same time a number of meaningful "sub-processes" were identified, in order to define those objectives more clearly.

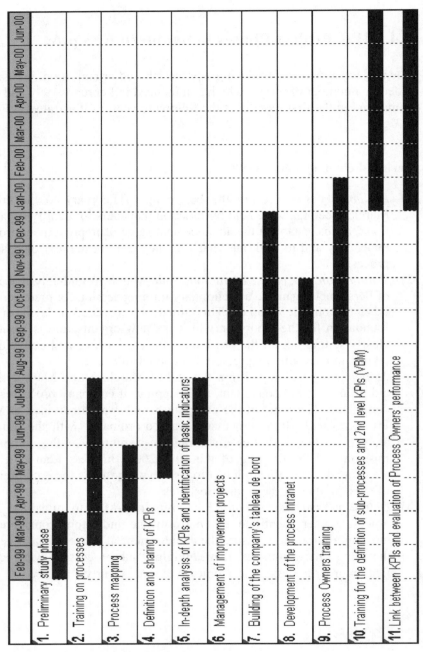

Fig 4.3   Snaidero's BPR project stage chart

5) *Examination of KPIs and identification of basic indicators.* From mid-June to the end of July, the definition of KPIs was examined. IT and non-IT sources were traced, methods of calculation established and managers of indicators, ideally not the process owners themselves, identified. Process owners were then informed of the basic indicators, that is the basic level of details expected to be used in the future to ensure a better understanding of KPIs. This activity was further improved when KPIs were incorporated in the IT system.

Period: September - December 1999

6) *Management system of improvement projects.* This is the implementation of what has already been illustrated in the previous paragraph, under the sub-paragraph "Organisational area: management of improvement projects".
7) *Building of the company's "tableau de bord".* This is a fundamental project step which, just like the above point, has already been illustrated in the sub-paragraph "DSS (Decision Support System) area: Business Intelligence software".
8) *Development of Process Intranet.* This is the last tool of the new organisation and has already been introduced when dealing with the "Communication area: the Process Intranet".
9) *Process owners training.* From September to January 2000, process owners attended a training course which was meant to be preparatory to the investigation and dissemination of the project. The latter envisaged the involvement of a further level of responsibility, that of sub-process owners or even of certain single process activities. This phase, where process owners are the main actors, is better described at point 10 which follows. Thus it is through this training phase that process owners must acquire the ability to analyse and subdivide the processes assigned to them (Process Building) as well as learn how to manage the Improvement Projects (Project Management) needed to improve their own performances (KPIs).

Period: First Semester 2000

10) *Training for identification of sub-processes and 2nd level KPIs (VBM).* A VBM (Value-Based Management) system is based on the creation of a set of performance indicators in line with the company's strategic objectives. These indicators (2nd level KPIs) must be detailed in order to be meaningful for each business area (sub-process) and specific

company personnel, and to allow integration with operating mechanisms, thereby ensuring coherence between the shareholders' target value and the actions required to achieve such value. The training session, which was supported by Eupragma consultants, enabled process owners to identify sub-processes and the related KPIs as well as to define actions to achieve improvement. This activity was carried out only in respect of the most significant/complex Major Processes, even though it involved a large number of staff. In any case introducing the new "culture" throughout the company was an objective which was to be attained. Process owners of processes excluded from training should carry on their activity autonomously with the support of internal resources.

11) *Link between KPI and evaluation of process owners' performance.* This stage is, in a way, the closing of a circle because, through the VBM, it connects the company to the process owners. An "incentive scheme" based on these assumptions completes the process owners' set of motivations, which include people's professionalism and the widespread sense of belonging to the company.

4.5   Main Difficulties and Immediate BPR Benefits

At the beginning of the chapter, we stated that it was our intention to transfer the experience gained on the project, in a direct and practical way, to all those currently implementing or about to embark on any such project. Therefore, at this point, it may be useful to stop for a second, look back, and make a list of the benefits achieved in the short term but also of all the main difficulties encountered by Snaidero in the initial stage of the BPR project. We shall start from the difficulties.

Main Difficulties

First of all it should be pointed out that the *cultural change* a BPR project calls for is a long process which must never be questioned and which sometimes appears to be *extremely* slow. Opposition will be strong and never really die down, therefore the company will experience a period of disorientation due to the radical change in organisational logics and dynamics, which are deeply rooted in the former function-based organisation. Coherence and tenacity by company top management, as the first sponsors of the BPR project, will guarantee that this phase is overcome.

As highlighted earlier on, the new way of *doing and being* in business may not suit everyone, however its basic principles must be accepted by everyone, even at the cost of loosing someone on the way.

The implementation phase requires the availability of ad hoc resources (especially people and time). Sometimes these resources may seem enormous even though they are proportionate to the size of the company. In other words, change always comes at a cost and top management must strongly believe in it to be willing to invest in return for sought-after though uncertain results.

At the beginning, when everything is to be *reengineered* or developed from scratch (e.g. new processes), managing priorities is a difficult task. On the one hand, bottlenecks must be managed as they are project-dedicated resources which have *limited capacity*. On the other hand, as regards the overall company structure, it should be pointed out that especially in the initial stage, reengineering will involve additional activities which imply some work overload. Thus, the use of *program management* tools, illustrated earlier on, becomes a requirement just as activities and strategic priorities must be carefully co-ordinated.

Finally, the new tools described above, though intuitively simple and effective, need time to be assimilated. Needless to say that changing one's own way of operating is not in the nature of human beings, therefore, only a clear advantage for users, easy to guess at the start and subsequently quick to achieve, and the determination and commitment of those promoting innovation can lead to change even the most deeply rooted working habits.

Reaping Benefits in the Short-Term

From a *quick win* viewpoint, thus ignoring any general benefits expected to accrue in the medium to long-term period, a BPR project has undoubtedly some advantages and, among these, the following deserve some attention:

- providing new and, sometimes strong reasons to operate in accordance with the principles inspiring BPR can help to remove historic and chronic reluctance to change, for example by encouraging people to promote unfulfilled improvement projects,
- by promoting team work and, at the same time, giving functions a secondary role, it is possible to achieve that dialogue which is the basic nourishment of any improvement and in particular of cross-process activities. Staff is no longer refrained from co-operating due to logic or

even physical constraints, on the contrary, they are encouraged to get together, at any level, in order to find ideas and effective solutions to problems,

- thus, whenever a decision or reasoning is made, customer satisfaction will be the company's top priority, as customers are the sole and only *super partes* arbiters of the company's population,
- if, on the one hand, some may dislike the new organisation and the risk may be that those who disapproving of this new model are lost on the way, on the other hand, experience tells us that the new structure is also an extraordinary opportunity to recover and increase the value of other people. This was the case of several members of staff who under the former, exclusively function-based, organisation had been placed in the wrong position, were undervalued, sometimes demotivated or, anyway, unable to express their capacity and potentiality to their best,
- it is the breaking up with the past which allows clear and coherent targets to be assigned to everyone, as it is evident that traditional logics (budgets to be adhered to, exaggerated competences, strict hierarchies) are no longer sufficient,
- finally, minor and more tactical improvement projects can be run in parallel, from the very start, with wider and more strategic projects, which characterise BPR, by taking advantage of this moment of great change, with the additional objective to achieve those *quick wins,* which represent the successful element of any project.

Initial Conclusions and Preface to the Following Chapters

So far we have described the distinguishing features of Snaidero's BPR project. The following chapters will examine the main operational processes which are typically found in medium-sized manufacturing companies like Snaidero.

Two final considerations are in order which, if on the one hand corroborate this model, on the other hand look at the projections of BPR future developments.

First, the so-called Vision 2000 regarding the new international standards issued to certify a company's quality systems consider BPR basic principles as a fundamental point of reference. This suggests that the company is on the right track. This statement is obviously based on the experience gained in Snaidero and assumes that the rules are interpreted and accomplished in a practical and operational way to achieve an effective rather than a superficial change within the company.

Finally, faithful to the tradition which says that once success is achieved one must go on and face new challenges, we wish to conclude by highlighting that this reengineering process is only the first step of Snaidero's organisational evolution which is currently heading towards the *extended company* concept. This however will be widely dealt with in the Third Part of the book (Chapters 8-9[2] and following).

2 Andrea Tramontano wishes to thank Ms. Gisella Piras for the translation of this chapter and chapters 8 and 9.

5. The Business Development and Sales-Service Processes

Stefano Tonchia

5.1 Business Development

The processes of "Business Development" are responsible for the changes and innovations that are made in a company; their primary scope is to supply new operative specifications to the "routine" processes (i.e. "Supply Chain", "Sales", "Customer Service"). More specifically (Figure 5.1) they serve to plan how the company should place itself on the market (both sales and services), the features of the product, how to manufacture it, and which suppliers and production system (= supply chain) to refer to.

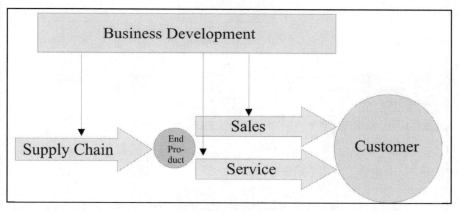

Fig 5.1   The mega-process "Business Development" as a source of working specifications for the other three mega-processes

The following major processes can thus be identified:

- *Marketing Strategy,* developing the typical "4Ps" of marketing (Product, Price, Place – intended as the geographical retail areas and distribution methods – and Promotion – including advertising and promotional activities in general),
- *Product Portfolio Definition,* whose task it is to provide and manage the best array of products, in relation to the different customer targets,

approve the development of new products or decree the removal of older ones from the market,

- *Product Input/Output Impact Evaluation,* which calculates the cash flow (revenues minus costs) of a product over its whole forecasted life-cycle, taking into account both the costs of design & development and those of "routine", which include both production and sales costs,
- *Design & New Product Development,* defining the specifications of the single products, their industrialisation and launch,
- *Research & Development,* concerning new materials, technical solutions and product technology, which are developed independently of specific products, but can be exploited in the short term when needed ("shelf innovation").

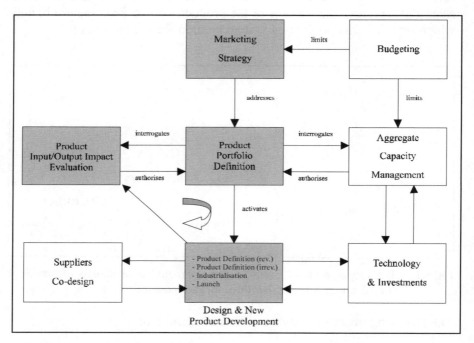

Fig 5.2 Linkages betweeen the major-processes of Business Development (grey)

All these processes are linked to each other, as depicted in Figure 5.2: Marketing Strategy inspires the Definition of the Product Portfolio, which must however be verified in terms of profitability (economic Evaluation of the Input/Output Impact of the products into and out of the portfolio). In the event of a positive outcome of this assessment, the definition of the portfolio activates the process of Design & New Product Development, articulated in the following sub-processes: 1) *Product Definition* (which in turn includes – as explained later in greater detail – a reversible and an irreversible stage), 2) *Industrialisation*, and 3) *Launch*. On the other hand, even when judged unprofitable, certain products are sometimes developed for strategic reasons, as they may be important for the company's image, complete the range of products or for a variety of other reasons.

The processes of Business Development are also linked to many others, the main being: Budgeting (a limiting factor for marketing strategies), Aggregate Capacity Management (verifying the compatibility of the portfolio with the necessary productive capacity over the months/years), Technology & Investments (the reservoir of competencies and funds required by the process of Design & Development).

5.2 Marketing Strategy and Product Portfolio Definition

An enterprise's process of *"Marketing Strategy"* combines and coordinates all those activities that are aimed at achieving marketing objectives, namely customer satisfaction (consumers or other companies – in this latter case it is more appropriate to speak of Industrial Marketing or Business-to-Business one), by offering product and services, and communicating ideas and values.

These are activities that set out how a company should interact with the sales market, thus the process can be classified among those of *change and innovation* known as "Business Development".

To achieve the marketing objectives, a vital prerequisite to is to analyse market opportunities, find the customers' "objects of desire", and define the market sector where the enterprise intends to concentrate its efforts ("customer target").

The typical marketing instruments are usually included in the so-called "4Ps" or *marketing-mix levers* (McCarthy, 1960):

1) *Product*, namely what the company proposes to its target, including variety, conformity to that ordered/described, reliability and durability, perceived quality (aesthetics, image and "status" communicated by the product – Garvin, 1988), packaging, type of delivery, assistance before, during and after the purchase, other services, payment method, etc.,

2) *Price,* which must be carefully determined, in relation to the features of the products, the competitors' prices, the company's structure of the costs, the expected profits from the investments,

3) *Place,* in the sense of the geographical area where customers and the company's distribution channels meet. It includes the organization of sales networks, transport systems, possible peripheral warehouses, type, number and area coverage of intermediaries, if present, and how the company relates to them,

4) *Promotion,* aimed at informing and communicating with the target customers, so as to persuade them to purchase the company's products. It can be carried out directly by the sales staff, through publicity and promotion, or indirectly, by means of PR activities, conferences, publications, sponsoring, and so forth (the activities aimed at promoting the company rather than its products or services are also known as "institutional communication").

The name of the process – Marketing Strategy – is according to the American Market Association (A.M.A.): "the process of planning and executing the conception, pricing, promotion and distribution of ideas, goods and services to create exchange and satisfy individual and organisational objectives" (Lambin, 2000).

Product variety can be expressed in three dimensions: width (= lines of product), length (= number of products) and depth (= models and variations). Product variety – which, together with the degree of innovation, makes the offer more or less complex (Clark and Fujimoto, 1991) – requires strict management, and therefore it is often preferable to investigate this aspect of marketing in the framework of a specific process, i.e. *"Product Portfolio Definition"*. The portfolio is generally represented by "product placement matrixes" that intersect the segmentation of the target customers with the price ranges of the products, placed inside the matrix and visualised as circles of a dimension proportional to the sales volumes. An example – referring to the Snaidero company – is reported in Figure 5.3.

In the case of Snaidero, the activities forming the process of "Marketing Strategy" can be summarised as follows:

- analysis of the consumers' trends (market analysis, etc.),
- comparison with the best competitors ("benchmarking"),
- definition of product features and reference price,
- selection of the designer,
- investigations/collaborations for market tests (with Barilla, Electrolux et al.),

- defining in general terms how to introduce it on the market and present it to the retailers,
- suggestions for the activities of external communication (publicity and other initiatives).

On the other hand, the activities referring to the process of "Product Portfolio Definition" can be summarised as:

- monitoring of the pre-existing portfolio (including the grouping into "families"),
- proposals for new entries (including the definition of the "name/wood-type" – in the case of Snaidero it is the elementary unit forming the portfolio and corresponds, respectively, to the model, with different versions, and the main material from which the product is made),
- restyling proposals,
- proposals for planned output of names/wood-types,
- final decision regarding product input/output.

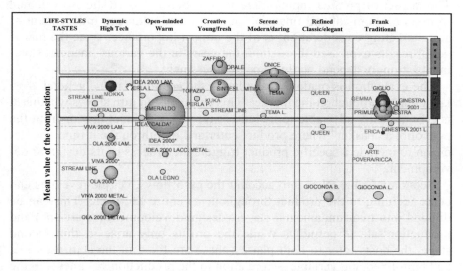

Fig 5.3 The "product placement matrix" of the Snaidero kitchens

It must be noted that, in the case of Snaidero, there is a major process called "Communication" that can be classified inside the (routinary) "Sales" mega-process, as it consists of activities aimed at adding value by means of marketing communications (brochures supporting catalogues, press releases, company magazine, updates to the web-site, publicity and promotion activities, PR work, sponsoring, and so forth), following indications and specifications made by the "Marketing Strategy" process.

Moreover, it must be noted that the "Sales" mega-process also includes two other major processes – "Trade Partnership" and "Show-rooms & Fairs" – respectively engaged (and always following the guidelines issued by "Marketing Strategy") in: a) relationships with retailers (external companies managing the sales outlets, both single- and multi-brand); b) designing the show-rooms at the sales points (Snaidero always selects the layout) and taking part in trade fairs.

5.3   Product Input/Output Impact Evaluation

The impact of product input/output into or out of a portfolio is evaluated from an economical and financial viewpoint and, although independent of any marketing consideration, is of the utmost importance, since the managerial results expressed throughout the years in the various financial statements strongly depend on this type of assessment.

The evaluation is made by calculating the *economic value* generated by launching a product on the market. This parameter in turn shows whether it is economically advisable to include or remove a product into or from the portfolio, a "basket" where product enter and exit throughout time; the decision to include a specific product triggers the process of its design & development.

Economic value takes into account the cash flows, i.e. the revenues and costs accruing to the product throughout its entire life cycle. This can be divided into two fundamental stages: design/development ("start-up") and production/sale ("routine"). While the profits only arise in this second stage, the costs refer to both phases: these are fixed in the start-up stage, and both fixed and variable – in relation to the production volumes – in the latter one.

The process of "Product Input/Output Impact Evaluation" acquires all necessary information from the different processes, calculates the economic value of a product during its entire life cycle, and hands it over to the process of "Product Portfolio Definition".

Table 5.1 shows a typical example, relative to Snaidero. It includes the following information-supplying processes:

- the process "Finance" supplies the cost of capital, for every year taken into account, so as to actualise the value of the financial flows (economic values, i.e. revenues and costs in different years, must all be considered at a given time, for example discounted in the present),
- the process "Sales" provides the revenues of the previous years, plus those forecasted for the following three years (those of the business plan, the first being that for which the budget is drafted) and estimates the overall cumulative proceeds for the years following that of the business plan, until the year when the product is expected to be taken off the market. Revenues from royalties are also included,
- the process "Show-rooms & Fairs", organising and managing exhibitions at sales outlets and in fairs, reports the costs of this activity for each of the previous years, that relative to the budget and the other two of the business plan, and an overall cumulative cost estimated for the remaining years. Moreover, it estimates the minimum cost of exhibiting a new product (at time zero), the expenses incurred in preparing the catalogue (for both retailers and customers) and presentation costs sustained when launching the product,
- the process of "Product Definition" supplies an estimate of the costs relative to investments for the new product, its designing, prototyping, testing and, possibly, restyling. These costs must take into due account other projects (both past and current, i.e. carry-over and commonalities), and possible co-design with the suppliers,
- the process of "Production Planning" estimates the level of stock required to start up production, the average stock-in-hand at full capacity (divided into: common materials, doors, wooden components, metal components), the average work-in-progress or WIP (for common and specific parts), and obsolete material at the end of the life cycle (divided into the same classes as the stock), all values depending on the stock management policies that the company intends to adopt. The interest rate (cost of capital) is added to the value of initial stock, stock-in-hand and WIP, in order to define their financial cost,
- the process of "Budgeting & Control" (B&C) considers the direct costs relative to materials (common materials, doors, specific wooden or metal parts) and labour (to manufacture common parts and doors – specific parts are purchased outside). This percentage is deduced from the bill of materials and manufacturing cycles. It furthermore supplies the

amount of fixed costs (relative to production, trade and general/financial aspects) that can be ascribed to the product.

It is easy to imagine that this type of information, and the precision/reliability of these calculations depend strongly on how advanced the process of product design/development is (the proceeds, for instance, estimated on a product that is still taking shape, depend on its sales price, which in turn depends on manufacturing costs). The impact evaluation is concurrent with the first stage of product design/development, namely the *reversible* one, and can determine remarkable changes in the project, if not indeed its termination. Subsequently, the Table 5.1 springs up while design/development evolves (as depicted by the circular arrow in Figure 5.2), until an economic value is reached that is considered sufficient to authorise the second, *irreversible* stage of design/development.

The sum of all the revenues, minus all the costs, determines the gross economic value that the business would gain from the new product. The net economic value is obtained by subtracting the amount of fixed manufacturing costs (plant depreciation, etc.), and fixed trade and general/financial costs. It is advisable to make a distinction between gross and net economic values, as the passage from gross to net is more sensitive to subjective criteria and thus the objectivity of the calculation is at risk.

Various levels of detail are taken into account: from the macroscopic one of "business unit" (the mother firm and the subsidiaries), to that of the "brand", the kitchen model, and the different versions and combinations. In the latter two cases, given the high level of detail, the inputs from "Sales" and "Show-rooms & Fairs" are not taken into account (they cannot forecast such a level of detail), nor that from "Product Definition" (costs do not increase in relation to the different combinations and versions), and therefore only an overall cost of the life cycle is calculated (which is important to identify the more expensive models).

The sum of the economic value of each product determines the *business profits* made throughout the years. In other words, each product is considered an investment, and the net economic value coincides with the Net Discounted Cash Flow (NDCF) of the investment. Revenues and costs are thus traced to the activities of the processes, as prescribed by the most advanced costing methodology, known as Activity-Based Costing – ABC (see Par. 7.3).

As the entire procedure of calculation is based on estimates, there can be considerable differences between budgeted and actual statements, especially over the long period (the life cycle of a kitchen is of many years). On the other hand, experience proves the strategic importance of reference values – even rough estimates – for business development. Besides the pro-

Table 5.1 Economic value (revenues minus costs) accruing to the product throughout its entire life cycle (informations from the various firm processes, by row): each column details that on its left hand side

		greater level of detail →					
		Business	Brand	Model	Wood	Version	Combin.
"Fin"	Annual Cost of Capital						
process "Sales"	Past Revenues (per year) Revenues (current year) Rev. bus. plan 2nd & 3rd year Rev. beyond bus. plan Taken-off the market (year) % Royalties/Revenues						
process "Show-room and Fairs"	Past Costs (per year) Costs (current year) Costs bus. plan 2nd & 3rd year Rev. beyond bus. plan First rooms minimum cost C. of the catalogue C. of present. events						
"Product Definition"	Specific Investments Design Costs Prototyping Costs Testing Costs Restyling Costs						
"Product Planning"	Financial Cost of Start-up Stock Fin. Costs of Stock (4classes) Costs of Obsoletes (4classes) Fin.Costs of WIP (2types)						
"B & C"	% C. Mat. / Rev. (4classes) % C. Dir.Lab. / Rev. (2types)						
	Gross Economic Value						
"B& C"	% Production Fix Costs % Trade Fix Costs % General Fix Costs						
	Net Economic Value						

profitability of the product portfolio (overall economic value in relation to business investments), it is possible to calculate its internal consistency by means of a Pareto's analysis of the various products; this analysis defines the contribution of each product to the overall economic value of the portfolio (the number of products responsible for the greater part of the overall economic value should not be too low, for in this case there would be too many products made for marketing reasons only).

5.4   Design & New Product Development

Rather than merely use the term *design*, nowadays it is considered preferable to substitute it with the expression "New Product Development" (NPD – Clark and Fujimoto, 1991): not only must this process design, but also develop, update and integrate the product, and for this purpose it can also use parts of pre-existing products' projects, or evolve them from similar ones manufactured by competitors. In other words, these are designs bearing a remarkable "carry-over" (percentage, in value, of the parts of a previous design that have been adapted and used for the new one).

There are three fundamental reasons for this:

- the high level of technological differentiation, and its constant evolution, increases the risk of investing in completely new products, namely those with low carry-over rates,
- the customers, ever more exacting and oriented towards customisation, and the market situation in general, recommend the development of new products sharing a common platform and not ones that are radically new,
- the strong international competition between many competitors and the adaptation to different local markets render practically inevitable the systematic use of carry-over and common parts when designing new products.

Today, there is a strong need to innovate the management of the product design/development process, and the term *Lean Design*, derived from the concept of Lean Production (Womack et al., 1990), has become popular to describe a global objective of design improvement.

An international research carried out by the MIT and coordinated by Cusumano and Nobeoka (1998) documents the need to "slim down" designs that are too "fat" both in terms of unnecessary parts and features, but especially in terms of efforts and resources invested in the single, often uncoordinated, projects. In short, lean design can be achieved by shifting the focus from single-project to *multi-project management* (by means of product platforms and modularity), in the context of a precise portfolio strategy, featuring a flexible team organisation, a high degree of concurrent en gineering, frequent exchange of information, co-design with the suppliers, in order to reduce expenses while preserving and improving product integrity. Internal and external customer satisfaction can be thus achieved by employing such techniques as the Variety Reduction Program (VRP), Quality Function Deployment (QFD), FMEA (Failure Mode & Effect Analysis), and so forth (Tonchia, 2001).

The product innovation process that, starting from the "concept idea" leads to the launch of production (by giving product and manufacturing specifications to the production process so as to start routine activities and execute customer or stock orders) can be divided into various stages. The typical stages forming the product design/development process can be generalised as follows:

1) The starting point is the *concept idea* (a mix of technological inputs and market needs/receptivity). The concept idea of the product is described by a small number of product key elements, and only at a later stage the product features and performances (i.e., those described in the catalogues) will be defined; it also includes the price range of the product, the image that the company wants to communicate, the way to present and sell it. It can be stated that a product is successful because the concept is good, just like a good portfolio of products is one that contains a good mix of innovative concepts required by the market,

2) It is impossible to deduce design specifications directly from the concept idea, in terms of size and features: an intermediate stage is required, where product functionality is examined in relation to the concept expressed. This stage is generally known as *product planning*; and leads to the definitions of the Product Function Structure (PFS), namely the breakdown tree structure describing the general features and functions that the product must have,

3) The following step of *product design* in a stricter sense, creates the main "deliverables" of the project, i.e. the product specifications. These include all the physical-dimensional features of the product and the bill of materials. The level of detail needed for these specifications must be such as to produce identical products, even when manufactured by different persons or groups; the specifications, in their final version, will determine the reference parameters for the measurement of product conformity, once production has started,

4)   The decisions made in the previous stage are not definitive, as they
     must be verified in practice, by means of *engineering*. While design
     can be an activity independent of the availability and use of machin-
     ery and plants, engineering requires at least laboratories and/or testing
     units or pilot plants. Engineering is aimed at testing the effectiveness
     of the solutions identified for the product (type of materials, geometry
     of the different parts, assembly, etc.) – *product engineering* – and at a
     second stage verifying work instructions and analysing manufacturing
     problems – *process engineering* – also by means of prototypes ("par-
     tial" products, in the sense that they have only certain functions),
5)   Engineering, and eventual prototyping, is still insufficient to define
     the final and definitive product and process specifications, as up to
     this stage it is primarily aimed at assessing the effectiveness of the
     product rather than the manufacturing process. Another stage is there-
     fore required, namely that of *industrialisation*, which leads to produc-
     tion on a vaster ("industrial") scale at low cost and with resource satu-
     ration, in other words with high productivity,
6)   At this stage it is possible to start ("ramp-up") mass production, pos-
     sibly preceded by a *pre-series*.

All these stages should benefit from continuous feed-back cycles, keeping
in mind the golden rule of design: the more changes are made at a more
advanced stage, the more expensive they become.

In order to endorse and enable this desired, constant exchange of information among the different activities so as to anticipate and prevent problems more or less simultaneously, process management – with its precise
identification of activities, input and output information, suppliers and recipients of the information – can be a very useful tool for improving the
performance of the design/development process in terms of quality, time
and costs.

In Snaidero, the "major process" *Product Design & Development* consists
of three "sub-major processes", which although sometimes overlapping,
develop one after the other, and benefit from constant feed-back cycles:

• *Product Definition* collects the ideas and demands regarding a certain
  product and prepares the design (initially in the form of drafts, and later
  as prototypes). If the project is approved, the process enters an "irreversible" phase, and the designs and prototypes at a more advanced
  stage of development, plus the complete criticality analysis and suggestions for future production planning rules, are passed on to the subsequent process of industrialisation,

- *Industrialisation* is in charge of carrying out production, testing before-hand the new product and manufacturing cycle, producing the technical catalogue and defining the purchase codes. It moreover releases the manufacturing BOM (bill of materials), including the automatic production programmes,
- *Product Launch* selects the combination of specifications, families and materials, prepares the bill of materials, takes care of the first orders (in particular those for show-rooms at the retail points, which will act as sales drivers), the publication of the information catalogue and the training of sales staff and workers who will install the kitchens.

The main outputs of the entire process of design & development are not only the product specifications and its manufacturing instructions, but also the definition of *production planning rules,* which are important for production scheduling and supplying (Table 5.2). According to these macro-rules (decisions regarding the lead time of the end product, defined with a "name/wood-type" that describe the kitchen model and material to be used, the "make-or-buy" for the families of items, and the management policies, distinguished into "policy A", or on demand, and "policy B", or on forecast), the sub-major process "Product Definition" is the key, decision-making process, while the others act as "consultant" processes. At a later, irreversible stage, other processes ("Relationship with the Suppliers" and "Production Planning") will play a decisional role, while "Product Definition" will act as consultant.

Tables 5.3 to 5.8 depict the input suppliers and output customers for the activities forming each of the above three sub-major processes (Product Definition, Industrialisation and Product Launch, respectively).

As described in Chapter 2, the method provides a formal identification of all the customer-supplier links and the goods/informations exchanged, as well as defining the procedures relative to each activity. In the Tables – made on Excel pages from an Access data-base – the *marked* internal *suppliers* and internal *customers* indicate the existence of "active links" with their process pages, while *marked activities* are linked to their respective *procedures*, and *marked inputs and outputs* to the formal *documents* describing them. The output of a supplier-activity of a process must necessarily coincide with the input of the corresponding customer-activity, and these will form the links between the various processes.

Table 5.2   Definition of production planning rules

Production Planning Rules	Central Process	Consultants Processes
about materials		
Lead Time proposal for Name/Wood-type	Product Definition	Pr.Plan., Sup.Rel., Sales, Ext.Log.
"Make-or-Buy" proposals for Items Families	Product Definition	Pr.Plan., Sup.Rel., Technol., Agg.Cap.
"A/B policy" proposals for Items Families	Product Definition	Production Plan., Suppliers Relations.
from reversible to irreversible		
Lead Times for external Items Families	Suppliers Relationships	Product Definition, Product. Planning
Lot Size & Frequency for external Items Families	Suppliers Relationships	Product Definition, Product. Planning
Lead Times for internal Items Families	Production Planning	Product Definition
Lot Size & Frequency for internal Items Families	Production Planning	Product Definition
Safety Stocks for Items Families	Production Planning	(from Information System)
Safety Lead Times for Items Families	Production Planning	Suppliers Relationships
Families of Items ("Group Technology")	Production Planning	Industrialisation, Suppliers Relations.
about capacity		
Calendars of available days	Aggregate Capacity Management	
Calendars of available work shifts	Aggregate Capacity Management	
Limits of flexibility and extra work	Aggregate Capacity Management	
Availability of temporary work staff	Aggregate Capacity Management	
Calendar of Preventive Maintenance	Aggregate Capacity Management	

Table 5.3   The "Product Definition" process: activities (by columns) and related suppliers (by rows) of inputs (in the matrix)

activity / supplier	1. Collection / definition of the project inputs	2. Realisation of the project proposals	3. Choice of the project proposals	4. Design studies & drafts
Strategic Planning	Business Plan		Project proposal choice	
Sales in Italy	Sales Plan (Italy)			
Internat. Market Develop. & Ctrl	Sales Plan (Export)			
Product Portfolio Definition	Product position, charact., time			
Marketing Strategy			Market Analysis	
External designer		Designer's proposal		
Detailed Capacity Mngt (CRP)				
Technologies & Investments				Feedback on studies & drafts
Aggreg. Capacity Mngt (RCCP)				Feedback on studies & drafts
Codesign Activation				Feedback on studies & drafts
Supply Activation				
Supplier Homol. / Certification				
Quality				
Product I/O Impact Eval.				
Production Planning				
External Logistics				
Packaging Ikea				
Packaging Rational				
Kitchen cabinets Finishing				
Custom. elements Finishing				

Table 5.3   (continued)

5. Product criticalities analysis	6. Prototyping	7. Check of price positioning	8. Proposal / check of planning rules	9. Decision on project continuation
		Sales price estimate		Gate #1 authorisation
			Consulting (Lead Time)	
			Consulting (Lead Time)	
Time-to-market	Comments on prototype			
	Comments on prototype			
	Comments on prototype			
		Prod. feasibility (int. & ext.)		
Criticality remarks	Comments on prototype / critic.		Consulting (Make-or-Buy)	
Criticality remarks	Comments on prototype / critic.		Consulting (Make-or-Buy)	
Criticality remarks	Comments on prototype / critic.	Costs & investm. estimates	Consulting (LT, M/B, Pol.A/B)	
		Supplying costs	Consulting (LT, M/B, Pol.A/B)	
	List of certified suppliers			
Criticality remarks	Consulting			
		Quantitative indications		
		Consulting (on estimates)	Consulting (LT, M/B, Pol.A/B)	
			Consulting (Lead Time)	
	Prototype test results			
	Prototype test results			
	Prototype test results			
	Prototype test results			

Table 5.4   The "Product Definition" process: activities (by columns) and related customers (by rows) of outputs (in the matrix)

customer \ activity	1. Collection / definition of the project inputs	2. Realisation of the project proposals	3. Choice of the project proposals	4. Design studies & drafts
Strategic Planning		Proposals (drafts, models, etc.)	Mini-Gate #1 report	
External designer	Project inputs			
Product Portfolio Definition		Proposals (drafts, models, etc.)	Mini-Gate #1 report	
Marketing Strategy		Proposals (drafts, models, etc.)	Mini-Gate #1 report	
Sales in Italy		Proposals (drafts, models, etc.)	Mini-Gate #1 report	
Internat. Market Develop. & Ctrl		Proposals (drafts, models, etc.)	Mini-Gate #1 report	
Technologies & Investments				Studies and drafts
Aggreg. Capacity Mngt (RCCP)				Studies and drafts
Purchase Marketing				Studies and drafts
Codesign Activation				Studies and drafts
Supply Activation				
Quality				
Product I/O Impact Eval.				
Production Planning				
Packaging Ikea				
Packaging Rational				
Kitchen cabinets Finishing				
Custom. elements Finishing				
Industrialisation				
Product Launch				

Table 5.4   (continued)

5. Product criticalities analysis	6. Prototyping	7. Check of price positioning	8. Proposal / check of planning rules	9. Decision on project continuation
		Product costs estimates		Gate #1 report
	Prototype			
	Prototype			Gate #1 report
				Gate #1 report
				Gate #1 report
				Gate #1 report
Request for critical. analysis	Prototype			Gate #1 report
Request for critical. analysis	Prototype			Gate #1 report
Request for critical. analysis				
Request for critical. analysis	Prototype; req. protot. suppl.		Decisions on LT, M/B, Pol.A/B	Gate #1 eport
			Decisions on LT, M/B, Pol.A/B	Gate #1 report
Request for critical. analysis				Gate #1 report
		Estimates (price, invest., design c.)		Gate #1 report
			Decisions on LT, M/B, Pol.A/B	Gate #1 report
	Request for tests / prototypes			
	Request for tests / prototypes			
	Request for tests / prototypes			
	Request for tests / prototypes			
			Decisions on LT, M/B, Pol.A/B	Design, protot., plan.rules, critic.
			Decisions on LT, M/B, Pol.A/B	

Table 5.5   The "Industrialisation" process: activities (by columns) and related suppliers (by rows) of inputs (in the matrix)

activity / supplier	1. Advanced design	2. Product & cycle testing	3. Def. of technical catalogue	4. Def. of supplying items	5. Photocatalogue supporting
Product Definition	Design, prot., pl.rules, crit.				
Product Launch					
Ext. services supplier		Market tests report			
Quality	Quality tests reports				
Photocatalogue					Photocompositions
Product Portf. Def.		Indicat. on compositions	Feedback on catal. draft		
Sales in Italy			Feedback on new items		
Int. Market Dev. & Ctrl			Feedback on new items		
International Sales			Draft translation		
Supplier Hom./Certif.	List of certif. suppliers				
Supply Activation	Purchasing feasibility	1st compos. for testing			Feedback on advancement
Production processes	Production needs; protot.	1st compos. for testing			Feedback on advancement
Technologies & Investm.	Consulting on new tech.				
Production Planning					
Orders Management					
Customer Satisfaction					

Table 5.5 (continued)

6. Def. of sale prices	7. Bill of Materials	8. Real. of technical catalogue	9. NC part program.	10. Product. cycles release	11. Indicat. on space requirem.	12. Mainten. / restyling
Decis. on LT, M/B, Pol.A/B						
Notice and tuning						
						Request for customist.
New items purch. prices						
				Production cycles/times		
				Production cycles/times		
				Production cycles/times		
						Errors; customisation
						Request for information

Table 5.6   The "Industrialisation" process: activities (by columns) and related customers (by rows) of outputs (in the matrix)

activity / customer	1. Advanced design	2. Product & cycle testing	3. Def. of technical catalogue	4. Def. of supplying items	5. Photo-catalogue supporting
Product Definition		Product. test report(MG#2)	Tech. catalogue draft		
Marketing Strategy		Product. test report(MG#2)	Tech. catalogue draft		
Sales in Italy		Product. test report(MG#2)	Tech. catalogue draft		
Int. Market Dev. & Ctrl		Product. test report(MG#2)	Tech. catalogue draft		
Customer Satisfaction					
Strategic Planning		Product. test report(MG#2)			
Production Planning	Specifications	Req. manufacure compos.	Tech. catalogue draft		Items for photo
Quality	Request for sample codes	Product. test report(MG#2)			
Supply Activation	Req. for purch. feasib.	Product. test report(MG#2)	Tech. catalogue draft	Purchasing items BOM	Items for photo
Technologies & Invest.	Req. feedb. on new tech.		Tech. catalogue draft		
On-line Catalogue			Tech. catalogue draft		
Purchase Marketing	Req. for new purch. item				
Supplier Hom./Certif.	Technical requirements				
Mat.&Ware. Management					
Coating application	Request for feasibility	Product. test report(MG#2)			Items for photo
Packaging: Ikea+ Ratio.					
Finishing: Cab.+Elem.	Request for feasibility	Product. test report(MG#2)			Items for photo
Product I/O Impact Eva.					
Product Launch	Specifications				

Table 5.6   (continued)

6. Def. of sale prices	7. Bill of Mate-rials	8. Real. of technical catalogue	9. NC part pro-gram.	10. Prod-uct. cycles re-lease	11. Indicat. on space requirem.	12. Main-ten. / restyling
Info on price positioning						
Info on price positioning						
Info on price positioning						
Info on price positioning						
						Technical info.
Info on price positioning						
			Info on load. & efficiency	Production items BOM	Info on new name/wood	
				Setup/meth. specificat.		
				Setup/meth. specificat.	Info on new name/wood	
		Definitive tech. catal.				
		Definitive tech. catal.				
			NC part programs			
			NC part programs	Setup/meth. specifica-tions		
			NC part programs	Setup/meth. specifica-tions		
Info on price positioning				Request for costs verif.		
		Def. tech. catal. + items	NC part programs		Info on new name/wood	

Table 5.7   The "Product Launch" process: activities (by columns) and related suppliers (by rows) of inputs (in the matrix)

activity / supplier	1. Combi. fam./mat.	2. BOM mngt	3. Man. data ass.	4. Man. data test	5. Def. compos.	6. Sales forecast	7. 1st purchase	8. Verif. raw mat
Product Definit	Dec. LT, M/B,A/B							
Industrialisation	Def.tech. cat.+item				Def.tech. cat.+item			Specifications
Technol. & Invest.								
Product. processes			Managerial data					
Product. Planning			Managerial data					
Informat. Systems				Data feedback				
Supply Activat.			Managerial data					
External suppliers								Specifications
Showroo. & Fairs					Type-composit.			
Orders Mngt								
Sales in Italy						Initial forecasts		
On-line Catalog.								

Table 5.7 (continued)

9. Object mngt	10. Order data-base	11. Order testing	12. Sh.-r. progress	13. ITcat. release	14. Sales instrum.	15. Verif. machin.	16. Verif. spaces	17. Training
	Def.tech. cat.+item					NC part programs	Info new nam. / wo.	
						Setups, methods	Space definition	
		Tested database					Space definition	
Type-objects		Tested database	Type-composit.					
		Tested database	Initial forecasts					
		Tested database		Tested catalogue				Training support

Table 5.8   The "Product Launch" process: activities (by columns) and related customers (by rows) of outputs (in the matrix)

activity / customer	1.Combi. fam./mat.	2. BOM mngt	3. Man. data ass.	4. Man. data test	5. Def. compos.	6. Sales forecast.	7. 1st pur-chase	8. Verif. raw mat
Industrialisation								
Product Processes		BOM et al.						Verified specific.
Product Planning		BOM et al.			Type-compos	Initial fore-cast	1st purchase	Verified specific.
Informat. Systems				Managerial data				
Quality								Verified specific.
Supply Activat.		BOM et al.			Type-compos	Initial fore-cast	1st purchase	Verified specific.
External Suppliers								
Showroom & Fairs								
Orders Mngt								
Sales in Italy								
Int'l Mkt dev. & ctrl.								
Internat. Sales								
On-line Catalog.								

Table 5.8   (continued)

9. Object mngt	10. Order data-base	11. Order testing	12. Sh.-r. progress	13. ITcat. release	14. Sales instrum.	15. Verif. machin.	16. Verif. spaces	17. Training
						Notice, tuning		
						Ok on machin.	Ok on spaces	Training
		Database						Training
								Training
								Training
Type objects								
		Database	Showroom Plan					
		Database						Training
			Showroom Plan					Training
								Training
								Training
		Database						

5.5   Sales and Service

The "Sales" and "Service" mega-processes carry out all those activities that, starting from the end product, reach the *customer*, throughout the stages of sales and assistance/support to that process (order management, delivery, technical assistance, etc.) (Figure 5.1). These two mega-processes are executed in compliance with the directives and indications given by the major process "Marketing Strategy" (a process that, given its features, belongs to the mega-process "Business Development").

The mega-process "Sales" comprises the following major-processes:

- *Trade Partnership* (aimed at identifying, monitoring and endorsing trade partners, organising training courses, joint activities of local promotion and publicity, planning/preserving the image of the sales outlet, supplying computer service to the retailers, etc.),
- *Sales in Italy* (which includes such typical commercial and routine activities as: preparing the sales budget and trade plan, training/managing the agents, public relations with customers/retailers, defining and revising trade agreements, supporting sales-related administrative activities, analysing, monitoring and reporting activities, etc.),
- *International Sales* (the activities described above, plus finding/ranking new agencies, importers, etc., and carrying out all those activities aimed at conforming to the different culture, technical-administrative aspects and language),
- *Contract Sales* (regarding, for instance, contracts to furnish entire buildings, particularly common abroad),
- *Show-rooms & Fairs* (together with the kitchen retailers, they plan the layout of the show room – an extremely delicate activity, which must be carried out in partnership, as it is one of the key factors conditioning the choice of the final customer),
- *Ikea* (selling ensembles for the renowned Swedish furniture multinational),
- *Communication* (activities aimed at adding value through communication to the market, via brochures enclosed in the catalogues, articles and press releases, the company magazine "News", updates to the Internet and the Extranet, publicity, promotion and PR activity, sponsoring, and so forth – in compliance with the indications/specifications made by the "Marketing Strategy" process).

The mega-process "Service" consists of the following major-processes:

- *Management of Kitchen Orders*, divided into *Italy* and *Abroad* (analysing, verifying and inserting the order, releasing of non-standard size items, managing variations, urgent orders, returned items – a subprocess called *Distribution* or *External Logistics* plans the deliveries, manages distribution constraints and loads formation, the accessories for the retailers, relationship with shippers, prepares the shipping documents, etc.),
- *Customer Satisfaction* (the management of the customer data-base, contacts, enquiries, complaints, queries regarding customer satisfaction with the purchased product, checking if problems are solved, managing warrants, etc.),
- *Management of the Orders concerning Ikea* (described previously),
- *Management of the Orders concerning Rational* (the Group's German partner),
- *On-line Catalogue* (called "Projet", and shared with the retailers and agents through Extranet – the activities concern both the insertion of the bills and their updating, government of the families and variances, building libraries and filters to create correct orders from the retailers and agents to the mother company and thus the factory, translation into different languages).

6. The Supply Chain Processes

Stefano Tonchia

6.1 Supply Chain

The "Supply Chain" mega-process is aimed at ensuring a continuous flow of materials, from the suppliers to the production processes, so as to render end products available to the "Sales" mega-process in the quantities, types and times required by the market (Figure 5.1).

The concept of "Supply Chain" is intrinsic to the theory of process management applied to the manufacturing area, and identifies exchange links between suppliers and customers, both inside and outside the company. Given the physical presence of materials, the concept in a certain sense is a precursor of the more general theory of process management, which also considers information as an exchangeable good.

Supply Chain Management is a discipline in which there is a growing interest, and it can be considered the natural evolution of *Logistics Management* and *Integrated Logistics*:

1) *Logistics Management* mostly focuses on optimising internal flows, during the three stages of acquisition, production and distribution (in-bound, internal, and distribution logistics, respectively). It is based on the definition of *logistics* as the *set of activities aimed at ensuring availability in time and space (where and when they are needed) of the goods (raw materials, parts or sale products) at the lowest overall cost* (Bowersox et al., 1986). In-bound logistics concerns the issue of orders, receipt and inspection of purchase goods and subsequent storage; internal logistics plans production, defines requirements of materials, manages stock and internal handling; distribution logistics concerns the management of the stocks of end products and their shipping/delivery to the final customer, via the appropriate distribution channels,

2) *Integrated Logistics* is aimed at smoothing out interventions in the above three stages, and promotes an integrated management of the physical flow of goods and information between in-bound, internal and distribution logistics,

3) *Supply Chain Management* broadened the horizon of activities and responsibilities to inter-enterprise logistics, as it was considered insufficient to merely integrate the logistics-related activities of a single enterprise. These activities must involve all the actors (supplier

companies, outside contractors, internal production units, distributors and retailers) who are crossed by the flow of materials and share the common aim of offering/selling the end product. It is thus important to find the correct methods and techniques to connect, coordinate and manage the overall logistics network that expands both inside and outside the company (this also includes the decision to centralise / decentralise the management of the entire network – See Chapter 3).

The term *"value chain"* has been coined to stress both the need to analyse and understand the various customer/supplier relationship links, and how the value of a product increases at each link (Porter, 1985; Schonberger, 1990).

The metaphor of the chain soon became very popular, but many objected to it, since it suggested a straight, unidirectional flow, that can somehow be associated with a pipeline. Reality is usually quite different: the supply systems feature bi-directional flows of materials and information, side links with other subjects, participation with other networks, and so forth. If on one hand it is more correct to use the definition *Supply "Network" Management*, on the other the term "supply chain" has become so widespread, that it is taken for granted that there is a web of relationships between the various subjects involved in these flows.

In the case of Snaidero (but this is also true for any manufacturing company), the major processes that ensure the correct functioning of the supply chain are the following:

- *Production Logistics*, including all production-aimed activities carried out both by internal units and external suppliers; in other words, these are the activities managing the logistic flow from a global "supply chain/network" viewpoint (it is defined Production Logistics to distinguish it from Distribution Logistics, which is placed downstream of production and concerns the end product),
- *Relationships with the Suppliers*, including the selection, activation (by contract), development and assessment of the suppliers (routine activities concerning the management of purchase orders are not included, they pertain to Production Logistics),
- *Manufacturing*, which includes all production processes,
- *Quality*, whose task is to manage/measure quality and preserve the standards (procedures) obtained through the ISO 9001 certification,
- *Plants and Safety*, aimed at managing the plants (maintenance, etc.) and complying to the rules of work safety and protection of the environment (ISO 14000 Certification),

- *Technology and Investments*, whose aim is the technological monitoring, analysis and assessment of the technological requirements, acquisition or development of technology through direct investments, etc.

Many of the above processes are quite complex and need to be broken down into several sub-processes. In Snaidero, they have been divided as shown in Figure 6.1. The breakdown representation can be compared to a tree, the leaves of which (the last level on the right) are the fundamental processes required to establish the supplier/customer relationships. These are characterised by an "active link" (as can be deduced from the underlined terms in Figure 6.1) that connect them to their process sheets describing their activities, suppliers, customers, inputs and outputs.

The processes forming the supply chain are described in greater detail in the following Paragraphs.

MEGA: SUPPLY CHAIN					
		other mega-processes			
Major		**Sub-major**		**Sub-sub-major**	
1 Logistics	1.1	Production Planning & Materials Management	1.1.1	Production Planning (MPS+MRP)	
				Management of Materials & Warehouses	
	1.2	Capacity Management	1.2.1	Rough-Cut Capacity Planning (RCCP)	
			1.2.2	Capacity Requirements Planning (CRP)	
	1.3	Shop Floor Control (SFC)	1.3.1	MTS Control	
			1.3.2	MTO Control	
2 Suppliers Relationships	2.1	Purchase Marketing			
	2.2	Suppliers Homologation/Certification			
	2.3	Co-Design Activation			
	2.4	Supply Activation			
	2.5	Suppliers Evaluation			
	2.6	Improvement of Suppliers' Performances			
	2.7	Purchasing Management Control			
	2.8	Price Analysis / Supply Estimation			
3 Manufacturing	3.1	Make-To-Stock Semi-finished Goods	3.1.1	Sectioning of raw materials	
			3.1.2	Squaring-Drilling	
	3.2	Make-To-Order Semi-finished Goods	3.2.1	Door Sectioning	
			3.2.2	Frame Sectioning	
			3.2.3	Linear Sectioning	
			3.2.4	Coating application	
	3.3	Packaging for Ikea			
	3.4	Packaging for Rational			
	3.5	Kitchens Finishing	3.5.1	Kitchen cabinets Finishing	
			3.5.2	Customised elements Finishing	
4 Quality					
5 Plants & Safety					
6 Technology & Investements					

Fig 6.1   The Supply Chain processes

6.2 Logistics

The major-process "(Production) Logistics" must ensure the availability of the materials in the appropriate place and time along the entire production chain, i.e. from raw material supply to the warehousing of the end products. The production system is thus considered in a more extended sense, and takes into account both internal manufacturing orders and the purchase orders issued to the suppliers.

All the activities revolve around the *Master Production Schedule (MPS)* which states:

- which end items are to be produced,
- in what quantities,
- when these are needed.

The Master Production Schedule is determined/driven by one or more of the following inputs (in particular, the forecasts will be constantly updated, until they become order entries) (Figure 6.2):

- sales forecasting,
- order entries,
- Distribution Requirements Planning – DRP.

The *Master Production Schedule* issued at this stage is still *tentative*. To ascertain its feasibility, it is necessary to check the production capacity requirements, which are considered at an aggregate level, i.e. only the gross requirement of resources per unit of end product (Rough Cut Capacity Planning – RCCP). Once this has been verified the schedule is *authorised* (Figure 6.2).

When advisable, it is possible to have two levels of MPS: the classical (relative to the end items) and one of a higher level (relative to the "families" of end products, as these feature a large number of final configurations).

At this stage it is possible to go into greater detail, separating the products into their parts and analysing the productive capacity in terms of departments, work centres, and so forth. Three production factors are required to formulate a production schedule: 1) materials, 2) machinery / equipment, 3) human resources. Since machinery/equipment and human resources form the productive capacity (and their mix determines the *level of automation),* what must be scheduled and managed are:

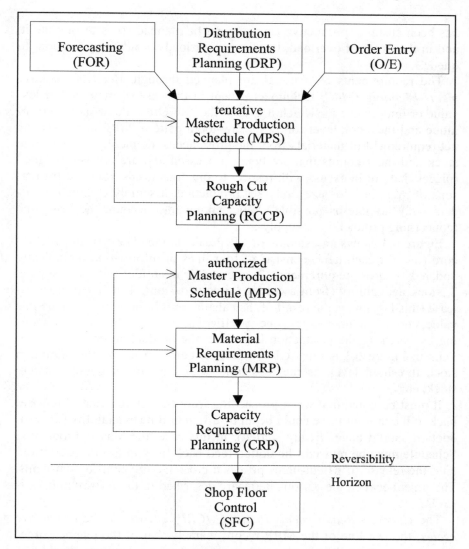

Fig 6.2   Logical flow for Production Planning & Control

1) the single items of materials *(Material Requirements Planning – MRP),*
2) the single work centre capacities *(Capacity Requirements Planning – CRP).*

From a logical viewpoint, materials and capacity can be considered on the same level: however, as it makes no sense to schedule the capacity in the absence of materials, material requirements are scheduled *beforehand*, and then those regarding capacity (Figure 6.2); once the presence of materials has been ensured, productive capacity can be planned so as to saturate it, and in the event of overload, levelling work loads or allowing material to queue.

The requirements of material are planned through *Material Requirements Planning (MRP)* technique, except in the case of materials of less value or importance for which it is used the "Re-Order Point" (ROP) technique and the stock level follows a saw-tooth pattern. MRP calculates the net requirement of materials from the gross needs, detracting the available stock and the amounts that are being processed and are not yet assigned (pieces that are in excess with respect to previous needs, released for reasons of minimum lot size), releases production, assembly or purchase orders with "as late as possible" logic, taking into account the lead time (concerning production or supply).

Figure 6.3 shows an example of MRP calculation. The typical MRP record (one for each item) consists of four lines of information periodically updated: 1. gross requirements, 2. open order quantities not yet assigned, 3. stock availability (from a certain "time zero" on), 4. planned order release (this last line is the result of the calculation). In order to calculate this value, certain parameters must be specified, such as: the lot size (if operating by batches), the production lead time (the production order of the 40 units in Figure 6.3 is released two periods before reaching the minimum stock threshold level, as the lead time is of 2 periods), possible safety stock, etc.

It must be noted that when proceeding from the future (time of release) back to the present there could be an insufficient time availability (i.e. production should have already started): in this case, the Master Production Schedule must be revised (the dotted feed-back lines in Figure 6.2). If extant, the release of parent-items primes a gross requirement for son-items. The links between the various items are described in the *bills of materials (BOM)*.

The *Capacity Requirements Planning (CRP)* occurs via the *productive cycles*: the last line of the MRP record, namely that of the planned order release, is translated from physical quantities to work loads or "backlogs" (the lower part of Figure 6.3), which are generally expressed in hours per work-centres where the product is processed, the latter being listed in the "routings". The CRP thus identifies the loads in the various work centres, formed by pre-existing and new customer orders. The "spreading" of the loads assumes centres of infinite capacity; in the event of capacity overload, it is necessary to level the work loads ("Finite Loading") and thus modify the MRP and, if required, even the Master Production Schedule (the dotted feed-back lines in Figure 6.2).

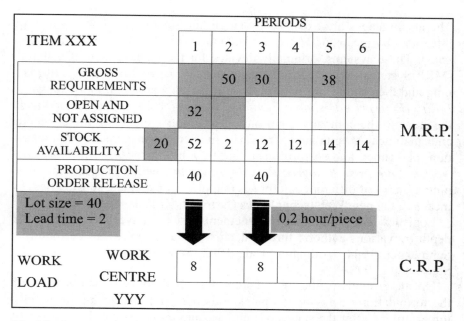

ITEM XXX		PERIODS							
		1	2	3	4	5	6		
GROSS REQUIREMENTS			50	30		38			M.R.P.
OPEN AND NOT ASSIGNED		32							
STOCK AVAILABILITY	20	52	2	12	12	14	14		
PRODUCTION ORDER RELEASE		40		40					

Lot size = 40
Lead time = 2   0,2 hour/piece

WORK LOAD	WORK CENTRE YYY	8		8				C.R.P.

Fig 6.3 An example of record M.R.P. (above) and C.R.P. (below): the data of the problem are highlighted, the other data are the solutions

Up to this stage, planning can still be changed: in other words, only a "what-if" simulation has been made to obtain an Available-To-Promise (APT) date of delivery. With the passage of time, it soon becomes indispensable to "freeze" the decisions that have been made, else it will be impossible to respect the delivery date of the customer order. This step leads to the *horizon of irreversibility* (Figure 6.2): all the orders regarding production, material purchasing, and processing by outside contractors are thus *placed*. Planning is over, and from this moment what has been scheduled need be performed. This stage is controlled by the *Shop Floor Control (SFC)*.

Shop Floor Control – often made with local software – has the following tasks: 1) to verify and enter the definitive production orders (by checking documents, quantities, presence of materials); 2) dispatching the single resources to each production works in compliance with the priority rules for *scheduling*, namely the definition of the start and completion time for each activity (De Toni, Nassimbeni and Tonchia, 1996); 3) collecting data, monitoring and tracking (i.e. constant traceability of the orders and their progress); 4) if required, interventions and corrective actions (e.g. extra work, alternative cycles, lot breakdown, subcontracting, etc.); 5) order reporting, until it is closed.

The above stages are executed by single information modules, which are integrated by means of *M.P.C.S. (Manufacturing Planning & Control Systems)*. These systems, originally devised for the management of materials (MRP Systems), widened to manage capacity, carry out first overall planning and then shop floor control. Nowadays they are commonly known as *E.R.P. (Enterprise Resource Planning) Systems*, because they extend to all the areas of the company – not only production – including trade, general and analytical accountancy, treasury, financial management, administration, personnel, and so forth. The latest evolution regards *N.E.R.P. (Networked Enterprise Resource Planning) Systems*, which integrate the planning systems of different enterprises (suppliers, customers, subsidiaries) by means of the new Web technologies (Extranet, XML language, etc.).

Logistics and production management systems have been analysed in depth by various authors; further details on these topics can be found in: Schmenner, 1984; Vollmann et al., 1992; Schonberger and Knod, 1997; Slack et al., 1998.

On the grounds of the logical flow described above, which starts with the formulation of production plans and ends with the closing of the customer orders, after the stages of purchase and production orders, materials and capacity management and shop floor control, it is possible to break down the (major) process of Production Logistics into sub-major processes, as intimated in Figure 6.1:

1) *Production Planning & Materials Management*, which in turn can be divided into two sub-processes (sub-sub-major processes): 1.1) *Production Planning* (MPS+MRP), 1.2) *Management of Materials & Warehouses* (responsible for handling and managing the stocks),
2) *Capacity Management*, divided between: 2.1) *Rough-Cut Capacity Planning* (RCCP), 2.2) *Capacity Requirements Planning* (CRP),
3) *Shop Floor Control* (SFC).

As can be seen, the first two classes of processes concern planning (and are thus placed in a reversible context), while the third concerns control (and is therefore positioned on an irreversible horizon). In the first class, MPS and MRP are considered together, since they both refer to amounts of materials (end items in the case of MPS, all other materials in the case of MRP); a sub-process specifically focusing on materials management (i.e. not in terms of planning but of handling) and warehousing is considered apart. The second class refers to units of capacity (for instance, labour-hours and machine-hours). Shop floor control is divided into two sub-processes, separately tracking production orders made-to-stock ("B policy") and those that have actually been placed and received ("A policy") –

as detailed in the Paragraph concerning the major-process "Manufacturing".

Figure 6.4 describes the activities of these "leaf-level" processes in Snaidero. Tables 6.1 and 6.2, as an example, describe the suppliers and customers, as well as the inputs and outputs, of the sub-sub-major process "Production Planning".

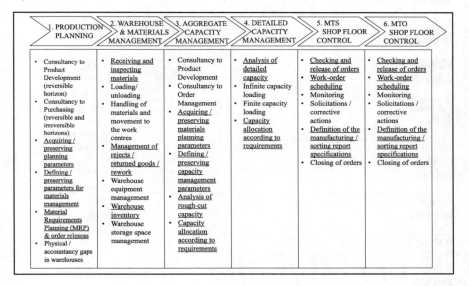

1. PRODUCTION PLANNING	2. WAREHOUSE & MATERIALS MANAGEMENT	3. AGGREGATE CAPACITY MANAGEMENT	4. DETAILED CAPACITY MANAGEMENT	5. MTS SHOP FLOOR CONTROL	6. MTO SHOP FLOOR CONTROL
• Consultancy to Product Development (reversible horizon) • Consultancy to Purchasing (reversible and irreversible horizons) • Acquiring / preserving planning parameters • Defining / preserving parameters for materials management • Material Requirements Planning (MRP) & order relescas • Physical / accountancy gaps in warehouses	• Receiving and inspecting materials • Loading/ unloading • Handling of materials and movement to the work centres • Management of rejects / returned goods / rework • Warehouse equipment management • Warehouse inventory • Warehouse storage space management	• Consultancy to Product Development • Consultancy to Order Management • Acquiring / preserving materials planning parameters • Defining / preserving capacity management parameters • Analysis of rough-cut capacity • Capacity allocation according to requirements	• Analysis of detailed capacity • Infinite capacity loading • Finite capacity loading • Capacity allocation according to requirements	• Checking and release of orders • Work-order scheduling • Monitoring • Solicitations / corrective actions • Definition of the manufacturing / sorting report specifications • Closing of orders	• Checking and release of orders • Work-order scheduling • Monitoring • Solicitations / corrective actions • Definition of the manufacturing / sorting report specifications • Closing of orders

Fig 6.4 The six *sub-sub-major processes* of "Production Logistics" and their activities

Table 6.1 The sub-sub-major process "Production Planning": activities (by columns) and related suppliers (by rows) of inputs (in the matrix)

activity / supplier	1. Consultancy to Product Development	2. Consultancy to Suppliers Relationships	3. Acquir./ preserv. planning paramet.	4. Definit./ preserv. mat. mngt paramet.	5. MRP & order releases	6. Physical /account. gaps in warehouses
Sales in Italy					Vol./t forecasts by name /wood	
International Sales					Vol./t forecasts by name/wood	
Contract Sales					Vol./t forecasts by name /wood	
Showrooms & Fairs					Vol./t forecasts by name/wood	
Orders Management					Finished products orders	
Product I/O Impact Eval.	Req. fin. costs lots & stocks	Req. fin. costs lots & stocks				
Product Portfolio Def.	Product I/O forecasts	Product I/O forecasts				
Product Definition	Gate #1 rep.; LT, M/B, Pol.A/B					
Industrialisation	Info on new name/wood			Specif.; Catal.; Load. & effic.	Specif.; Req. comp.; For photo	Production items BOM
Product Launch			BOM et al.; Verified specif.	Database	Ty.comp.; Init. for.; 1 pur.; Training	
Aggreg. Capac. Mngt (RCCP)					Authoris. MPS	

Table 6.1   (continued)

Detailed Capac. Mngt (CRP)				Conf. / mod. MPS	
Mat. & Wareh. Mngt					Materials Stocks
MTS Control			Planning param. modifications	Delays; Plan. par. modif.; Report	
MTO Control			Planning param. modifications		
Codesign Activation	Req. for suppl. volumes et al.				
Supply Activation	Req. for suppl. volumes et al.	Item LT, lot, freq., pol. A/B		Supply contract	
Suppliers Evalutation			Info calcul. safety LT		

Table 6.2   The sub-sub-major process "Production Planning": activities (by columns) and related customers (by rows) of outputs (in the matrix)

activity / customer	1. Consultancy to Product Development	2. Consultancy to Suppliers Relationships	3. Acquir. / preserv. planning paramet.	4. Definit. / preserv. mat. mngt paramet.	5. MRP & order releases	6. Physical /account. gaps in warehouses
Product I/O Impact Eval.	Financial costs of lots & stocks	Var. of fin.costs of lots & stocks				
Product Definition	On estimates; On LT,M/B,A/B					
Industrialisation				Production cycles/ times		
Product Launch				Manager. data;D/B; Space		

Table 6.2   (continued)

Aggreg. Capac. Mngt (RCCP)			Req. for MPS feasibility	
Detailed Capac. Mngt (CRP)			Req. for MPS modifications	
Mat. & Wareh. Mngt				Req. for stock verification
MTS Control			Order releases; Urgencies et al.	
MTO Control			Order releases; Urgencies et al.	
Codesign Activation	Prop. of suppl. vol. et al.			
Supply Activation	Prop. of suppl. vol. et al.	Req. info calcul. safety LT		
Suppliers Evalutation				

6.3 Relationships with Suppliers

This process concerns external procurement, whereas the cycle of purchase orders is managed by "Logistics": in fact, from a logistics viewpoint, there are no differences in materials management from internal units or external suppliers (i.e. juridically independent). The process "Relationships with Suppliers" is therefore aimed at ensuring – but not carrying out – the procurement from the suppliers. The term *Procurement* indicates a set of activities resulting in the stipulation of the contract between vendor and purchaser for the supply of goods or services required by the enterprise to carry out its processes of transformation or trade. *Purchasing,* on the other hand, indicates those activities aimed at ensuring a regular flow of goods and services according to a pre-established schedule. In the framework of process management, the business function "Purchases" (sometimes defined "Procurement") acts as a reservoir of competencies and a point of reference for the suppliers; the main processes executed by means of its resources are those here defined "Relationships with Suppliers" (for their selection, stipulation of the contract, development and assessment) and "Logistics" (more precisely, "In-bound Logistics", whereas the production planners take charge of "Internal Logistics"). Obviously, one person belonging to the function "Purchases" may contribute to both processes.

The relationships with the suppliers have become increasingly important over the last few years, as it became more evident that a synergy with the suppliers – for the management of the production cycle and during the stage of product design/development – could greatly improve performances in terms of time, cost and quality; another cause has been the increasing incidence of purchase costs on the price of the end product.

The main novelties concerning the evolution of relationships with suppliers regard the *models* and *types* of relationship.

With reference to the *models*, these mainly consist in (De Toni, Nassimbeni and Tonchia, 1994a):

- a *revision of the traditional antagonistic model of the customer/supplier relationship*. The closer interdependence between the different units of the supply chain have transformed the transaction of goods into a relationship of cooperation, which has also become more exclusive, reducing the number of suppliers. In advanced relationships, these have evolved into "single sourcing", "dual sourcing", "parallel sourcing", featuring, respectively, one supplier per component, two in competition with each other, or again, only one, but with the possibility of changing the supplier with another who produces a similar part and/or one that can be used in another model,
- a *reconfiguration and integrated management of the supply chain*. The broader area of customer-supplier interaction re-defines the profile and role of the upstream interlocutor. In particular, privileged suppliers are those who manage whole sub-assemblies that are not critical for the purchasing company, thus allowing the latter to reduce the relational effort arising from a larger number of supplying interlocutors. In other terms, the advanced company interacts with a smaller number of suppliers than in the past; these are often tier-1 suppliers managing tier-2 and tier-3 suppliers, who in the past would have interacted directly with the purchasing company (Cusumano and Takeishi, 1991),
- an *extension of the traditional geographical area for procurement*. These changes arise from the world-wide competition that exists in certain sectors, and the need for a company to acquire distinctive features on the global market.

Regarding the *types* of relationship with the suppliers, it is possible to distinguish between (De Toni, Nassimbeni and Tonchia, 1995a):

- a *traditional relationship,* featuring negotiation of each order, incoming inspections, need for safety stock,
- an *operative integration,* with medium- or long-term relationships, the possibility of agreement on changes in prices and volumes throughout time, quality warranted and certified, responsibility for entire assemblies or modules, frequent supplies in small lots (in the framework of so-called "open orders"), direct "pull" supply according to the needs of the production departments (Just-In-Time Purchasing – Ansari and Modarress, 1990), continuous improvement in quality and constant cost reduction, offers of "service packages" (De Toni, Nassimbeni and Tonchia, 1994b) by the suppliers, advising and training of the suppliers by the company,
- *partnership*, which results in cooperation since the stages of design ("co-design" – Hartley et al., 1997; Ragatz et al., 1997), common investments in technology, research and development, constant exchange and sharing of information, and in general, coherence of strategies.

Due to relevance (cost) of the materials and complexity (risks) of the supply market (Kraljic, 1983), not all the suppliers are destined to establish partnerships; however, for the key suppliers, these types of relationships represent the different stages of an evolution that ends in a partner supplier being the single source for a particular type of items and often ensuring the management of tier-2 suppliers (thus becoming a supplier of entire sets of items – modules).

In Snaidero, the following strategic priorities are considered the critical factors of success in the Purchasing Area:

- a marked and continuous reduction in the overall purchasing costs,
- a constant warrant of quality for the purchased products,
- improvement of time-related performances (lead times and reliability of delivery, and consequent lower stock levels).

These priorities determine objectives, precisely measured, leveraged on:

- the organizational structure of purchases (separating the activities inherent in the order cycle from those regarding the object of the purchase),
- assessment of the vendors' competencies (including quality issues and Vendor Rating),

- the development of "purchase marketing" (with appropriate market segmentation into classes and the creation of a repository of current and potential suppliers),
- research and assessment of innovative and pro-active suppliers (including policies of competition and price control, with costs breakdown and consideration of the experience curves),
- development of partnerships (agreements, open orders, etc.),
- negotiation with the suppliers (making deal sheets, keeping a data-base of the purchase bills, defining of the end-of-year bonuses, etc.),
- development of an inter-functional purchasing team (with the manufacturing, industrialisation, etc.).

Snaidero has approximately 245 suppliers, 36 of which (15%) account for roughly 80% of the purchase invoice, and form the so-called "class A" suppliers. Class B (22 suppliers) and Class C (187 suppliers) each account for about 10% of the invoice. The classes of purchased items have also been analysed according to ABC logics (Pareto analysis), and 15 categories have been identified, five of which account for 90,2% of the purchases.

Partnerships are consolidated through actions of: a) update/revision of contract specifications; b) shared monitoring of competitiveness throughout time; c) common projects of performance improvement. Moreover, the issuing of tenders and their rating are subject to regulation, both in the case of partners and normal suppliers: they contain information concerning times (deadlines, duration of the contract, lead time of delivery, when payments must be made, etc.), costs (pricing formula and composition of the costs, changes in prices/quantities, penalties for delays, quality) and delivery (packaging, assortment, ensured safety stock, etc.).

In Snaidero, "Relationships with the Suppliers" is a major process consisting of the following sub-major processes – Figure 6.5:

- *Purchase Marketing*, to seek and catalogue suppliers, preparing "minimum requirement profiles",
- *Suppliers Homologation/Certification*, aimed at providing an "homologation profile" (more detailed than the previous one, as it also takes into account the potential requirements) and subsequent "audit profile" (with information verified by carrying out visits and examining samples),
- *Co-Design Activation*, which acts as consultant for the internal process of product design/development, and receives from it requests to involve the suppliers in design activities,

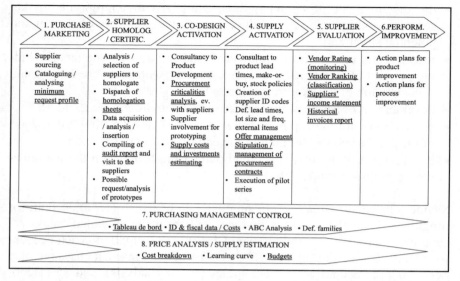

1. PURCHASE MARKETING	2. SUPPLIER HOMOLOG. / CERTIFIC.	3. CO-DESIGN ACTIVATION	4. SUPPLY ACTIVATION	5. SUPPLIER EVALUATION	6.PERFORM. IMPROVEMENT
• Supplier sourcing • Cataloguing / analysing minimum request profile	• Analysis / selection of suppliers to homologate • Dispatch of homologation sheets • Data acquisition / analysis / insertion • Compiling of audit report and visit to the suppliers • Possible request/analysis of prototypes	• Consultancy to Product Development • Procurement criticalities analysis, ev. with suppliers • Supplier involvement for prototyping • Supply costs and investments estimating	• Consultant to product lead times, make-or-buy, stock policies • Creation of supplier ID codes • Def. lead times, lot size and freq. external items • Offer management • Stipulation / management of procurement contracts • Execution of pilot series	• Vendor Rating (monitoring) • Vendor Ranking (classification) • Suppliers' income statement • Historical invoices report	• Action plans for product improvement • Action plans for process improvement

7. PURCHASING MANAGEMENT CONTROL
• Tableau de bord • ID & fiscal data / Costs • ABC Analysis • Def. families

8. PRICE ANALYSIS / SUPPLY ESTIMATION
• Cost breakdown • Learning curve • Budgets

Fig 6.5 The eight *sub-major processes* of "Relationships with Suppliers" and their activities

- *Supply Activation*, which acts as a consultant for the process of production planning, and activates supply relationships by issuing tenders and subsequently stipulating contracts (there are reference standard forms for offers, their assessment, cost breakdown structure, business deals and agreements),
- *Suppliers Evaluation*, including the areas: *service* (% delayed deliveries, average delay, % and no. of missing items, under-stock times, plus problem-solving, availability, flexibility), *quality* (returned items upon reception and from the market, re-works), *costs* (price per unit, full price, etc.), *contractual conditions* (days for payment, stocks, lead times, packaging, transportation),
- *Improvement of Suppliers' Performances*, affecting the products and/or the manufacturing process,
- *Purchasing Management Control*, which controls all the costs of the items listed in the BOM, makes ABC analysis, etc.,
- *Price Analysis / Supply Estimation*, including the supplier's cost breakdown structure and its "learning curve".

Table 6.3   The sub-major process "Co-Design Activation": activities (by columns) and related suppliers and customers (by rows) of inputs and outputs respectively (in the matrix)

ACTIVITIES	1. Consultancy to Product Development (reversibility)	2. Procurement criticalities analysis	3. Supplier involvement for prototyping	4. Supply costs & investments estimating
SUPPLIERS				
Product Definition	Studies & drafts	Request for criticality analysis; Decisions on LT, M/B, Pol.A/B	Prototype; Request for supplying prototypes	Gate #1 report
Production Planning	Proposal of supply volumes and LT, lot size & freq. indications			
Supplier Homologation / Certification		List of certified suppliers	List of certified suppliers	
External supplier		Criticalities / alternatives sheet compiled	Prototype; Prototype costs	Volume/time forecasts
CUSTOMERS				
Product Definition	Feedback on studies & drafts	Criticality remarks; Consulting (LT, M/B, Pol.A/B)	Comments on prototype and criticalities	Costs & investments estimates
Production Planning	Request for supply volumes and LT, lot size & freq. indications			
Purchase Marketing		Criticalities; Necessity of searching new suppliers		
External supplier		Informations and drafts; Critic./altern. sheet to be compiled	Request for prototype; Request for prototype costs	Request for volume/time forecasts

Figure 6.5 depicts the activities relative to each of the above sub-major processes; the underlined activities have links to formal-procedural documents describing how these activities are carried out.

All these sub-major processes exchange inputs and outputs with each other and with other last-level processes (i.e. the "leaves" in the process breakdown trees) of the company. Table 6.3 shows, for instance, the inputs and outputs exchanged by the sub-major process "Co-Design Activation". The underlined inputs and outputs have links to formal documents describing their structure and contents.

6.4   Manufacturing

At first sight, manufacturing is the easiest major-process to map, as its breakdown structure into sub-processes and activities is indicated/suggested by the bonds of the production cycle and handling of the materials, which simplify the identification of internal customers and items exchanged. However, often for these reasons this major process risks being broken down in correspondence to production stages and units. These must be taken into account, but other, "softer" criteria should not be neglected, such as how the (internal or external) demand is met, or the different business/customer targets of the production.

For instance, in Snaidero the "Manufacturing" major process has been divided into production of semi-finished goods (upstream stages) and final operations (finishing and packaging) – Figure 6.1.

The upstream stages are distinguished according to how the demand is met: 1) "Semi-finished goods made-to-stock" (when it would be inconvenient or there would not be enough time to manufacture the batches upon receiving the customers' orders); 2) "Semi-finished goods made-to-order" (which follow established pathways and are labelled with the name of the customer). This situation can be schematically represented as two conical frusta – the first, larger one, having its smaller base coinciding with the larger base of the second frustum – which converge at the end in a "tube" where the final operations occur (the concept of "tube" representing a "pull" production, i.e. driven from downstream, was conceived by Bonazzi, 1993, and is one of the key concepts of *lean production* – De Toni and Tonchia, 2002).

The coinciding axes of the two cone frusta follow the evolution of time, whereas the size of their bases can be considered proportional to variety: therefore, a limited number of models can be obtained from a large number of components (in Snaidero, the models are identified by name/wood-types – there are approximately 40 names, each of which is available in 3-5 different types of wood). From a certain point onwards (coinciding with the smaller base of the smaller cone) the "tube" starts, where each name/wood-type is rigidly bound to operations of finish/packaging, thus pursuing top efficiency and timeliness.

Make-to-stock (or "B"-type) purchasing policies are associated with the larger cone frustum, whereas make-to-order (or "A"-type) purchasing policies with the smaller one: purchase orders can in fact be inserted into both frusta. With the passage of time, the forecasts are either confirmed or not into order entries ("progressive freezing of the options").

Moreover, a distinction is made between processes pertaining to the various companies of the group (such as, for instance, packaging for Ikea or Rational products), but only when specific managerial choices must be made.

6.5 Quality

The issue of quality concerns on one hand ISO 9000 quality standards (described in Paragraph 1.5), and on the other its management, which will be discussed in this Paragraph.

Quality management is often associated with Total Quality Management – TQM practices (Flynn et al., 1994), where the adjective "Total" refers to the extension of these methods and instruments to the entire company (thus the other similar term, "Company-wide"), and not only to the manufacturing areas or inspection of materials. Despite the number and variety of opinions concerning TQM both in the literature and at a consultancy level, there are four common key elements:

1) the involvement of the *entire* company, including the management, who must ensure the necessary *commitment* and endorsement to quality policies,
2) the focus on *customer satisfaction* (rather then mere compliance with the required conformity standards), a customer who can also be *internal*,
3) the concept of *continuous improvement* (a company must also improve during the period that runs between the issuing of two official specifications),
4) the *reduction/elimination of variability* in the manufacturing processes as a source of quality conformance (the qualitative level depends on the design process, which should have released specifications ensuring conformity of quality).

Process management can be considered pivotal for quality management in the new production contexts, and acts as a powerful catalyst for the deployment of quality programmes.

Figure 6.6 illustrates how the concept of quality has evolved, and the current relationship existing between quality and process management:

- From quality based on standards, we have passed to quality intended as customer satisfaction (quality as a means of meeting customer requirements, by supplying an adequate level of service too: quality coincides with value, which in turn is decreed by the customer). All *processes generate value*, and consider customer visibility of the utmost importance (both final and the internal customers).
- From quality control, we have reached the "trilogy" consisting of *planning* (to meet increasingly severe standards), *control* (along the entire pro duction line, carried out in real time and using sophisticated statistical techniques) and *improvement* (by training, coaching and accepting suggestions). Improvement by learning can indeed be considered as the objective of the processes.

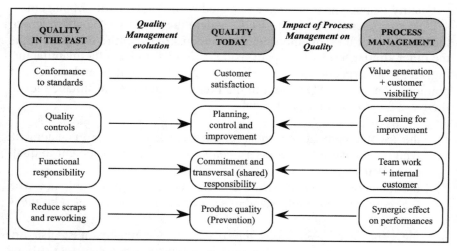

Fig 6.6   Total Quality Management and Process Management

- Functional responsibility has become shared responsibility, with integral management of the quality factor even during the first stages of design and production (the concept of "upstream quality management"). In process management, the existence of internal customer/supplier relationships and team work are at the roots of shared responsibility.
- The inspective approach, with its measurement and control of rejects and re-works costs, has been replaced by a preventive approach, aimed at achieving "first-pass quality" so reducing/eliminating the above costs

before they occur. As mentioned previously, process management features a more precise measurement of the performances, which are synergic when considered jointly (costs and quality are the two faces of the same coin, as described at the end of this Paragraph).

In short, process management and TQM are reciprocally functional. Process management ensures the achievement of all performances and the focus on the final customer by creating an organisation oriented towards the creation of value, learning and integration; these are the prerequisites for high performances in terms of quality. At the same time, the orientation towards "process capability", the continuous improvements, prevention of defects just from the first stages of design and development, translate the typical features of process management into TQM requirements. It could be stated that a *process-managed organization* is basically a *quality-aimed* one, its core resource being human ones (both along the production line and as support), exploiting quality instruments (statistical, problem solving and involvement ones, etc.) to concretise potentials and ideas.

As mentioned previously, in order to manage it, is necessary to measure: the quality performance dimensions must be identified so as to carry out measurements during processing. In particular, quality can be divided into (De Toni, Nassimbeni and Tonchia, 1995b):

1. *Perceived quality and customer satisfaction,* both in terms of product and services:
    1.1 for the *product*, Garvin's eight dimensions of quality (1988) can be used: basic features, secondary features, performance or operating characteristics, conformance to specifications/catalogue, reliability (absence of failures over time), durability (of the life cycle), aesthetics, perceived quality,
    1.2 for the *service*, it is possible to use the instrument "ServQual" (Zeithaml et al., 1990; De Toni and Tonchia, 2004). The dimensions are defined as follows: tangibles (physical facilities, equipment, personnel), reliability (ability to perform the promised service), responsiveness (competence and promptness), assurance (courtesy and trust), empathy (the caring attention given to the customer).
2. *Quality offer*, which can be divided into:
    2.1 *in-bound quality* (quality of supplies – indicators such as Vendor Quality Rating),
    2.2 *internal quality*, which in turn includes:
        2.2.1 *product design* ("design capability"),

      2.2.2 *engineering of the production processes* ("process capabil-ity" – C_p and C_{p_k} indicators),

      2.2.3 *production* (conformance – warranted by control charts),

   2.3 *output quality* (quality regarding distribution and delivery).

3.   *Quality-related costs*:

   3.1 *prevention/maintenance costs* (including the management costs of the quality procedures and improvement programmes),

   3.2 *quality control and final inspection costs,*

   3.3 *non-quality costs* (or "negative quality"), including the following costs: rejects and waste material, scraps, re-working, non-conformities at final control, products returned by the customers, and interventions covered by guarantee (staff and spare parts).

6.6 Plants & Safety and Technology & Investments

Typically, there are two processes supporting manufacturing: "Plants & Safety" and "Technology & Investments".

The major-process "Plants & Safety" is responsible for managing plants and their proper use, so as to ensure safety in the work place. Plant man-agement must comply with the *maintenance* policies, stating on which parts of machinery and equipment maintenance is to be carried out, the type of maintenance (preventive or corrective, and, in the former case, whether calendar-scheduled or in relation to certain parameters), who is in charge of carrying out the interventions (external or internal maintenance, and in the latter case, centralised or decentralised at the various depart-ments), the structure of maintenance costs (hours/person, instruments, spare parts). The effectiveness of these activities is monitored by indicators for *reliability* (Mean Time Between Failures – MTBF), *maintainability* (Mean Time To Repair – MTTR) and time *availability* of the plants. This major-process is also responsible for safety, i.e. compulsory activities regulated by law decrees, and in general, any act that improves the work conditions of the employees.

The major-process "Technology & Investments" focuses on manufac-turing technology and the investments required to innovate the manufac-turing processes (not to be confused with the major-process "Research & Development", described in the chapter on "Business Development", which concerns new materials, technical solutions and product technology, and precedes the stage of "Product Design/Development"). The major-process "Technology & Investments" is considered part of the "Supply Chain" mega-process, since the efforts to innovate the process usually follow and depend on those regarding product innovation (Abernathy and Utterback, 1978; von Hippel, 1988). Although it is not strictly necessary to have new products in order to improve the plants and manufacturing processes, the changes are usually less expensive or frequent. On the other hand, different production lines or machinery may be required to launch a new product; in such a case this major-process carries out activities of technological monitoring (studying available literature, attending technical fairs and conferences, etc.), analyses the technological requirements for the new products, assesses costs and benefits of new technologies (including "make-or-buy" decisions, i.e. subcontracting certain parts and processes), proposes alternative investments to the management, and finally sets up the new machines/plants.

7. The Directive and Support Processes

Stefano Tonchia

7.1 Strategic Planning

The three paragraphs of this chapter focus on the main directive and support processes of a business, namely "Strategic Planning " and "Human Resources Management" (directive processes), and "Budgeting & Control" (supportive). Other directive and support processes are reported in Figure 4.2.

Strategy can be considered in terms of "content" and "process". The "content" concerns both the *competitive priorities* (performance macro-objectives that can become Critical Success Factors – CSF) and the *intervention choices* (*technological* levers regarding product/process and information/communication, internal *organisational* levers and those to interface with suppliers/customers, and *managerial* levers ascribed for example to Just-In-Time, Total Quality Management and Project Management/Concurrent Engineering), made to achieve the above-mentioned priorities. The "process" regards the *formulation* and *implementation* of the strategy.

Traditionally, corporate strategy mainly relies on three options: cost leadership, differentiation, and segmentation (Porter, 1980). The current trend to overcome performance trade-offs questions this distinction (Filippini et al., 1998): the aim is the joint achievement of multiple performances, at least giving them different importance throughout time (the "sand cone model" – Ferdows and De Meyer, 1990).

Nowadays, strategy is above all defined in terms of priorities, which are not standard, but more of an "order-winning" and "qualifying" type (Hill, 1989): the former make it possible to steal customers from the competitors, the latter simply allow the company to enter into a certain competitive arena. Both are equally important, and when analysing its current situation, a company could need to invest in one or the other type.

Recently, Porter (1996) declared that "the 'essence of strategy' is deciding to carry out activities in a *different* manner from the competitors". This is made possible by the so-called "core competencies", which in recent years have been the object of the debate in order to renovate the traditional "structure-conduct-performance" strategic scheme, typical of the Industrial Organization. The latter scheme has been hugely criticised because of the differences in profitability found between companies operating in the same industry/sector; furthermore the classic five forces (intensity of competition, potential new entries into the industry, threats deriving from substitute products, contractual power of the suppliers and the customers) often failed to explain the sustainability of the competitive advantage. The criticism is advanced by supporters of the theory according to which *resources and competencies* are the real source of advantage for a company (and not an adequate strategic behaviour for the industry, as maintained by the traditional theory of the Industrial Organization). Theories such as Resource-Based View and Competence-Based Competition – which share some of the concepts expressed in the Enterprise Evolutionary Theory and Organisational Behaviour Theory) – are approaches that have many features and principles in common, so that it is possible to speak of a "Competency Theory" (De Toni and Tonchia, 2003).

According to the Competency Theory (Grant, 1997; Collis and Montgomery, 1997) strategic analysis can be schematically described by the sequence: analysis of the resources/competencies possessed; assessment of their profitability potential; consequent definition of a suitable strategy to exploit, valorise and consolidate them; strategy implementation by means of appropriate policies of resources management.

So the process of *strategic planning* should take into account both the sequence of analysis typical of the Industrial Organization, and that characterising the Competency Theory, identifying the principal point of contact when comparing *competitive priorities* on one hand and *resources/competencies* on the other (shaded in Figure 7.1 to highlight this link): competitive priorities cannot emerge only from an analysis of the industry; the resources/competencies possessed must also be taken into account, having analysed their potential of profitability in a certain industry. Moreover, it must be kept in mind that the typical resources/competencies of a company have a value *in se,* when compared to the outside world (the environment and the industry, this latter increasing difficult to identify with precision nowadays), but also in relation with the company's competitive priorities.

The link between the internal i.e. the company perspective, typical of the Competency Theory (inside-out approach), and the external i.e. the market/competitors perspective, typical of the Industrial Organization (outside-in approach), can be summarised by the so-called "S.W.O.T. analysis"(analysis of Strengths & Weaknesses + Opportunities & Threats).

SWOT analysis is usually carried out once the management has made its mission and vision clear. A company's *mission* is the answer to the questions: who are we? what do we do? how? why and for whom? Conversely, the company's *vision* answers questions regarding the future: where will we be? what will we be? Mission and vision should be communicated both inside and outside the company.

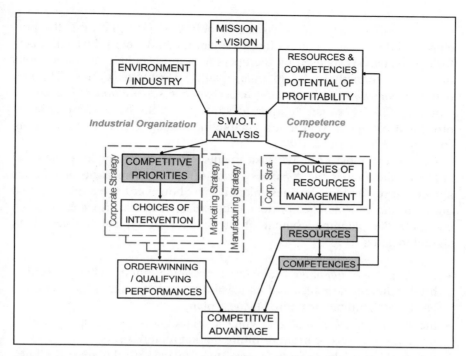

Fig 7.1 Strategic planning according to Industrial Organization and Competence Theory

Mission, vision and SWOT analysis lead to the definition of a strategy (depicted in Figure 7.1 by dashed lines), in terms of competitive priorities, intervention levers and resources management policies. The latter policies affect the competencies, which are placed at a higher level of aggregation in respect to resources, and assess the capacity of an appropriately managed set of resources to carry out an activity or pursue an objective: competencies can explain how two companies, having the same aims and resources, can perform differently, or have the same performances when possessing different resources (De Toni and Tonchia, 2003).

The strategic decisions concerning competitive priorities, intervention levers and resources management, are made at a corporate level ("corporate strategy"), but are then further detailed for business unit and function, usually proceeding from the trading area ("marketing strategy") to the operative one ("manufacturing strategy").

According to Corbett and Van Wassenhove (1993), all customers typically consider three things: 1) the price; 2) the product and/or the service (external i.e. perceived quality); 3) its availability (external performances throughout time, such as rapidity, punctuality and reliability) and accessory performances (such as assistance before, during and after the purchase, product/mix customisation, payment methods, etc.). Instead, a performance analysis focused on the operations must include the dimensions of: 1) cost/productivity; 2) (internal) quality; 3) (internal) times. The link between *operation performances* and *customer satisfaction* is indeed the "missing link" between "corporate strategy" (with its performances of profit and profitability in time), "marketing strategy" and "manufacturing strategy" (Wheelwright, 1984).

One of the most effective instruments for formulating the process of strategic planning is the *Business Plan*. Although there is no unanimous agreement on the ideal business plan, it must however have a multi-annual duration and not merely consider economical-financial aspects, so as to complete the planning content of the budget. A typical business plan should include:

- an *"executive summary"*, aimed at obtaining funds, which describes briefly the business idea and its feasibility, and stimulates the interested parties to examine the entire business plan,
- the *product/market analysis*, which explains how the company's offer responds to precise current or future market requirements,
- the *analysis of the industry/competitors,* to identify the areas for business development, the levels of profit and the rates of profitability realistically achievable in the coming years,
- the *distinctive and winning factors* of the idea and the competencies possessed,
- the objectives of the *sales plan,* throughout all the stages,
- the *work plan* (infrastructural and operative decisions),
- the necessary *technical and human resources*, and the forecasted *organisation and management* (including a description of the company structure and its management),
- the definition of the *financial requirements* and the analysis of the *funding sources*,
- the *economic-financial plan,* including the expected cash-flow throughout time.

The process of Strategy Planning supplies the most important inputs to the processes forming the mega-process Business Development (Figure 4.2).

7.2   Human Resources Management

Human Resources Management, although mainly carried out with the contribution of the Personnel function, is a typical example of process because of its transversal nature and the variety and multitude of inputs and outputs that characterise its activities. For the strategic importance of its decisions, it can be classified as a directive process.

Human Resources Management includes activities of a juridical, administrative, relationship, planning and organisational nature. These in turn can be grouped into two sub-major processes, each of which is formed by a number of sub-sub-major processes, such as those listed below:

- *Work Rights and Industrial Relationships*:
  - staff management (remuneration, taxation, social security),
  - trade-unions (relationships with trade unions, contracts, disputes, etc.),
  - individual litigations,
  - social life within the company (canteen, child care, recreation, etc.),
  - internal relationships (introducing the staff, divulging information, etc.),
  - external relationships (social initiatives, subventions, grants, etc.),
- *Organization Development:*
  - recruitment/selection and staff turnover,
  - manpower planning,
  - salary scheme and wage levels,
  - salary and bonus policies,
  - training (professional and managerial),
  - relationships with external consultants,
  - analysis and assessment of the work (tasks, roles, responsibilities, etc.),
  - management by objectives and assessment of staff performance,
  - assessment of staff potential and career plans,
  - competency analysis,
  - evaluation of the organisational climate,
  - organisational planning and revision (flow-chart, processes, etc.).

More information on these sub-processes, and, in general, organisation and management of human resources, is widely available in the literature (for instance: Becker et al., 2001). Our intent is merely to supply a few definitions to clarify other parts of the book.

The *competencies* of the personnel not only define what the persons know or are able to do, but also their behaviours: different "competitive" competencies must be provided, possessed and developed, which regard:

1) *knowledge*, i.e. what the person knows, acquired by education and/or learning in organised contexts (a knowledge concerning: techniques, technology, methodology, instruments, product or process design, standards and procedures, etc.),
2) *abilities*, namely what the persons are able to do, thanks to the experience matured and the practical application of knowledge (abilities to analyse, understand and make models, to assess alternatives, make decisions, forecast problems and solve them, be self-controlled, plan and control, be result-oriented, play different roles, etc.),
3) *behaviours*, namely how the persons act, both as individuals and in a group, because of their aims, values, ideas and habits (reflected in their attitudes, motivations, their taking or delegating responsibilities, flexibility, sense of initiative, talent for negotiation/persuasion, leadership skills, ability to work in a team, communicate, etc.) (Hunsaker and Cook, 1986).

These competencies are *individual* – and can be classified, respectively, as: 1) technical, 2) managerial and 3) relational. They should not be confused with the *organisational* competencies, described in the previous paragraph about strategy.

7.3   Budgeting & Control

Also the process "Budgeting & Control", although mostly carried out through resources of the "Administration & Control" function (or similar), is a typical example of process, due to its pervasiveness and the great number of inputs and outputs exchanged with all the other processes of the company.

Its activities can be summarised as those of the following three sub-major processes:

- *Budgeting*, i.e. the definition of the objectives and actions for the coming year, at different levels of detail, area and time. The main output of this process is the "budget" (consisting of asset and liability statement, income statement, and cash flows – all three estimated) (Anthony, 1997),

- *Control*, including general accountancy (having as main output the balance sheet, in terms of asset and liability statement, and final income statement) and analytical accountancy (aimed at calculating margins, analysing variance, choosing between alternatives, etc.) (Anthony et al., 1999),
- *Measurement of the Performances*, by designing, managing and maintaining the Performance Measurement System (P.M.S.) and the Balanced Scorecard (the name derives from the most famous one, developed by Kaplan and Norton in 1992); this latter depicts the key factors of success and synthesises the performance results collected by the whole P.M.S. The P.M.S. takes into account both cost-related performances (costs, productivity, capacity saturation, stock & work-in-progress levels) which determine the economical-financial results in an explicit way, and "non-cost" ones (quality, service, times, flexibility); the P.M.S. must permit to translate into practice and verify strategic plans and intervention programmes, benchmark competitors, coordinate and control work activities, assess and involve the human resources (Tonchia, 2000; De Toni and Tonchia, 2001).

In Chapter 2 we described how process management can greatly affect the business organisational asset and its P.M.S.; process management however is also a prerequisite for the application of the accountancy method illustrated below, namely *Activity-Based Costing (A.B.C.)*.

A.B.C. was devised as an alternative to the traditional technique used to calculate the *full cost of product*, according to which labour-hours, or other direct parameters such as materials amount or machine-hours were the allocation bases for assigning indirect costs, or overheads, to products (Morrow, 1992). However, when direct costs represent only a small part of the overall costs, to consider the overhead as proportional to "direct" costs (assumed as "variable") may determine remarkable distortions.

Already in 1985, Miller and Vollmann observed that "indirect" ("fixed") costs cannot depend on production volumes. In their opinion, overheads derive from *transactions*, which in turn can be distinguished in: logistic transactions (e.g. customer or handling orders), balancing transactions (i.e. all those activities related to the availability in space and time of the materials, and labour and machinery needed to face the demand), quality-ensuring transactions (control and prevention) and change transactions (arising when new projects are started or extant ones are modified). On the other hand, Cooper and Kaplan (1991) believe that indirect costs are "driven" by *complexity*, while direct costs are "driven" by production volumes; they identify four types of cost-generating activities, each of which has different "drivers": plant management supporting activities, product development supporting ones, activities related to lot management (such as machine set up), and volume-related ones (direct labour, materials and energy, "driven" precisely by the production volume).

A.B.C. is a technique aimed at calculating the full product cost starting from the cost of the resources used. In brief, traditional accounting methods allocate direct costs (that can be attributed objectively) directly to the products, or to the (direct) cost centres, whereas indirect costs are first referred to common and auxiliary centres, and then allocated, following certain criteria, to the direct cost centres; the cost of the direct centres, inclusive of these allocations, is then spread to the products. The main problem with this type of approach is that these allocation criteria are based on "variable" costs (production volumes, labour-hours, machine-hours, etc.), which are often "direct".

In A.B.C. the costs of the resources are not directly allocated to the various products (or contracts) as in the past, but pass through the *activities* (Figure 7.2): it is the activities that use the resources, whereas the products do not consume resources but rather activities. Two moments or stages can be thus identified:

- during the first, the costs of the resources are allocated to the activities by means of "first-stage drivers" (also called "cost drivers" or "resource drivers"),
- during the second, the activities are related to the products by means of "second-stage drivers" (or "activity drivers").

Among the more important "activity drivers" are: the number of orders (customer-, manufacturing and purchase orders), parts (common and not) and levels in the bills of materials, amount of handling, set up, non-conformities, complaints, etc. On the other hand, the number and type of "resource drivers" used depends on the accuracy desired and the variety of products and manufacturing processes.

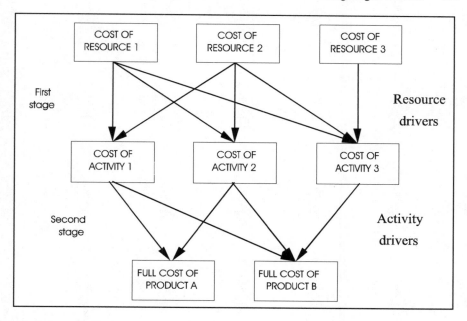

Fig 7.2 Calculation of full product cost according to Activity-Based Costing

Part Three

From Processes to the Extended Enterprise

8. The Knowledge Extended Enterprise: An Innovative Business Model Suggested by Snaidero

Andrea Tramontano

8.1 An Evolving Business: The Process-Based Company Becomes a Knowledge Extended Enterprise

The contributions of the previous chapters focused on the ways and reasons, which from both a theoretical and application viewpoint, lead the company to completely question itself and thereby radically change its way of doing business.

As we have already seen, not only does a BPR project involve an organisational change, it creates also havoc, shaking the company right down to its foundations and, if the project is successful, a revamped company will emerge with considerably new trends, employees' mentality, structures and working tools. Thus, for companies of a certain size and operating in specific sectors, the transition from being traditional to becoming process-based, is in itself a real and nonetheless remarkable competitive advantage.

At this point, some questions arise: is what has been achieved so far enough? Has the way of doing business adopted by the company reached its zenith and, if not, can the company relax for a while? In other words, are these processes the finish line or just an intermediate stage, or perhaps even the starting point? What else could there be?

This chapter and the following ones will try to provide answers, based yet again on a practical and real case, that is Snaidero, and will be related not only in the first person, but also by the main partners involved in the project called "Knowledge Extended Enterprise".

The Opportunity and Need to Proceed With Change

Even before attempting to relate how the process-based organisational and business model could further evolve, a clarification is required with respect to Snaidero's context and the pressures which forced the company to continue along its path to change. In this case, too, we believe that readers will be able to identify context elements common to their own interests or activities and, once again, they will be able to make comparisons with their own business realities.

The first major boost to change is, as it happened with the introduction of the process-based organisation, the need to further increase customer orientation. If the company recognises the customer as the sole and real arbiter of its strategic decisions, then its organisation must be even more streamlined and flexible, able to respond dynamically to any needs that may arise. However, whereas the goal of a BPR project is to reorganise the company's internal activities, flexibility should be sought externally as well.

Companies wishing to achieve this objective should pursue policies aimed at enhancing the value of their know-how, mainly by shedding their tangible assets and increasing the value of intangibles.

In the first case, for instance, the company may opt to outsource some of its activities or adopt business alliance strategies involving other players along the product chain. In the second case, instead, the company may decide to take steps to increase brand-awareness, optimise its distribution network, enhance the value of its human resources and adopt a knowledge extended management.

The second boost, is represented by what may defined as Snaidero's own curse, that is the duty to act as a reference point for the entire product chain whilst attempting to remove the gap between the company and the end consumer.

The company's core business is, in fact, the production of modular kitchens for distribution to the medium-high and high market segments. At the beginning and at the end of Snaidero's product chain we find mostly small if not very small suppliers and distribution companies. On one end there are the suppliers, even craftsmen, and on the other the small and medium-sized retail outlets, which are often family run businesses. Generally these businesses adopt a short-term strategic focus, are poorly organised and rely on basic IT tools. Therefore, being a point of reference means sustaining these companies by guiding them to share Snaidero's strategic choices whilst pushing them to organise themselves in order to improve their overall service quality and, hence, end customer satisfaction.

This last point is particularly important if we delve into a more technical context: the product. For a company such as Snaidero, which has chosen this element to distinguish itself in the market (with regard to any aspect of the product: design, quality, innovation but also service), the proper communication of all the products' peculiarities is fundamental. Specific knowledge held by Snaidero or its suppliers and distributors should be accessible by all those within its product chain, including the end consumer.

Company's Processes: Where Are Their Boundaries?

The two main driving factors of change illustrated in the previous sub-paragraph highlighted an important fact: carrying out a business process reengineering project is crucial but it may not be sufficient.

An enterprise can and should aim at improving its internal processes, but at the same time it should realise that these stretch beyond their theoretically established boundaries. The quality of the product and services provided depends in great part, if not decisively, on activities carried out by resources external to the company. The inability to positively influence the latter, may lead even an extremely organised, consumer-caring company with the right products to struggle to express its full potentialities, since it is further removed from its end consumers and surrounded by partners (or would-be ones) with whom it is unable to share not only strategies and information, but also culture and knowledge (meaning, in its broader sense, specific knowledge about product/market as well as professional skills).

If *an enterprise may be defined as a set of assets organised by the entrepreneur to carry out an economic activity with the aim of achieving specific economic goals* then, based on the observations made earlier on, the question is to ascertain the actual size of its field of operation. Should the set of assets relate to the resources of several and legally separate entities which are however united by a common objective? Can the term entrepreneur, be used to mean "a company acting as a point of reference for the entire product chain"? Should the entrepreneur bear the responsibility for the organisation of all of its partners (at this point, real ones)? Can the specific economic goals be really common to all product chain participants?

Partnership Policies

In the past, Snaidero had already tried to answer all these questions. The fact that both the beginning and end of all business processes extended well beyond the enterprise's physical boundaries had, since long, stimulated the company to develop partnership policies with other product chain partners.

The first step was to involve the company's network of sales agents which comprises of small organisations (with a minimum of two people up to a maximum of ten), as the first link of the supply chain. These organisations are separate legal entities and operate under non-exclusive agency agreements, dealing with a variety of other furnishing companies (exclusivity being for kitchens only). These sales agents were involved by giving them full responsibility, therefore common trading agencies were transformed into real physical extensions of the company over the territory. Snaidero took responsibility for the full training of all their personnel and for their software (client/server) in order to establish a remote connection with the company and thereby simplify a whole range of activities based on information flows which, until then, had been managed traditionally (using fax and telephone).

A second step aimed at developing partnership policies was to involve the proprietors and salesmen of the various retail outlets. Permanent training was organised in order to ensure that they acquired the necessary skills and knowledge to perform their roles. A fully equipped room for multimedia training was arranged at the Majano offices, and suitable teachers selected in order to develop different subjects (ranging from the financial management of retail outlets to consumer knowledge) and for different skill levels (basic and advanced courses). Another important aspect of these meetings is that they represent an opportunity to develop deeper human and professional relationships through which the company may better convey its principles and values, some of which actually developed through the reorganisation by processes (cooperation, customer care, output-orientation, etc.). Sharing the above with the partners will help spark renewed business relationships. Old colliding interests will be replaced by the awareness that better results and real customer satisfaction may be achieved by working together.

Therefore the company continues to run these training courses which, over the years, have involved hundreds of people coming from all over the world. Similar activities have also been carried out, though less frequently, for some categories of suppliers.

The success of these initiatives which attempted to achieve deeper involvement, strengthen relationships and even make the whole chain grow was evident from the start. The partnership, at any level, became one of Snaidero's strengths and, therefore, one of the pivots of its strategic lines.

However, it was soon clear that supporting these activities, especially from a physical point of view, would be a difficult task. The space available, in fact, limits each training session to 30-40 people. The geographical distance, especially for retail outlets located overseas, reduces the possibility of attendance to one or two courses each year. When people return to their daily activities it is often difficult for them to continue to apply what they have learnt during the course, unless the newly introduced concepts are constantly refreshed. Even vision and strategy confrontation and sharing, being diluted over time, loose their efficacy. In other words, a partnership is generally positive however, if it is carried out in this way, it becomes extremely demanding and, perhaps partly ineffective.

New Technologies for New Business Models

As it sometimes happens, initiatives stemming from apparently different assumptions and with totally different timings, can converge in a single context, in such a logical way, to seem almost a natural evolution of things. This is the case of customer orientation, the process-based organisation, partnership policies and, finally, new technologies. In Snaidero, all these initiatives merged into a single project named "Knowledge Extended Enterprise". The advent of new technologies, based mostly on Internet, in fact, represented for Snaidero an extraordinary opportunity to close the circle, to conclude a journey which, as we have seen so far, had started quite far away.

Let's take a step back and look at the year 1999. Even if a lot of things happened since then, we cannot forget the atmosphere prevailing at the time. Everybody, from the private citizen to the big company, sized with enthusiasm for Internet, asked themselves how to take part to this extraordinary gold rush set off by the new technologies. In Snaidero, too, countless consultants knocked on the company's door to recommend the introduction of new business models, new distribution systems, services or even products. In short, everyone was lured by risky ventures (it seemed that soon everyone would have bought kitchens exclusively on-line).

Fortunately, a sort of entrepreneurial (and a little bit "Friulian") pragmatism prevailed and the temptations turned into a serious strategic study which, by taking into account the three-year Business Plan, would have established the potential favourable overall impact of the new technologies on the company's activities. In other words, the aim was to find out if, and how, these technologies could have helped a typically old economy enterprise. This automatically implied giving up the possibility that new tools could lead to a change in strategies, instead, their use was meant to help achieve a smoother running of the company's business.

This strategic study, carried out with the help of a major consulting company such as IBM Consulting, defined and assigned priorities to more than fifteen different projects, of different scale and complexity, but all of them very coherent with the company's trends and strategies, which represent the framework of all Snaidero's e-business activities.

Company management immediately realised how important initiatives, such as those mentioned at the beginning of this paragraph, found an equally important common element in this project programme. The company was facing the extraordinary opportunity to proceed along the path outlined, with renewed energy: the new Internet-based technologies, in fact, allowed the company to reach, in a more timely fashion, all the companies in the chain, thereby effectively extending and integrating the processes of every participant. This would have permitted a continuous and exhaustive transfer of knowledge and, would have led to the creation of operational information flows among companies, eliminating a whole range of "non-value-added' activities, with ensuing benefits for Snaidero, but also for all the actors in the chain.

Therefore, the new challenge was to adopt a business model which enabled the company to combine its strategic choices with new technological opportunities and therefore significantly improve, yet again, the ability to meet the end-customer real requirements.

8.2   The Knowledge Extended Enterprise: Main Features and Comparisons

Main Features: Not Only Operational Communication Flows but also Knowledge Management (K-Commerce)

This paragraph will first attempt to explain the evolution process which led Snaidero not to stop at the "process-based company" and take a step further by extending this business model, where possible, also to the company's partners, then it will try to clarify the concept of knowledge extended enterprise. The above is obviously Snaidero's free interpretation of various models and trends. In the following pages terms like Knowledge Management, Business-to-Business (B2B), Electronic Data Interchange (EDI), Extended Enterprise, E-Commerce, etc. will recur frequently. The real novelty is that we are actually facing the real application of all the above trends into a single business model, carried out by a medium-sized company and generated by real competitive needs. Generally theory comes first and the practical applications later, in this case the opposite is true and theory is elaborated as a result of the need of the internal workgroup to give the project solid reference points and to find an overall coherence in all new initiatives, with respect to the consolidated business reality.

A first reference point is represented by the integrated enterprise, first embryo of the Extended Enterprise. In fact, technical-logistic networks based on the integration of operational information flows between different legal entities belonging to the same productive chain had been already carried out in the past, especially by large companies. Through EDI technologies, in particular, the company's output is coordinated so as to automatically become another company's input. Processes are therefore integrated but only partially as their integration is restricted to technical-operational aspects. In addition, even if knowledge is mutually accessible by everyone, accessibility is limited and the need for it to become totally accessible has not yet been fully justified and explained. Finally, integration may also be defined as static, as the elaboration of divergent strategies by the various actors, may lead to the need to reshape the product chain, thwarting common investments and loosing the advantages deriving from the fact partners know each other.

In the early '90s, Snaidero tried to advance in this direction, but it soon clashed with reality: the IT integration with companies which were mostly small-sized was a really hard task. In addition, the volume of information flows had not appeared to be so important, as although Snaidero was a manufacturing concern its production was very fragmented and focused on product customisation. Moreover, this kind of integration did not solve Snaidero's main problem that is collaborating with suppliers and distributors also with regard to strategic policies and the spreading of market and product knowledge.

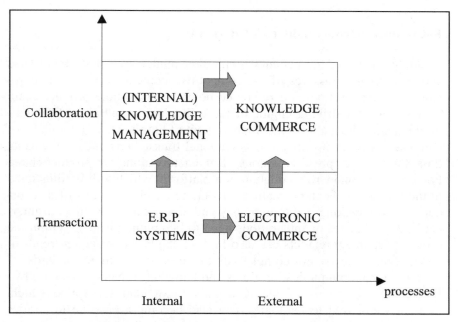

Fig 8.1 Convergence of E-Commerce transactional processes and Knowledge Management collaboration processes [source: R. Kocharekar]

A second theoretical reference point for the Knowledge Extended Enterprise comes from an article by R. Kocharekar published in Brint.com, a US portal dedicated to new technologies and knowledge management. This article is about K-Commerce (Knowledge-based Commerce, see also Figure 8.1), meaning by this term the synergistic convergence path between two trends, E-Commerce and Knowledge Management (KM), which characterised the evolution of many companies in the last few years, especially as a natural completion of important projects dedicated to the implementation of ERP (Enterprise Resource Planning) systems.

In fact, whilst the main objective of the latter had been to optimise internal transactions, the introduction of E-Commerce activities, in all their accepted meanings, led the company to use web-based technologies to carry out transactions with external parties. At the same time, the development of KM projects, instead, concerned the performance of internal collaboration activities aimed at sharing experience and knowledge. The combination of these two concepts generates a business model, called K-Commerce, which, through the web, allows to carry out transactions with external entities (the "stakeholders" or interested parties) but also collaborations in a wider sense, and eventually achieve mutual sharing of knowledge.

K-Commerce from Snaidero's Viewpoint

Snaidero identified immediately with this model. We have mentioned above the main pressures of the competitive context in which the company operates. Acting as a reference point for the whole product chain means being the driving engine of the technological but also of the cultural change which allows the improvement of both quality and volume of communication flows linked to operational transactions and, at the same time, knowledge spreading among all the actors along the product chain. For example, Snaidero's collaboration platform, which will be illustrated in the following chapters, enables retailers to check the status of their orders ("order tracking") autonomously and at any time as well as to interact in case changes or integrations need to be communicated. Within the same environment retailers can also find out the latest consumer trends or verify if their showrooms comply with Snaidero's exhibition standards.

Operational communication flows and knowledge management are two fundamental elements of the Knowledge Extended Enterprise which, through web-based technologies, can also become accessible to entities which are poorly or differently structured from both an IT and an organisational point of view. No specific IT knowledge or even the setting up of complex environments for data transfer are required, in fact a common PC, a browser and a traditional telephone connection are quite sufficient.

This is the integration of processes of legally separate companies, however, the development of shared knowledge allows to support collaboration also with regard to vision and strategies. The periodical "customer satisfaction" surveys carried out by Snaidero on a sample of customers who purchased a kitchen in the previous six months highlights, for example, which of the services provided by Snaidero or its retailers, are the ones where the customer has the highest expectations and what is the level of service provided. Sharing the results of these surveys is the best way to re-direct, both tactically and strategically, the activities of all the actors involved.

Table 8.1   Comparison between Knowledge Extended Enterprise, current Extended Enterprise, and traditional enterprise

Traditional Enterprise	The enterprise is viewed like a "black box" where raw materials and labour are input and products and information are output.
Current Extended Enterprise	It is achieved by creating a logistic/technical network of the enterprises chain, where one enterprise's output is another's input (in a coordinate way).
Knowledge Extended Enterprise	The network, which consists of logistics, technical information and knowledge in a broader sense, is reshaped so as to recreate the structures of a single enterprise at network level.

From a cultural viewpoint, the company should aim at developing an industrial and common market culture, and integration could complement professional skills and abilities in order to compensate for any lack or low level of professionalism on the part of the actors in the chain. A clear example could be built-in or panelled electrical appliances. Retail outlets staff is, by profession, more competent about the technical-aesthetic features of furniture. On the other hand, nowadays consumers are more and more alert, they often seek information on the web via Internet and before purchasing a kitchen they become real experts on all its technical aspects, electrical appliances included. Thus, being able to foresee, within Snaidero's collaboration platform, whether the salespersons can complete their knowledge by drawing on information sources made available to the public at large by electrical appliance manufacturers becomes of fundamental importance.

Table 8.2   Aspects of the company's evolution towards the Knowledge Extended Enterprise (first part)

	Traditional Enterprise	**Current Extended Enterprise**	**Knowledge Extended Enterprise**
Strategic Focus	Objectives centred on the company with ensuing difficulty in obtaining direct feedback from the customers	Objectives centred on the customer with continuous feedback and development of customer loyalty	Objectives centred on the transmission and sharing of knowledge with the customer and the other actors in the chain
Production Focus	Integrated internal production, with ensuing difficulty in managing product range and customisation	Integration of the company's production processes with the external parties, thus widening product range and customisations offered	Integration of production processes with external parties, supported by vision and strategy sharing
Information Systems	Local and closed information systems	Open information systems, connected with all the other systems in the chain, but only with regard to transactions	Knowledge is distributed to all the information systems in the chain, by relying on the extensive use of the New Technologies
Knowledge Management	Internal knowledge management, limited by functions	Knowledge only partially accessible by suppliers, distributors and customers	Full participation by all actors in the chain in the development of shared knowledge

This is also a dynamic integration since it evolves, over time, thanks to the strategic coherence of all participants who, as previously explained, can thus share vision, strategies and even organisation. This can be defined as a real community made up of members having at their disposal all the elements to co-ordinate their own decisions regarding future growth and investments.

Table 8.3 Aspects of the company's evolution towards the Knowledge Extended Enterprise (second part)

	Traditional Enterprise	Current Extended Enterprise	Knowledge Extended Enterprise
Organisation Structure	Integration between the various production processes and the company internal processes	Operational integration of processes, both within the company and with external parties	Complete integration of processes, supported by the sharing of vision and strategy
Cultural Approach	Spontaneous and internally structured	Exchange of information, especially technical-operational data, between different parties	Integration and complementing of the professional abilities and skills in order to make up for any shortcomings and limitations of the actors in the chain; development of a common industrial culture
External Relationships	Continuous reconfiguration of the actors within the chain (selection of suppliers and distribution channels; difficulty in retaining customers loyalty)	Static integration, i.e. differing strategies may lead to the need to reconfigure the chain	Dynamic integration, i.e. it consolidates over time thanks to the coherent strategic evolution of the participants in the chain (with the sharing of vision, strategies and organisation)

Comparison Between the Traditional and the Current Extended Enterprise

In order to summarise the concepts explained so far, we will rely on a number of tables which will provide a clearer comparison between the Knowledge Extended Enterprise, the enterprise with no external integration (defined as "traditional") and the current Extended Enterprise (i.e. the one stemming from the integrated enterprise).

The first is a summary table (Table 8.1), while the following two (Table 8.2 and 8.3) focus on some of the main distinguishing features.

8.3   The Collaboration Platform: Its Target Addressees and Main Benefits

As already highlighted, the Knowledge Extended Enterprise would have been a nice concept, void of any practical applications, if the Internet phenomenon had not developed.

Once the illusions of the bygone New Economy were cast aside, the opportunities offered by the so-called B2B started to be taken into greater consideration, and the new technologies came to be used to achieve improved integration between companies. This occurred to such an extent that the business context was renamed Net Economy.

Snaidero's project, with all its abovementioned peculiarities, takes its rightful place in this trend. Therefore, a web-based collaboration platform is the technological engine of this business model, as a valid alternative to traditional ways of communicating (personal contact, letter, telephone, fax, e-mail) and providing information (human memory, reports and books, data-bases also in electronic format but insufficiently shared, attendance at training courses), used by all the participants.

In this paragraph we shall illustrate the various platform collaboration areas dedicated to the different actors in the chain. As adhering to the Extended Enterprise concept means that these parties will have to deeply change their working habits (and this is the highest investment required) we shall try to illustrate its advantages in order to encourage them to proceed strenuously (yet, not without difficulty) with change.

The best way to show how the platform is logically made up is by providing a diagram (Figure 8.2).

Collaboration Platform Areas: Employees' Intranet

The central part of the platform is represented by an area dedicated to Snaidero's employees and is called Intranet.

It arises as a primary need of process reengineering which, as already described in the previous chapters, requires the development of specific tools aimed at collaborating, expliciting and sharing the know-how held by the company and its knowledge workers.

The first Intranet embryo was entirely dedicated to the BPR project and therefore it developed as a supporting tool for all company's activities, according to four guiding principles:

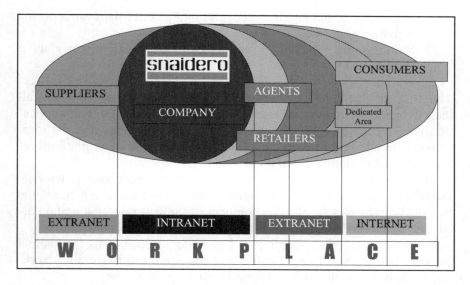

Fig 8.2   The Collaboration Platform

- Collaboration
  - Team work,
  - Project management,
  - Managing and sharing of information and documents (in any format),
  - Company knowledge management,
- Communication
  - Improving internal communication in order to improve external communication,
  - Communicating with all company departments and their personnel,
  - Using various communication tools and at the same time standardising the information flow to/ from others,
- Productivity
  - Quick retrieval of information required to perform tasks,
  - Simple arrangement of the tools required to perform tasks,
  - Awareness of what happens in one's own department and in the whole company,
  - Avoid loosing time in low-added-value routine and administrative activities,
- System administration and security
  - Intranet customisation according to specific requirements,

- Possibility of having different roles and profiles depending on the activities performed,
- Working under maximum security (without having to worry about ... security).

Thus, for all Snaidero's employees, Intranet is the starting point of all their everyday activities and enables them to be connected with application software running on the central information systems and the local network. In addition it allows an easy connection with other platform areas dedicated to suppliers and distributors.

In this area, as well as in the entire Snaidero's Extended Enterprise, knowledge management and operational work flows management are the two main guidelines for the development of the various collaboration areas and of the services made available to the company's employees.

In the first case, the collection and indexing of documents for internal use only is organised using a publishing application software, thus working towards the creation of a company knowledge repository.

In the second case, as it will be illustrated in more detail in the following chapter, the main work flows are reengineered with the support of a "workflow" tool, which is the real engine of the activities performed within the company's main processes.

Collaboration Platform Areas: Suppliers' Extranet

Earlier on we briefly touched upon some of the context features of Snaidero's logistic-production chain. The current trend is to make this process as flexible as possible, through the strong involvement of the partners chosen for outsourcing entire production or processing phases. This will enable kitchens to be outfitted with a wider range of built-in components (from very heterogeneous product areas, such as marble, aluminium, stainless steel, etc.) but also timely deliveries and a reduced time to market (both in case of normal orders and requests due to a poor service level). However, partner-suppliers can be effectively involved only if they work in close cooperation with Snaidero, acting in some cases as if they were the latter's own departments. Thus the platform envisaged a number of specific areas for the management of the main information flows aimed at improving the synchronisation and efficiency of operational activities, in particular, keeping in mind poorly organised suppliers, or even craftsmen, which represent a significant part of the industries linked to Snaidero. In the platform development stage, due consideration was also paid to the (few) large-sized partners such as electric appliance multinationals, as in that case the main goal was to make the processing of large volumes of data more efficient.

The sharing of vision and growth strategies with the company's production partners should not be disregarded either. In the medium-term this allows to identify areas for mutual investment with regard to structures, organisation and human resources. This is why, also in this field, collaboration areas dedicated to the mutual exchange of knowledge about the market situation, mutual research & development activities to develop new products, etc. are particularly important.

Tab 8.4 Main areas of the Suppliers' Extranet

	Area	**Phase**	**Further use**
Strategic	Purchase marketing and sharing of knowledge on the modular kitchen sector and Snaidero	Initial approach and acquaintance phase	Once the partnership has been established, also for the mutual verification of the evolution of strategies and context
Tactical	Awarding of supply agreements and evaluation of performances	From the negotiation to the definition of a general agreement	The evaluation of performances is carried out with a view to decide upon the renewal of the agreements in the following years
Operational	Management of the purchasing cycle	General activities linked to the supply of goods and services carried out as part of the general agreement	Joint planning of production activities

The platform thus envisages approximately 30 collaboration areas, subdivided into three sectors which correspond to the main phases of a typical relationship with a partner (see Table 8.4).

The platform allows Snaidero to rationalise also its internal activities, particularly those connected with the last step of the purchasing cycle. In this way, any resources released can be regularly assigned to tactical and strategic activities which, in the past, used to be sacrificed in favour of everyday activities, despite their unquestionable importance.

In this context, the collaboration area dealing with performance evaluation becomes particularly important. This area was developed through the Business Intelligence tool which had already been used in other areas of the collaboration platform. With regard to supplying activities, some of the performance indicators measured relate to the timeliness of deliveries or the compliance of supplies with agreed standards, etc. Through the use of two tools, namely "Rating of suppliers" and "TCO (Total Cost of Ownership)", Snaidero and its partners can constantly verify the trend of performance indicators in order to be able to identify improvement projects which could be carried out in co-operation and with mutual benefit. TCO becomes also the basis for the renegotiation of all contracts, enhancing all aspects of the relationship and not just those linked to the purchase price of goods. This area is important not only for the undisputed benefits accruing to all the actors, but also because it is extraordinarily coherent with the conviction that the Knowledge Extended Enterprise is the natural evolution of the process-based organisation. Here too, the process is considered in its entirety (regardless of any physical or legal boundaries, represented by the various companies), performances are measured, improvement projects are carried out and the teams involved become transversal (i.e. affect more than one process or a number of companies). In a way, this is what was originally intended by Snaidero's definition of the Extended Enterprise, that is a network involving logistics, technical information and knowledge in a broad sense, which tries to rebuild, through a network, the structures of a single enterprise.

A significant contribution to the development of the suppliers' Extranet was Snaidero's participation to a European research project called "Main-e" (Ref.: Growth 2000). The industrial result of that project was the Extranet, however, benefits came undoubtedly also from the cultural enrichment and the broad-mindedness arising from being in contact with the Main-e project partners, important research centres (both private and public), universities and other manufacturing concerns, all of which pursued the same goal, i.e. the experimentation of new business forms based on the concept of collaboration.

Collaboration Platform Areas: Agents' and Retailers' Extranet

As already underlined earlier on, the strategic study carried out by IBM Consulting at the start of the project had highlighted, among other things, the priorities to be assigned to the various initiatives based on the benefits generated by each initiative and the degree of complexity in carrying it out. The platform area dedicated to distribution received the highest priority, in fact, that is where Snaidero's Extended Enterprise begun.

The objectives were extremely clear. The issue was to find a way to connect Snaidero, quickly and directly, with the other partners (agents and distributors-retailers) in order to improve the service level provided to consumers but also reduce time and costs required to gain access to information to be shared.

Earlier on we briefly described the distribution situation of the furnishing sector in Italy and in most of Europe. In particular, the high and medium-high market segments are characterised by a myriad of small shops, which are mainly multi-product (selling kitchens as well as other type of furniture and accessories) and multi-brand (selling more than one brand of kitchens) outlets. The IT level of retail outlets is one of the lowest, and the general slump in the economy has eroded much of the sales margins. A gradual generational turnover is also taking place, with the business founder being replaced by the second generation. This means that some of the entrepreneur's typical peculiarities are lost (technical skill and knowledge of the product, business flair, knowledge of the consumer, etc.).

All this leads retail outlets to seek the support of manufacturing companies which may help them to improve their knowledge of both the product and the market, optimise operational activities (in an effort to achieve greater efficiency and therefore higher margins) and, finally, to be better prepared for the end consumer.

Also the manufacturing companies involved, being closer and more in touch with their own distributors, can significantly improve all these aspects.

The Extranet addressed to the distribution network (30 agents and 800 retailers worldwide), therefore aims at:

- sharing Snaidero's knowledge about the market, the company, etc. in order to improve the effectiveness of its retail outlets and to provide them with a higher quality of service to be capitalised for the benefit of the end consumer,
- making information exchange tools available to all users (both internal and external) so that the status of each transaction is visible to all the parties involved thus eliminating unnecessary archives (especially the paper-based ones) and avoiding activities with no added value,
- sharing operational experiences between company's personnel and retailers but also through the creation of a sort of (private) marketplace, between the latter and Snaidero's suppliers of certain types of products (electric appliances, accessories, etc.) which are an integral part of kitchens and require specific technical instructions,
- being closer to retail outlets by enhancing the quality (and the availability) of Snaidero's services.

In order to meet the requirements of users (retailers), and to compensate for their lack of Internet skills, the project was implemented by paying particular attention to the ergonomic and functional qualities of the tool.

In this area, the two main features of Snaidero's Extended Enterprise were also examined, namely communication flows and knowledge management.

With regard to the first feature, which is also the more operational of the two, the goal was to achieve a higher level of service by creating information flows supported by appropriate and special technological tools ("workflows") so as to guarantee definite answers within a defined timeframe. The wireless system supporting external logistics, developed within the European research project called "Main-e", is worthy of note. The partner-carriers, supported by palmtop PCs connected to the collaboration platform, can do their unloading while automatically checking that the goods being delivered comply with the delivery documents or the customer's order and communicate any anomalies to the company or, in case of delay, inform the retail outlets of any changes to the scheduled time of deliveries.

With regard to the second feature, the goal was to create, through the Business Intelligence tool, organised content databases which were easy and fun to search as well as areas with statistical information analyses, so that the entire distribution network could share the knowledge created by the company. The integration achieved by carrying out the optical archiving of documents in collaboration with Postel (the Italian Post Office) was also extremely interesting and innovative.

All this resulted in the development of an operational portal where these two sides merged and intersected thereby generating a single integrated "work place". Retailers can count on approximately 60 types of services which have all been designed and developed by taking into account their requirements and any type of information or service which the retailers and the modular kitchen manufacturers may need to exchange. The services fall under the following categories:

- orders,
- show rooms,
- communication,
- marketing,
- technical,
- training,
- administration,
- agencies.

Collaboration Platform Areas: Consumers' Dedicated Area

Can the Knowledge Extended Enterprise reach the consumers too? And can the consumer play a leading role in the purchasing process and thus be a collaboration platform user? Naturally! And now we shall attempt to illustrate how this can happen.

The main consideration, which may be valid for various industry sectors is that manufacturing companies are often too removed from the end consumer to be able to put into practice the "lesson learned" according to which companies must become more and more oriented to listening and responding rather than to producing and selling. In other words, a powerful distribution system can act as a heavy filter between the consumer and the manufacturer and thus hinder the latter from establishing a beneficial two-way contact aimed at affecting market and product strategies and to permit the newly acquired customer to be treated as a company asset and be fully capitalised (in the furnishing sector, for instance, grapevine is one of the most effective forms of advertising).

On the other hand, consumers purchase a modular kitchen on average every 15 years and are seldom furniture connoisseurs, however, considering the entity of the expense (note that Snaidero sells mainly to the medium-high market segments) they try to make wise and responsible decisions. The purchasing process is therefore very expensive (on average the customer visits 4 retail outlets and takes 6 months to decide on the purchase). It is only lately that the purchasing process has speeded up, especially in its initial phase, thanks to Internet which has allowed potential customers to visit companies' web sites.

Also in the after-sale phase, consumers have service expectations which at times retailers cannot fully satisfy.

In the light of the above issues, the Knowledge Extended Enterprise intends to make use of its collaboration platform to support consumers in each phase of the purchasing process. A set of ad hoc services have therefore been devised which gradually aim at (Table 8.5).

Internet-surfing consumers who visit the company's web site or peruse the main furnishing virtual magazines are offered the opportunity to enter a dedicated area of the platform where they can find consumer-dedicated information and services (some totally innovative). In this way consumers feel free and consent to be guided on their tour of the company's products and services, interacting with Snaidero's Extended Enterprise to acquire and return knowledge and experiences and to make use of operational information flows aimed at facilitating their purchasing activities, thus eliminating all those with no added value.

Tab 8.5   Objectives of the services supplied by Collaboration Platform

Purchasing process phase	Objectives of the services supplied by the collaboration platform
Initial approach to the "kitchen product"	Making the consumer fully knowledgeable on "kitchen products" to enable them to make a well informed purchasing decision
Analysis of the overall market supply	Making the consumer fully knowledgeable on Snaidero, explaining all brand and product advantages
Field research	Directing consumers towards Snaidero's partners, by promoting contact and evaluation activities
Deciding and Purchasing	Supporting consumer and retail outlets, by facilitating the purchasing decision
After-sale	Supporting consumers and retail outlets, by providing assistance with the solution of problems concerning the use and maintenance of goods, eventually gathering information on the quality of product and services supplied, and by interacting in order to stimulate customers to convey their satisfaction to other consumers

Advantages, Training and a Lot of Perseverance Over Time, for Everyone

This chapter provided an outline of this new business model, both from the point of view of its inspiring principles and real applications. The reader might find these two aspects to be more or less convincing, but evidence of the model validity can only be provided by the parties involved through acceptance of the model and effective use of the collaboration platform.

Changing our working activities is not at all easy. By nature, people tend to stick to their old healthy habits and it is only when faced with enormous advantages that they are willing to take into consideration the possibility of change.

The Internet phenomenon also, has confirmed these rules. Those who believed that by offering anything new with an e- prefix, was enough to induce people to change their way of living, eventually understood that reality was quite different, and many web-based initiatives failed because they did not make life easier and therefore did not offer real benefits.

The Knowledge Extended Enterprise, instead, was conceived to provide benefits to all the participants, based on a "win-win" model (i.e. one where someone's advantages do not correspond to someone else's disadvantages, on the contrary, these advantages add up and benefit the other party as well). This model had been theorised by gurus of the new technologies (often also disowned), on more than one occasion, and in this particular case it seemed that it would have worked.

The potential platform users' ability to use Internet was yet another aspect which was given due consideration. Despite the platform required a basic knowledge of the tool, it envisaged also a number of working areas expressly devised for these basic users both in terms of ergonomic qualities and appeal.

If changing the working habits, mentality and tools within a traditional company is in itself a difficult task (though some sort of leverage still exists), attempting to achieve such undertaking with external parties (the partners) may appear to be a crazy objective, and it often is.

Since the very beginning, when the first meetings were held with retail outlet owners or suppliers to illustrate the platform and ask for their formal acceptance, Snaidero aimed at highlighting all the advantages of this new way of interacting with the company and the other actors in the chain and eventually tried to persuade them to make a small investment: some of their time to try and change.

Among the main benefits, accruing to all the users of the various platform areas, the following are worth noting:

- *non-stop service*: 24 hours a day, 365 days a year: in this way problems due to different working hours and time zones are solved and both information and operational areas can be accessed at any time of the day,
- *easy and quick use*: different ways of navigating have been envisaged so that searching for information could be facilitated for all users regardless of whether they are Internet-proficient or not,
- *no real costs*: a basic PC, a traditional telephone line (though alternative and more technologically advanced lines would be better) and the browser supplied with the PC operating system (thus no license and plug-in costs) are quite sufficient,
- *constantly up-to-date information*: all the companies in the chain share the same level of knowledge existing within each company, with no delay or incompleteness,
- *integrated information flows*: a lot of information is generated only at the inception of a business process, afterwards it is transferred from one company or department to another without having to be re-entered, with obvious benefits both in terms of data quality and speed of transmission,

- *elimination of physical paper-based archives*: there is no more need to file documents in physical archives as they can be easily retrieved in digital files and printed, exceptionally, only when the need to peruse them arises,
- *requests answered within specific deadlines*: the operational "workflow" mechanism dictates the time taken by the various activity flows, thus it enables users to have a complete picture of the status of any file still open and hence press for it to be dealt with,
- *full access to knowledge held within the chain*: a lot of examples in this respect have already been given as this aspect is of utmost importance for the new business model,
- *exclusive services*: some collaboration services/areas are available only because they can be accessed via the collaboration platform as neither Snaidero nor any other participant could have provided them following the traditional route.

The above mix of advantages aims at gaining both efficiency and effectiveness and at re-building logics which, also in this case, had been developed at the single company level as part of the BPR project.

A further analogy with the latter comes also from another aspect linked to the introduction of the Knowledge Extended Enterprise: training. Unfortunately, as in the case of the BPR project, highlighting all the advantages accruing by introducing change is not enough to persuade people to modify their old healthy habits. It is necessary to take people by the hand and ensure that the initial "change acceptance" phase is followed by actions aimed at supporting the change of mentality and the introduction of new tools which the company hopes to achieve.

Thus Snaidero equipped itself with resources and means to provide proper training to all the parties involved including employees, suppliers and retailers. An on-line tutoring service was also envisaged for consumers in order to involve even the least expert or laziest Internet surfers.

Snaidero, however, is fully aware of the fact that both advantages and training may not be sufficient to guarantee that a radical change will take place shortly after the introduction of the Knowledge Extended Enterprise. Involving all the participants of the entire production chain, i.e. the company's partners and the consumers who, through the purchase of a modular kitchen, hope to obtain the same quality service they get when purchasing other items, is a medium-term process which is probably more similar to a marathon than to a 100 m. flat race.

Thus, reconfirming its role as a reference point for the whole chain, Snaidero undertakes to proceed with the project, as the real driving engine of innovation and change for the entire "community", in a coherent and resolute way.

9. The Web-Based Collaboration Platform: Implementation Phases, Tools and Architecture

Andrea Tramontano and Samanta Franz[1]

9.1 Basic Principles for Implementing the Collaboration Platform

In the previous chapter we introduced the web-based collaboration platform by presenting it as a real *enabling factor* of Snaidero's extended enterprise. The four application areas which the platform comprises of are as follows:

- INTRANET – dedicated to the COMPANY and the GROUP,
- EXTRANET – dedicated to suppliers,
- EXTRANET – dedicated to retailers,
- INTERNET – which provides also a consumers' dedicated area.

The following pages will illustrate the principles guiding the choices made with regard to the overall plan (external and internal company users), the main phases of the implementation project, the tools developed (the so-called "Toolbox") and, finally, the logical and physical architectures (software and hardware) of the collaboration platform.

The various project partners will be mentioned too, as, thanks to their specific skills and features, they allowed the development of this complex and varied working environment. In the following chapters, some of them will closely examine the area they are specialised in, by introducing various aspects and viewpoints relating to the topic under consideration: the extended knowledge enterprise and the subsequent implementation project.

Since the various application areas were at their initial design stage, it was clear that important decisions had to be made regarding two main assumptions:

- users (suppliers, retailers, but also employees) were to be gradually introduced to the innovative elements of the project, from both a logical and technical point of view,

---

[1] New Technologies Resp. – Snaidero R. S.p.A.

- the company had to make a gradual investment over time, growing progressively as it registered positive feedback from users accepting the new tools. This is why the company wanted to avoid a massive project (carried out perhaps with just one partner) and preferred instead to develop a set of projects which would be co-ordinated and yet independent of one another.

This last assumption was indeed a difficult task as it required the various sub-projects to dovetail just like the pieces of a puzzle. The objective was nonetheless successfully achieved despite the projects were carried out by different partners and the solutions and technologies they contributed were diverse yet all web-based.

The assumption made about the users led to the development of various applications based on some fundamental principles, some of which deserve a closer look:

- *graphics consistency*: all operational areas should be developed using the same graphics so that users perceive the collaboration platform as a single environment. Thus, despite the Extranet dedicated to retailers comprises of 6 different "application blocks" (illustrated in the following paragraphs) which were developed in different software environments, users do not realise that they are moving from one to the other and navigating is easy and smooth,
- *operational integration*: the same objective was set for the functionalities of all applications so that, also in this case, moving from one "application block" to another would not be perceived,
- *ergonomics*: all applications and functionalities were conceived to promote an easy and intuitive approach by web surfers. As already mentioned earlier on, often collaboration platform users are not sufficiently IT literate (generally websites are addressed to advanced net users and, in this case, Snaidero's partners decided to approach the web for the first time mainly because they were encouraged by the high degree of user-friendliness), therefore it was immediately clear that this aspect should be particularly taken care of in order to get the web users' attention. As a result, every single page was designed trying to predict the web-users' reaction to the tool and also their expectations. Therefore, before publishing any part on the web, tests were carried out on a sample of potential web-users and their feedback evaluated.

So far, users involvement in the project has only been briefly touched upon. If the goal was to develop a tool capable of solving real problems and generating the extraordinary advantages which would convince people to change their way of working, the focus was nevertheless on those who would have eventually used the tool. Their participation was thus crucial if all of the abovementioned points were to be satisfied. But there was also another aspect: their close co-operation was required for the macro definition of the services and collaboration areas which were to be made available. Internet's short but rich history demonstrated that only what arises from real needs is subsequently put to use, and our platform in fact was created in an effort to combine its proven usefulness and user-friendliness. Every single function of the Extranet dedicated to retailers was discussed with the personnel affected by the process and then tested with a sample of users before it was finally published. Similarly, all the functions of the Extranet dedicated to suppliers were discussed with a sample of selected suppliers, whereas the functions of the area dedicated to consumers were discussed with a research institute specialised in web process validation and tested using various "focus groups" represented by a few significant samples of Snaidero's potential customers and net users. The deliverables of these listening and sharing phases carried out with potential users provided clear-cut specifications for the project partners to actually develop a tailored tool for any future member of the Snaidero's Community.

After illustrating the basic principles of the project from the user's viewpoint, we shall briefly review those regarding the company. In the initial phase, the study for the definition of services and collaboration areas was carried out alongside the analysis of the platform software and hardware architecture. The requirements to be met were clear from the start:

- a single working environment: if for the user this stands for uniformity of graphics and ergonomical use, for the company it means the identification of a solid yet flexible basic technological platform (Oracle was chosen for both the database and the application server) where the various and heterogeneous applications can run and integrate. This was a particularly strategic choice as it was meant to be a final infrastructural investment, valid also for all future sub-projects, regarding collaboration areas already envisaged but which were still in the pipeline,
- easily scalable software and hardware solutions: in the light of the magnitude of the project and, taking into account the possibility that, over time, new application areas would be added, it was of fundamental importance to move towards an easily scalable platform,

- a platform open to different project partners: the platform should be open, easy to integrate with applications developed also in different environments and platforms. With regard to an Intranet solution, for example, being able to integrate in a new environment also applications developed with different logics and at different times could be of fundamental importance.

The above considerations were then used by Snaidero and its main project partners to carry out an analysis of the solutions which appeared to be the most interesting ones.

Now we shall try to go briefly through the main phases of the project, but first we shall illustrate the features and explain the role played by the consulting and IT companies which helped Snaidero to develop the collaboration platform.

9.2   Why Not Just One Project Partner?

As it was already highlighted in the previous paragraph, the strategic study carried out by IBM Consulting at the initial stage, had shown the extent and the complexity of the whole plan of e-business projects. The options available were two: either identify a single partner to entrust with the development of the entire plan, or create a team of companies, each specialised in a particular area of Internet technology. In the first case the advantage lay in having one point of reference but a limited range of infrastructural and application solutions, in the second case in having a number of web experts to choose from depending on the specific problem at hand but facing difficulties of integration, synchronisation of activities and uniformity of choices.

The final decision was to run the latter potential risks mentioned above and create a team of partners, where each of them would be specialised in a particular area of Internet technology, as follows:

- E-Tree (graphical and ergonomical aspects, identification of technological platforms and content publishing),
- TXT e-solution and its partner Multigraphics (development of applications linked to the Supply Chain and catalogue management),
- Oracle (database, application server and Workflow tool),
- SDG Consulting (business intelligence),
- Wind/ITNet ("web-farm" and connectivity),
- Postel (remote optical filing),

- Powerhouse Arredamento.it (supply of contents regarding the furnishing sector),
- Atos Origin (development of wireless applications).

With regard to the consulting assistance received, in addition to the abovementioned IBM Consulting, a significant contribution was provided by Cegos Italia which designed the entire area dedicated to suppliers.

TXT was appointed system integrator in charge of solving and even anticipating all partner integration problems, starting from infrastructural hardware and software choices.

The project team was completed and integrated by actively involving also a number of key company personnel. In fact, in addition to the authors of this chapter, namely the Project Leader and the manager in charge of the New Technologies process, also people from the Information System department, of the Organisation and of other company departments contributed greatly with their professional skills both at the initial study phase and subsequently with the introduction of the new tools.

For the entire duration of the project, the same team spirit expected from Snaidero's extended knowledge enterprise prevailed: great professionalism, the right amount of anxiety towards the attainment of goals, willingness to find the best solution rather than the culprit when problems arise (even at the hardest times). Dozens of people alternating on the project have been *virtual colleagues* as the platform building site was physically located at the "web-farm" (which incidentally was in Genoa but could have been anywhere else in the world for that matter) whereas each of them worked from their own offices (Milan, Treviso, Verona, Naples, Turin, Rome). The only visible trace of the *virtual building site* was the list of e-mail addresses to which messages were automatically sent to keep everyone constantly updated on the latest developments and to ensure the coordination of all activities, even trivial ones such as switching on and off of a server located hundreds of miles away.

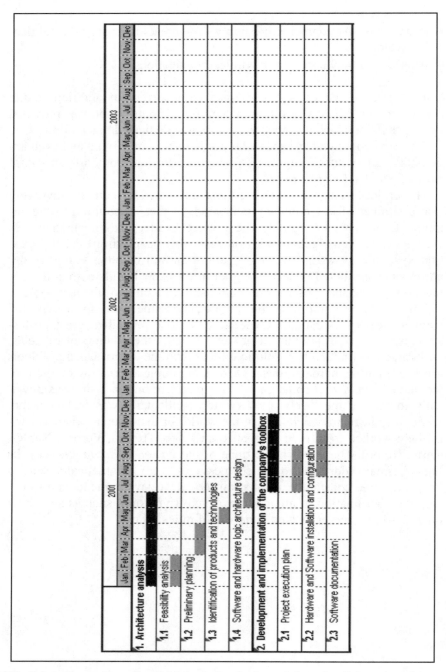

Fig 9.1   Gantt chart of activities relating to the web-based collaboration platform project

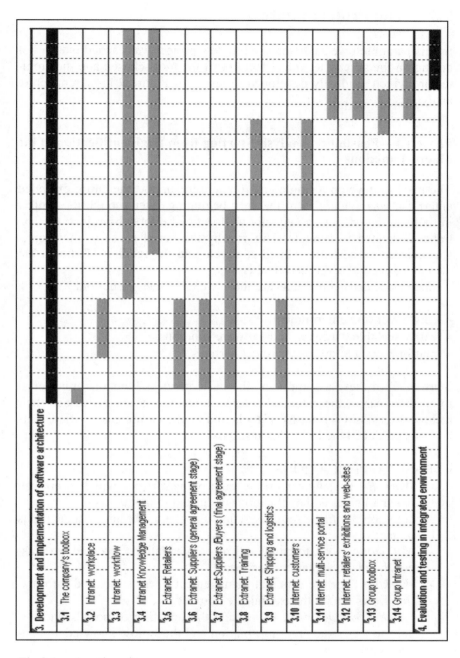

Fig 9.1   (continued)

9.3   The Project Phases

In this paragraph we shall analyse how the project was carried out, by focusing on the strictly technical features of the tools chosen and the architecture which gradually developed (Phase 1 of Figure 9.1 – Architecture analysis).

Phase 1.1 – Feasibility Analysis Starting from the Identification of the Macro-Functions

The need to develop a single environment to support the entire extended enterprise was evident from the very beginning, even though the project initially stemmed from an equally well-defined pilot sub-project: the Extranet dedicated to retailers. This is why the initial phase of the project was centred on activities aimed at developing the retailers' Extranet but also more general and transversal issues.

The basic needs/constraints are those we have seen earlier on:

- single working environment,
- easily scalable hardware and software solutions,
- platform open to different project partners.

Starting from these assumptions, the basic services/functions transversal to all the areas of the extended enterprise were to be identified and their technical feasibility in terms of tools and application areas verified. This analysis produced the following results:

- BASIC APPPLICATIONS:
    - *Work Place*: single working environment, from which users can reach all areas and applications dedicated to them,
    - common *Profiling* tool, to define users and administer their rights of access,
    - *Notification* tool, to handle all recommendations received from users and make the latter operational,
    - *Workflow*, for the efficient management of all structured information flows within the extended enterprise,
    - *Content Management*, to manage the updating of portals with regard to less structured information and thus allow knowledge management,
    - *Knowledge Management*, to manage and spread knowledge throughout all the areas of extended enterprise.

- CUSTOMISABLE APPLICATIONS (these are application areas which have different uses depending on the various environments):
  - *Business Intelligence*, to manage statistical reports for all users of the various environments,
  - *Technical catalogue* and *price list* management,
  - *Photographic brochures*, using photos to show the company's products,
  - *Order tracking*, to enable users to check, for example, the status of their orders at any point in time,
  - *E-learning*, in an extended knowledge enterprise the module for distance learning is a must,
  - *Shared work* to manage activities carried out by actual or virtual workgroups or project teams,
  - *Document storage*, to file a huge number of documents.

These tools (which together are called "Toolbox") have been found to be transversal to all the platform areas. An in-depth analysis of their content will be made in the last part of this chapter.

Additional ad hoc applications were developed at a later stage in order to meet the specific requirements of each area: for instance, the Extranet dedicated to retailers includes a section specifically designed for the management of receivables.

The fact that these additional applications were identified at the initial stage of the project was extremely important as it later affected the type of software and hardware to purchase. Moreover this solution allowed the project to be extended to other companies of the group, by selecting and customising the most interesting modules (an approach which is particularly valuable for some project environments, such as the Group's Intranet).

Phase 1.2 – Preliminary Planning of Possible Solutions for the Software Platform

Based on the constraints and software macro-requirements identified and analysed in the previous phase, it was decided to evaluate different software platforms operating, in some cases, on different systems.

We tried to explore different options, from "open source" to more sophisticated products, trying to satisfy performance and service requirements as well as economical and other needs, dictated by the company size and the expected number of users to be connected: the objective was to start with a technological solution which would not be disproportionate to the abovementioned requirements.

One of the decisive elements of the final choice was the identification of an "application server" with built-in applications capable of satisfying some of the previously illustrated requirements, then allowing the easy plug-in of other tools from the Toolbox. Project planning was focused on searching the right combination of customised and ready-made solutions.

Phase 1.3 – Identification of Products and Technologies

The choice made in phase 1.2 led to the solution proposed by Oracle which supports also environments of other solutions. Oracle solutions were chosen both with regard to the Application Server (Oracle 9iAS Enterprise Edition) and the DataBase (Oracle 8.1 Standard Edition).

This technological platform was the starting point to search for solutions to the other modules and meet the application requirements identified in the first phase. Was it better to use applications already built in the suite, develop "custom-made" solutions or use programs currently being sold in the market (even by already identified partners)? A different solution was chosen depending on each case.

Initially, project objectives were matched with offers received by the main partners identified by Snaidero. These offered customisable products which had already been developed in different environments or on other operating systems. Thus not only the flexibility of the platform allowed for significant economies of scale, but experiences gained in other contexts could be re-used on the project. In one case, for example, one of the partners identified for the retailers Extranet recommended a product for catalogue management, developed in a Linux environment and customised on the basis of the company's requirements, whilst a product already built in the Oracle suite was used for the workflow.

In other cases, solutions were sought in the market and not from project partners (who, however, had the task to integrate them) or alternatively they were developed from scratch and totally "custom-made". This is the case of the areas relating to messaging and order tracking (both purchase and sale orders). The product chosen for Content Management was recommended by E-Tree and permitted us to have a tool which was transversal to the various environments, with the possibility to instruct different workflows for creating, approving and editing the various contributions. The decision was to buy an average quality product which was more than adequate for our needs and not too complex for the management of these phases, this being a requirement of businesses whose core activity is news management. In other words, as the range of web solutions available on the market and their costs vary greatly, attention was made to ensure purchase decisions were cautiously evaluated. Therefore, it is only after careful initial planning that it is possible to take the right path and make a decision which takes into account actual requirements.

In identifying the most suitable products and technologies, Snaidero's internal IT structure was taken into account, aiming at integrating the latter with the collaboration platform. This was the case of Web Board as regards business intelligence, and of Biz Interiors as regards the management of catalogues.

In the case of Web Board, i.e. the Business Intelligence module, we chose the web version of a product already used by the company. In this way it was possible to use the same database, information and pageviews (though these needed to be reconverted for the web-based solution) and the reports currently used to monitor company's *Key Performance Indicators (KPIs)* were re-designed for the benefit of all external parties. Once the alignment of internal and external data had been achieved, Snaidero commenced to train these parties to develop the same mentality existing within the company, i.e. evaluate events in order to understand them and then act accordingly. The extended knowledge enterprise is based on these very tools which are the assets and the culture of its participants. Moreover, internally, Web Board has become the tool used to disseminate information towards to an ever-greater number of company areas, with an easy and timely interface (however, this information will not be as detailed as the one provided by the LAN version of the program which is used internally).

In the second case, i.e. the module for the technical catalogue, Biz Interiors was almost a natural choice, because it represented the web porting of part of the tool already used by the sales force to process orders ("Projet 2000"), with which it integrated perfectly. Here too, the use of the same database, a very similar interface and web navigation system were elements which influenced favourably the choice made.

The Business Intelligence and the Technical Catalogue will be dealt with in more depth in the following chapters, by SDG Consulting and TXT e-solutions respectively.

Phase 1.4 – Final Design of the Software and Hardware Logical Architecture

At this point a final verification from a logical viewpoint was required: a diagram was made of the logical architecture of the software and hardware needed for the environment to operate. The identified solution was extremely simple: a database server, two application servers to manage the applications, and a web server (Figure 9.2).

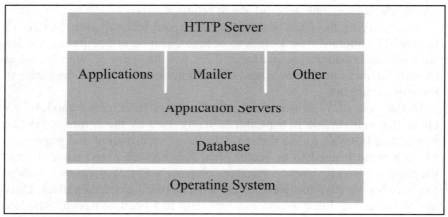

Fig 9.2   Reference diagram of the software logic structure

It was clearly opted for a simple solution which tried to avoid a complex architecture. The choice made was based on the assumption that the project would grow over time as the activities of the collaboration platform developed, and therefore the hardware and software structure could be expanded accordingly at any time. Further details on the identified structure will be provided in the following paragraph.

Once the architecture was outlined, the analysis could be completed only after deciding the physical location of the servers needed for the project. On the company's premises or somewhere else? Managed internally or with the help of third parties? There are pros and cons in both solutions which have been carefully weighed before arriving to the final decision.

On the one hand, having the servers on the company's premises is convenient and economical, however, on the other hand, maintaining a very high quality of service (i.e. checking that the servers operate properly and are visible as well as ensuring that there is no service interruption) is of the essence and this is particularly true for medium-sized companies with Information Systems which cannot guarantee a 24-hour service. In order to guarantee this quality of service the company should be able to rely on a wide range of technical skills (hardware and network maintenance, security policies, databases and single applications) and succeed in guaranteeing a 24-hour, round-the-clock coverage.

Other aspects regard the need to guarantee connected users an appropriate bandwidth (hence adequate response times) to enable them to work, but also the security of the company's network and of the data stored in the servers which can be accessed through Internet in order to prevent servers from being accessed by unauthorised or illegal means.

Finally, specific application software (Intranet in particular) runs much faster if it is located on the company's premises and bandwith costs can consequently be reduced (as there is no external web connection).

In the light of the numerous aspects involved which are specific to the project as a whole, the choice was rather difficult.

In brief, the main aspects to be examined were as follows:

- security,
- guaranteeing a level of service adequate to requirements,
- hardware and software response time adequate to requirements (number of users connected, type of transactions),
- economical solutions.

The final choice was an external supplier (ITNet, a company of the Wind group), which would provide us with both connectivity and a web-farm to house our computer infrastructure. A decisive element was that the project started with the launch of the retailers' Extranet, a service which needs an extensive and non-stop service (Snaidero's retailers operate in several time zones and need to be connected throughout the day). It was thus decided to postpone the creation of internal servers (except for the development environment and the testing thereof) necessary for a more flexible management of the Intranet (less demanding in terms of service level: it does not require, in fact, a 24-hour service as all employees operate from the same premises and with the same working hours). They would be developed in the following phase. With regard to the hardware, we had to choose between housing and hosting and eventually we opted to outsource the first option.

As regards the company's connectivity to the web farm, a 512 Kb VPN connection was established which would allow internal users to have quick access to published data.

9.4   Development and Implementation of the Company's Toolbox and Software Architecture

The following phases (2 and 3 of Figure 9.1) involved the detailed definition and the subsequent development of individual applications, starting from the transversal modules which are part of the infrastructure, and then moving to the specific applications and their customisation in the various environments. All interviews and verifications carried out directly with the expected potential users of the tools, in the phase dealing with the definition of detailed specifications, became particularly important: crucial aspect to guarantee the success of the project.

Now we shall examine the final result of the development phase, excluding the technical aspects which will be dealt with by our partners in the following chapters.

The results can however be examined under two different points of view:

- *Software* (functionalities and virtual environment), which can be further subdivided into:
  1) reference tools (functional analysis),
  2) applications (analysed by areas/processes),

- *Hardware* (physical environment), subdivided into:
  3) "layers" (structural analysis),
  4) logical & physical infrastructure diagram.

1) Reference Tools (Functional Analysis)

Now we shall try to describe the project architecture and its tools, according to the high-level functionalities used (WM, KM, SCM, CRM); the following description will be user-oriented and is particularly effective to identify the objectives to achieve.

Each high-level functionality is a logically distinct unit but it cooperates, to a lesser or greater extent, with all the other functionalities of the system producing a Work Place supporting the users in all their activities.

- *Workflow Management (WM)*: a WM system is a software system allowing the exchange of documents within the extended enterprise. The objective is to optimise workflow management through encoded and organised approval routing rules which guarantee a higher level of security and fast information exchange (requesting, sending and filling up forms with attachments, if any) notification of the various steps of the process and automatic reminders to ensure timely delivery,

- *Knowledge Management (KM)*: KM systems allow to create, store and manage the knowledge inside the extended enterprise, trying to achieve a greater degree of information sharing and increased co-operation, thus optimising people efficiency and productivity,

- *Supply Chain Management (SCM)*: SCM systems allow to obtain an integrated and process-oriented approach in terms of purchases, production as well as delivery of products and services to clients. This type of management aims at improving efficiency both inside and outside the company, by reducing operational costs whilst keeping stock levels to a minimum. Moreover, customer satisfaction can be increased by guaranteeing a supply of products which are constantly up-to-date and in line with market trends and development, and productivity can be improved through a more efficient use of resources, increased data security, less input errors when entering orders or faster communications,

- *Customer Relationship Management (CRM)*: CRM is oriented to the management of customer relationships, in order to achieve the customer's loyalty by improving the level of service offered.

2) The Applications Developed (Analysed by Areas and Processes)

We have previously mentioned the applications (both basic and customised) that we considered necessary to carry out the project. Now we shall examine their features and functions and how they interact with the various environments making up the portal of the extended enterprise.

- *Basic Applications:*
  - *Work Place*: single working environment from which users can reach all the areas and applications dedicated to them,
  - common *Profiling* tool: a single profiling tool was created to cater for the different environments and to define the necessary authorisation levels to gain access to the various applications and data stored therein. Each user is assigned to one or more groups with different roles, even transversal to the different existing environments (for instance, the same user can access the retailers' Extranet as a member of a Commercial Service Team or as a co-ordinator, but, at the same time, he can access different areas of the Intranet, depending on the processes or the workgroups he is part of, his

rights being linked to his function within each group). This basic concept fostered the development of a powerful and flexible profiling tool, capable of managing the manifold requirements arising, particularly in an Intranet, where the same person could have different roles and authorisation levels depending on the role,

-   *Notification* tool: in each environment users can take advantage of a notification tool devised to support the specific operation activities of individual users. This tool is connected to other tools generating messages and notices, and allows users to check at a glance all communications reported by other users by accessing a single environment. This is the foundation first core of a unified communication tool, which would provide a single location where all the messages generated by one or more environments (either Intranet or Extranet) or by different tools (e-mail, workflow or even fax) could be easily retrieved,

-   *Workflow*: this particular Oracle platform was chosen because it included this module. This shows just how important this tool was from the very beginning, when the whole project was still at the design stage. Workflows are essential to ensure the smooth and proper operation of processes (these being structured flows of data, knowledge and documents) both within the company and the entire extended enterprise. Without such tool it is very difficult, in fact, to be able to guarantee that information (or requests for information) reach the right person at the right time. This is particularly true for the extended enterprise, where the actors involved cannot always be easily reached (even physically) or do not feel they have to abide to company procedures,

-   *Content Management*: also this tool is essential for the creation, approval and publication of the contents generated by the different environments. Content Management, together with the Workflow, covers the two most important theoretical aspects of the extended knowledge enterprise and the environment which was about to develop. On the one hand the infrastructure should enable the creation of operational processes and ensure their smooth running (hence the workflow), on the other hand it should become an instrument for the gathering (also through other channels) and above all for spreading knowledge towards all the users of the different environments. This is why we considered a flexible tool, permitting to publish a contribution in different environments, by taking into account the visibility to be given through profiling (not everybody can access everything, of course!). This tool should have supported also the publishing phase, by identifying different routes, through a creation, approval (the related request must be notified and checked) and publishing workflow. All this should be linked to the database, so as to facilitate the retrieval of information by users (to quote just a simple example, in the retailers' Extranet a search engine was added to enable the search of the database and the retrieval of all the contributions linked to a key word),

- *Knowledge Management*: in this area, a set of tools was necessary for organisational purposes and knowledge management, thus tools enabling the gathering of company knowledge (possibly explained beforehand) and its organisation in a database easily accessed by users and, finally, tools supporting the creation of new knowledge.

- *Customisable applications:*
  - *Business Intelligence*: it was felt that users needed a tool which would enable them to verify a number of performance indicators on the trend of their trading activities and the quality of service provided (order quality). As we previously mentioned, the decision was to employ the same Business Intelligence tool used by the company to analyse the trend of KPIs and other internal indicators (sales analysis reports, for example), by adapting it to be employed on the web,
  - *Technical catalogue* and *price list* management: the end of the product chain (agents, retailers and, partly, consumers) requires a module for the management of the catalogue and the price list, but also as a support for potential purchases (in our case, this requirement with regard to suppliers is less important). Navigating through the catalogue should be user-friendly and allow information and product technical data to be easily retrieved (especially if the catalogue is huge and structured, as in the case of modular kitchen catalogues). The solution we opted for was twice as successful because, and we explained this earlier on, it was derived from a program which, for the last few years, had been successfully used by the sales force for processing orders made using the catalogue,
  - *Photographic brochures*: this is a tool supporting the presentation of Snaidero's products. Consumers require increasingly more customised material capable of meeting their requirements and helping them in their purchasing decisions. This requirement cannot be met using traditional tools without incurring in prohibitive costs; web-based tools, in this case, too, allow communication to be easily customised, thus making it more targeted,
  - *Order tracking*: this tool is essential to manage both the purchasing and the sales cycles, to find out the status of an order, the steps to

follow but also the person who will carry out the required transactions and when. In addition to the above, a document management system linked to the order tracking was developed in order to allow access to the entire order history and related documents, so that users could have everything under control without having to resort to the paper-based archives,

- *E-learning*: a very important module considered to be crucial for the development of a feature linked to the creation and management of knowledge, as well as to its re-distribution within the product chain is that which permits to manage on-line courses with multimedia content. This is a wide-ranging topic, however we shall try to simplify it by saying that courses can be provided in two ways: asynchronously or synchronously. In the first case the trainee decides the timing of the course, whilst in the second case on-line courses are run by teachers directly through the web ("virtual classroom"): we opted for the first method as we believed it was important to give users the possibility to attend our courses at any time of the day,

- *Shared work*: especially where an Intranet is concerned, teamwork supporting tools are essential and should aim at overcoming the fact that people may be physically based in different locations. These tools range from shared folders where all group members can retrieve any document they require, to tools which allow for web conferencing (all the steps involved from the calling of the meetings to the time they are actually held), or project management, both in terms of times and costs,

- *Document storage*: this is a tool for the remote optical archiving of great quantities of documents. For example, a dedicated environment was developed to facilitate the retrieval, by internal users as well as by users of the retailers' Extranet, of all invoices issued by the company and indexed according to different data fields (for example: client, invoice number, agent, etc.).

The following Table 9.1 shows how these applications were used in the various collaboration areas. As the software of the first group is transversal, it supports all other applications.

Finally, a brief note on processes. We frequently asked ourselves where company's *processes* actually started and ended, first in the introduction to the book, then in the chapters which followed. From the point of view of the business model, the extended knowledge enterprise is the answer, whereas the web-based collaboration platform is the way to achieve it. The tools and applications illustrated above can be used indifferently by the external partners' processes and the company's internal ones, thereby improving their respective effectiveness and efficiency. Table 9.2 below highlights the processes and the external partners using them.

Table 9.1   Comparison between applications and collaboration areas

Environments / Applications	Suppliers' Extranet	Intranet	Group's Intranet	Retailers' Extranet	Internet consumers' dedicated area
Workplace	X	X	X	X	X
Profiling	X	X	X	X	X
Notification	X	X	X	X	X
Workflow (procedures)	X	X	X	X	X
Content (publishing)	X	X	X	X	X
Knowledge Management	X	X	X	X	X
Technical Catalogue / Price List	X			X	
Tracking	X	X		X	X
Brochure	X			X	X
Business Intelligence	X	X	X	X	
E-learning	X	X		X	
Workgroup shared tasks		X	X		
Document Archiving	X	X		X	

Table 9.2 Applications are transversal not only to collaboration areas, but also to processes (both internal and external)

Applications	Final Customer	Assembler	Distributor	Agent	Carrier	Management	Sales Italy/Abroad	Customer Service	Product Development	Support Processes	Supply Chain	Suppliers
Workgroup shared tasks			X	X	X	X	X	X	X	X	X	
E-learning		X	X	X			X	X	X	X	X	X
Business Intelligence			X	X			X	X	X	X	X	X
Brochure	X	X			X	X	X	X				
Tracking		X	X	X	X	X	X	X			X	X
Technical Catalogue and Price List		X	X	X	X	X	X	X	X	X	X	X
Knowledge Management		X	X	X	X	X	X	X	X	X	X	X
Content (publishing)		X	X	X	X	X	X	X	X	X	X	X
Workflow (procedure)		X	X	X	X	X	X	X	X	X	X	X
Notification		X	X	X	X	X	X	X	X	X	X	X
Profiling	X	X	X	X	X	X	X	X	X	X	X	X
Workplace	X	X	X	X	X	X	X	X	X	X	X	X

Actors

3) The "layers"

Now we shall attempt to analyse the development of the environments representing the structure of the extended enterprise from a different viewpoint: a more engineering-type representation (so-called by "layers") which represents the enterprise architecture by overlapping layers, where the upper level uses the services offered by the immediately preceding level. This diagram can help us to get a better understanding of the complexity of the environment and the relation between the various parts it is made of.

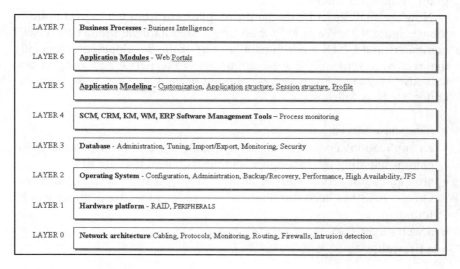

LAYER 7	**Business Processes** - Business Intelligence
LAYER 6	**Application Modules** - Web Portals
LAYER 5	**Application Modeling** - Customization, Application structure, Session structure, Profile
LAYER 4	**SCM, CRM, KM, WM, ERP Software Management Tools** – Process monitoring
LAYER 3	**Database** - Administration, Tuning, Import/Export, Monitoring, Security
LAYER 2	**Operating System** - Configuration, Administration, Backup/Recovery, Performance, High Availability, JFS
LAYER 1	**Hardware platform** - RAID, PERIPHERALS
LAYER 0	**Network architecture** Cabling, Protocols, Monitoring, Routing, Firewalls, Intrusion detection

Fig 9.3   Snaidero's solution "layers"

0 Level   *Network Architecture*: this is the network hardware. It enables the portals to be visible in the network and allows the exchange of data packages,

1st Level   *Hardware Platform*: this is represented by the servers (and peripherals) on which the following software levels are installed, and which relies on the first level to have network services,

2nd Level   *Operating System*: this is represented by the operating systems installed on the servers (the first software layer),

3rd Level   the *Database* used by the applications to save all data,

4th Level   *basic applications* (software management tools) described earlier on,

5th Level   custom-made applications (*Application Modelling*)

6th Level   *Application Modules*: applications are integrated in a single Work Place (grouped in three environments); these are the actual web pages which allow the applications to be used,

7th Level   *Business Processes*: monitoring of the Work Place, by optimising and executing the business process in real time.

4) Logical & Physical Diagram of the Infrastructure

Finally we shall examine the solution identified with respect to the technical aspect, i.e. the one relating to the logic and physical (hardware) diagram of the infrastructure.

Now we shall describe the hardware platform from the logical point of view (Figure 9.4). We opted for an Intel-based hardware rather than SUN computers and UNIX environment, as part of the development, especially that related to some of the applications, was to be performed using Microsoft ASP language. From a physical point of view, the hardware of the architecture is as follows:

- a database server,
- an application server with Linux operating system, on which the applications handling the catalogues and the technical lists are run,
- an application server with Windows 2000 operating system, on which Oracle 9iAS has been installed and where the other applications can be found,
- a web server,
- a firewall.

This environment, hosted in the ITNet web-farm based in Genoa, is interfaced via FTP with the servers located on Snaidero's premises which are dedicated to data preparation and loading to which it is connected by a VPN line (Figure 9.5).

The next chapters, edited by our main project partners, will examine in depth some of the issues already dealt with in these last pages, paying particular attention to the reasoning and providing further information on the Snaidero's extended enterprise project.

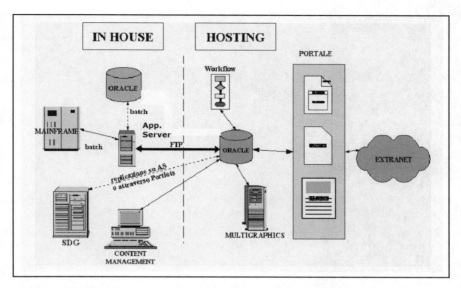

Fig 9.4   The hardware platform from the logical point of view

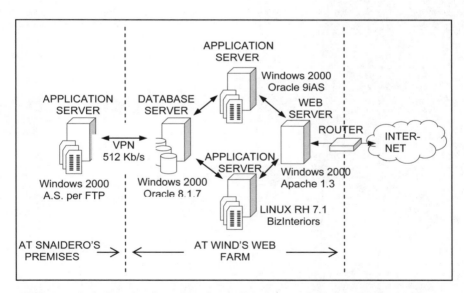

Fig 9.5   Web-farm hardware configuration and connections with Snaidero's environment

10. The Management Intelligence Methodology: From Process and Capabilities Redesign to the Development of Knowledge Management

Luca Quagini[1]

10.1 SDG Consulting

An organization can be defined, in business and sociological terms, a complex organism based on the respect for what is shared explicitly and implicitly by its actors. Organization is a synonym of sharing and agreement, but also of the possibility to create links between practices and effects, as well as the ability to modify practices so that they can produce better effects.

This paradigm, taken from modern social science, clearly expresses the meaning and importance that business initiatives of process reengineering and knowledge management have on the development of our companies.

To create links means to build a series of relationships. This activity often requires the breakdown or disarticulation of some links in order to build or rearticulate others. The Management Intelligence approach represents the practice and tool to implement these activities and to insert them in a context of continuous and gradual evolution. This facilitates the links with the external environment an, as a consequence, extends the sources and recipients of the organization's knowledge.

In meetings or business conferences of the last years, it is difficult to remember a president or CEO who did not highlight the strategic importance that human resources have in the success of their organizations. Likewise, it is even more difficult to recall a clear application of mechanisms which facilitate an improvement in collaboration, that can be implemented rapidly, and at the same time, is of effective and incremental support during it's development.

The challenge that SDG Consulting accepted in 1989 was to specialize its offering as a solution to these issues which are of critical importance for organizations that aim to grow and compete in the information and knowledge society.

The offering, which has grown symbiotically with the development of the multidimensional OLAP technology (one among several strategic

---

[1] CEO & Managing Director – SDG consulting S.p.A. (www.sdgconsulting.net)

partnerships for the development of the Board Management Intelligence project), has been enriched, as a result of the projects and experiences shared with the clients, with new potential and new applications, making SDG become one of the most innovative European leaders in the area.

Management Consultants who are able to "manipulate" powerful tools of knowledge management, planning and controlling, process redesign, and performance monitoring and improvement, become the principal facilitators of these fundamental mechanisms.

The meaning that SDG attributes to the concept of Management Intelligence is not only that of a working methodology, but also that of a project to design and implement information solutions which support business processes. This new management consulting frontier, which executive teams of several companies – small and large – are calling to support their projects of organizational innovation, started in Milan and is currently present in Italy with two other offices in Verona and Rome. In Europe SDG is present with six offices: Barcelona, Madrid, London, Paris, Stuttgart and Paderborn.

SDG Consulting boasts more than 80 professionals, who combine superior business management competencies with advanced skills in Business Intelligence. They are used to taking innovative approaches, are specialized in projects of performance monitoring and knowledge management. In the last 3 years more than 300 projects have been completed and over 100 active clients are the evidence of a courageous choice made ahead of time, which now allows SDG to take advantage of the virtual marketplace potential in projects of knowledge-based extended enterprises.

The theme of knowledge and human resources development issues tends to go against another major organizational trend of concentrating activities around the core business and reducing, if not outsourcing, the secondary activities.

The interpretation that should be given to these apparently contrasting trends can be found in the concept of extended enterprise. A concept that explains how virtual marketplaces become the central location promoting training and knowledge-sharing without having to dedicate physical structures.

Creating effective and relevant relationships among key players, both inside and outside of the organization, is SDG's primary objective today.

The abundance of processes that are attainable and supportable today are no longer limited to the exchange of data and information, but are enriched with new forms of collaboration that contain a large degree of interaction and dialogue. Take into consideration e-learning solutions, remote conferences and web forums, and integrate them with typical sessions of Management Intelligence. The result is, in a single channel, that one can intercept and manage the primary needs of planning and controlling without losing the important requisites of personnel interchange (agreement of concepts, suggestions) and knowledge sharing in general (both at the individual and organizational level).

In this context, the staff areas of organization, coordination and controlling have a double advantage:

- the convenience of not having to increase the organizational structure solely for the logistical requirements of decentralization,
- they are able to verify the increased velocity and quality of those key processes that impact the organization of the business and development of human resources.

This is not an insignificant goal if we consider the broadening of frontiers and personnel that managers have to coordinate, plan and above all, from whom they hope to be able to obtain new knowledge and new opportunities.

10.2 Management Intelligence and the Extended Enterprise

The recent project experiences seem to confirm to a great extent that companies, slowly but inevitably, are starting to understand that Business Intelligence environments represent the cornerstone for effective collaborative process management and for extensions of their own business processes (CRM, marketplace, Knowledge Management, etc.).

With the emphasis and increased goals focused on clients and on the continuous exchange of knowledge, the concept of *extended enterprise* is evolving from the simple integration of internal and external processes, to the extension of the monitoring, simulation, and planning practices to key business players, that are increasingly external, not only physically, to the central headquarters.

Clients and Sales Force, Suppliers and Partners, Managers and Workers, logically, are able to better conduct their efforts if the information used is directly linked to the person or persons who are responsible for the actions that originally generated it. The degree of reliability of a forecast or trend is unquestionably increased when it is "shared" beforehand, even if just as a hypothesis, with the players who determine its realization.

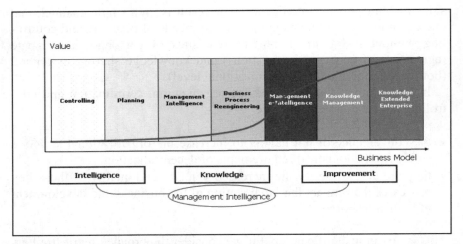

Fig 10.1 "Value Intelligence Chain": matching incremental business needs with up-to-date intelligence practices

Undoubtedly, the fluidity and speed of information exchange is an essential part of its value. Regarding this issue, the Web has been the revolutionary element that has allowed the practicability of models which otherwise would have been extremely difficult to accomplish. For example, it would have been impossible to even consider the idea of collaborative planning for procurement or sales because all the actors would had to be continuously called for several budgeting or controlling meetings. Now, complete collaboration is possible without having to leave their office.

Nonetheless, e-Intelligence does not only mean the remote sharing of planning and controlling practices. Its highest value is expressed in new forms of integration between *operational and strategic levels*:

- from operational automation to the shared analysis of business processes,
- from passive/ reactive relationships to proactive and collaborative planning,
- from the acquisition of new clients to the growth of the existing top clients,
- from transaction-oriented mechanisms to dialogue-oriented mechanisms,
- from product proposals to customized services proposals.

As an example, the Snaidero's project fully represents this model because the objective of the Intelligence Process Reengineering launched is not the management of the information, but the change in the relationship rules along the whole value chain.

In conclusion, information on it's own does not create value, but it can do so when it induces change and stimulates the development of improvement actions. In other words, the objective is no longer to take the best decision, but to improve the entire decision making process starting from business models and the useable knowledge.

Management Intelligence projects are not easy. On the other hand, if they were, the main competitive advantage of the company, its knowledge, would be structurally weak.

Therefore, let's try to draw up a decalogue, a sort of roadmap of the conditions which, when applied, determined the achievements of the project goals and increased their impact to the point of inducing radical changes in the management of organizations.

These criteria are the summary of several experiences, developed over a decade of projects, both in complex environments as well as in simpler ones. Each criteria should be intended as a guideline which has to be adapted to the specific aspects of each organization.

1. *Spiral approach*: short, quick steps which are controllable and offer the possibility to obtain immediate feedback. This feedback is then used to develop the model gradually and incrementally,
2. *Application building:* "Creation, not personalization". The right solutions are never pre-built. They are designed and developed to meet company-specific requirements,
3. *Maximum six-month project duration*: based on the objectives, one must define project modules that are finite and achievable. It is very important to avoid diluting the project's "critical mass" which could result in a loss of control and direction,
4. *Multidimensional modeling*: the analysis are multidimensional and data is the principal object of the analysis. It would be difficult to respect these basic principles if the data could not be structured in its proper dimensions and if models for the automatic definition of navigational and drill-down paths were not present,
5. *Intelligence process design*: if a Business Intelligence project does not require the creation of new models or new analytical metrics, what is its purpose? Often, reporting projects are considered Intelligence projects: I hope this book contributes to clarify their differences both in terms of the tools used and of the goals achieved,

6. *Team member skills*: we too have participated in projects with other consulting teams, often with some of the larger multinationals of this sector. In special projects like these, the brand credentials count a lot less than the skills that each team member can contribute to the specific project,

7. *No more than 5 members per team*: competencies and skills are the main selection criteria: a team member should be able to participate actively in every phase of the project: from the initial assessment to the final implementation. Entropy and "passing the word on" reduce value,

8. *A lot of time designing the business model*, and spend a lot of time with users: those projects that are "protected" by presumptuous pre-analysis or rigid organizational "filters" have almost always produced a loss of impact and effectiveness in the solutions implemented,

9. *Redesign autonomy*: the duplication of the existing system, innovating only the reporting tools and models currently used, may result in the repetition of existing "bad habits". Management Intelligence projects should represent the opportunity to challenge the "status quo",

10. *Web enabled*: Talking about extended enterprises means creating the necessary conditions to facilitate the access and management of intelligence processes remotely, hence, via the Web.

10.3   The "Adapt - Case" Approach

The idea which originated this approach was the need of a *modus operandi*, that, while transforming the Business Intelligence processes, would, at the same time, serve to accommodate the particular requirements of each project phase.

Adapt Case, an acronym which stands for A*nalysis*, D*iagnosis*, A*pply*, P*iloting*, T*utoring* and C*apturing*, A*dding*, S*haring*, E*ducating*, represents the synthesis of two complementary sets of skills. The *Adapt* phase corresponds to the sessions of management consulting focused on designing the ideal business model, while the *Case* phase characterizes all the steps regarding the implementation of the supporting tools.

- *Analysis*: analysis of the "as is" model: assess the current environment of practices and supporting tools. It includes finding the "intelligence workers", categorizing business processes according to their relevance and studying the critical issues related to these processes,

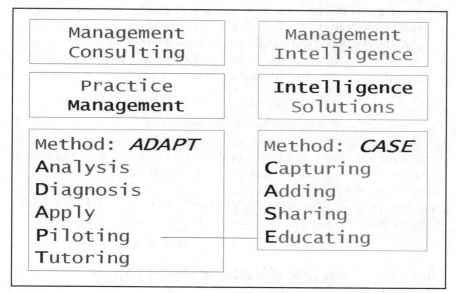

Fig 10.2   Adapt-Case©: the balanced approach for intelligence process reengineering - from design to implementation

- *Diagnosis*: identify development paths and events that will have the greatest impact on bettering the business processes that have been identified in the design of the new business model: together with the organizational and informational support architecture,
- *Apply*: application of the new model via an initial test period which verifies its practicability. At the same time, definition of those indicators that measure the impact,
- *Piloting*: guiding the business processes in their initial stages,
- *Tutoring*: coaching of the new "process owners" regarding the new context, relationships, and the new business model that the Intelligence System will now monitor,

- *Capturing*: selection and integration of the available information sources (internal and external),
- *Adding*: creation of Intelligence environments where data is "redimensioned" and the new model is enriched with the new information from the simulation, planning, and briefing processes,

- *Sharing*: creation of the architecture that allows the connection and communication of the various players, with dynamic, precise profiling, and the maximum simplicity from the supporting systems,
- *Educating*: training of the methodology and technology for all users regarding the new Intelligence environment and the new information tools.

These two series of activities have to be adapted according to the individual characteristics of each company, project, and module. It is not possible to have a preconceived recipe or formula. The experience and professionalism of the consultant must serve, above all, to mix and match the interventions according to the particular needs and requirements. Furthermore, the consultant should adapt them to the organizational culture of the working team in particular and the company in general.

10.4   The Creation of Value in BPR Projects

Management Intelligence is also a technique, or better yet, a supporting tool. As such, some of its principal modelling characteristics have been transferred into the *Board* Management Intelligence toolkit. This is the tool that SDG applies in the development of BPR or IPR (Intelligence Process Reengineering) projects as the main facilitator for the creation of a knowledge-based extended enterprise.

Management Intelligence must contribute to narrow the gap between controlling processes and the operational lines. The controlling practices must permeate the strategic, commercial, and technological cycles. The controller is one of the figures predestined to become an "intelligence worker" inside the company, but paradoxically, it is the Controlling area which usually presents the most process gaps.

Consequently, it becomes imperative to:

- move from the use of *lagging* to *leading* indicators,
- link measurements to strategies (KPI's – *Key Performance Indicators*); in other words, to create new measurements, if useful, that represent the convergence between actions and the general and specific goals,
- distribute goals in each area of competence to induce all the players to promote the performance improvement of the whole organization,
- allow the navigation of analysis models to permit process owners to fully understand the process result and subsequent gaps (should they exist) from the goal,

- eliminate the inefficient activities of data collection and data entry in order to free resources for the identification of knowledge and value sources that might be hidden inside the organization.

Management Intelligence must facilitate the formulation of hypothesis and the generation of non-linear budgeting processes. In fact, the planning activity adds value only if it is:

- *flexible*, adapts easily to changes and variations of the diverse business processes while it consents to plan the unexpected, or at least, to modify the budget without having to start from the beginning when the hypothesis change,
- *multidimensional*, to encourage the synchronization and circular approach, facilitating the creation of a clear and participative budgeting process during the definition of targets and their allocation,
- *up-to-date*, render each decisional process fast and reliable. It means to be "on-line" in every place and at every moment; for controlling or highlighting new opportunities or threats,
- *entrepreneurial*, in the sense that it stimulates the highest performance possible and avoids behaviours like: "I have reached the budget, I can rest now!", given the new visibility on the building of results and the possibility to redefine targets and goals; both general and personal.

Management Intelligence should facilitate the search of the *informational sources*, which are usually qualitative or unstructured.

Knowledge is not always explicit, or it cannot be rendered explicit with measures, dimensions, and relationships. Often, it is necessary to dig deeper to find its subtler components, which are usually hidden inside comments or contextual conditions.

It is fundamental to collect and make this variegated kind of information available, thus, it is important that:

- not only measurements are important, but also the factors which have caused them (*components*), and above all, the stories and the people who have determined the positive results (*best practices*) and the failures or problems (*lessons learned*),
- once the information has been found, it must be possible to contact the person who has originated (*chat, e-brief*) it. On one hand, not always is a result self explicable. On the other hand, it is unthinkable to establish a meeting for each required analysis. Thus, notes and comments should transit as fluidly and easily as numbers and graphics,

- it is also necessary to allow the management of unstructured information and to render it contextual (*forum*). Knowledge originates when contextual meaning is assigned to the received information. Such activity is a social process: we all know that sometimes we learned more from our classmates than from the courses attended,
- it is essential to make "the best practices" and "the best knowledge workers" visible. Knowledge sharing is fundamental during highly competitive or crisis periods. To find and to empower the best talent present in the organization is the only way to discover the best solution to any problem.

The Supporting Technology

The introduction of Management Intelligence must be transformed in a constant practice in the organizations that have launched it. Thus, it is necessary to implement an *applications generator* which can catalyze the diverse requirements and allow the gradual development of the entire BPR design.

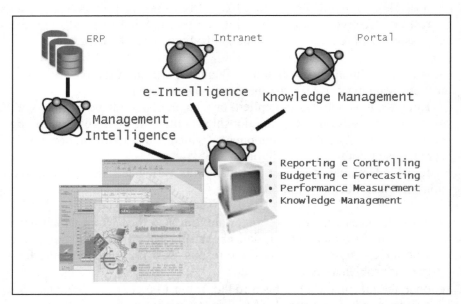

Fig 10.3   Management Intelligence: main components and connections supporting Extended Enterprise model

SDG, as stated before, has always believed in the need of having tools which could render the proposed models "concrete" right from the first phases. They should allow the collection of feedback, changes and constant development. These technological environments must be very powerful in that they should consent the realization of ambitious and unique projects and at the same time, remain highly user-friendly.

The principal characteristics of these tools must be aligned with the philosophy of a *BPR and Extended Enterprise* project. Therefore, the following values must be respected:

- *speed*: both in terms of modeling and transaction times (i.e. Multidimensional Engine, On-Line Visual Modeling),
- *simplicity*: the design and use should be intuitive. A complete set of tools for the management of information must be available (i.e. synchronized Tool-box, development without the need *of programming),*
- *versatility*: an applications generator that should support all the business areas and functions, several user profiles and their distribution inside or outside the company (Horizontal, Vertical, Dimensional),
- *feasibility*: complete access to modelling and Intelligence functions which permit the construction of complex solutions (i.e. Read & Write Multi-user, Automatic Consolidation, Splitting & Splatting, Graphic Data-Entry, Drill Anywhere),
- *cost effectiveness*: maximum containment of development time and costs related to the acquisition and use of the technology.

10.5 Snaidero Case: SDG's Contribution to the Creation of KPI's and the Knowledge-Based Extended Enterprise Through Web-Intelligence

In advanced management systems, one of the first requirements is to converge all business activities towards a single strategic coherence. When this becomes a goal for the entire organization, including its external environment, planning, controlling, and knowledge management processes assume a central role.

The idea is to always have the different areas of the organization under control hence enabling the identity of the *performances and improvement targets,* and at the same time allowing the *filing and sharing of best practices and lessons learned,* which determine the real diffusion of knowledge.

The project was developed with a series of interventions that covered a vast area, but at the same time, was gradual and always synchronized with changing business requirements.

Phase 1: Process Reengineering

The Snaidero-SDG project started with the following premises: modelling of the company in "Mega" Processes (Directive, Support, Business Development, Customer Service, Sales, and Supply Chain), identification of Process Owners and identification of Key Performance Indicators (KPI's) for each Process, from "Mega" to operational ones.

The KPI's are algorithms that elaborate information related to processes, or to their parts, resulting in a parameter that represents the trend or a significant component of the cause that determines it.

The *repository system* of the company's information and related KPI's was created with *Board M.I.T.,* and was entitled "DSA – Decision Support Area". To achieve this result, it was necessary to revise several internal procedures and to modify "old habits".

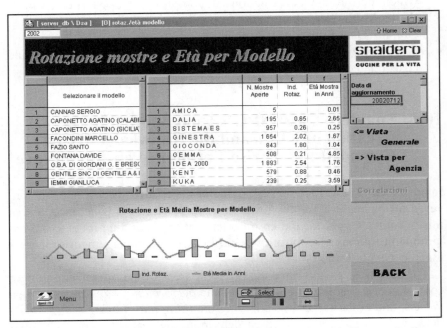

Fig 10.4 Decision Support Area: Showrooms KPIs and graph (Source: Italian Snaidero Portal screenshot)

The first activities were focused on the main generators of business information, Marketing and Operational Controlling, and on the new contexts related to the reorganization by processes. As a result, the first KPI's, mainly quantitative, were introduced in the company's *Balanced Scorecard*.

The project, *developed as a "pilot" in Italy,* is assuming an international dimension. The model is being implemented in the other European offices to facilitate the sharing of best practices through the use of a single Intelligence environment for the whole Group.

During the implementation, the *early warning* aspect was privileged. In other words, immediate priority was given to critical indicators; to their components in detail, to their relative causes, and via guided "drilldowns" (synchronized information paths). The extensive use of *colour coding* was also fundamental as it expresses immediate and intuitive judgement regarding the global process performance with respect to the set targets and becomes the privileged signal for issues that should be analyzed precisely through specific reports.

Equal relevance was given to the phase of results interpretation, which was facilitated by the possibility each Process Owner had to include, next to the single KPI's, a qualitative comment which indicated the possible motivations of results or the meaning of the indicator itself.

The Work Team, comprised of SDG consultants and Snaidero *knowledge workers* (i.e. people responsible for collecting information and generating reports for top managers), concentrated its activities on an initial group of economic and financial KPI's. Such indicators provide a updated vision (daily or weekly) of the sales trend, orders, customer satisfaction level, banking accounts and credit/cash cycle.

The activity of *Capturing* base information for the calculation of indicators highlighted that:

- the majority of data existed, but was not contained integrally in the transactional system or was not directly accessible,
- the Process Owners dedicated a lot of time looking for and collecting data from the different transactional systems, normalizing it through filtering and selection. They were trying to converge the massive "multidimensionality" of the sources within the limits of the required reports. This activity usually implied time-consuming manual collection of data and the related data-entry.

The *Adding* phase, the consolidation and normalization of all the existent and relevant information together with the storing and filing of data in a single and shared environment, has increased the value of the Snaidero's informational asset. What initially circulated informally in the company, today resides in a centralized, integrated and synchronized model. This allows the people who are responsible for the processes to access it and analyze, at established time intervals, the "TOCS" trend of the day, the sales trend, the bank accounts, etc.

As planned in the project design phase, the conclusion of this first phase provided the normalization of the information necessary for the construction of diverse KPI's.

Quality, Marketing, and Controlling have been the first to benefit from the value and advantages of this new approach to business knowledge. The various Process Owners, after familiarizing with the model and its indicators, have started to ask for more information and details in order to face several questions which up until now had been unanswered.

Fig 10.5 Decision Support Area: Geomarketing KPIs (Source: Italian Snaidero Portal screenshot)

The final goal which has been achieved is the construction of an *Enterprise Balanced Scorecard*; a summary of the actual 120 indicators related to the various *processes*. The Scorecard levels are basically two: one, more synthetic, contains four/five KPI's, and an analytical one, with a dozen KPI's. To support these KPI's, there are several measurements and specific reports which allow the analysis of their operational determinants.

Today, more than eighty company players, from all levels, consult and utilize the DSA on a daily basis with the most diverse objectives: from the support of strategic decisions, to the budgeting process, analysis of sales, and quality controls.

Phase 2: The Extended Enterprise

Snaidero's journey towards the knowledge-based extended enterprise has passed through careful management of the business knowledge. First, it was collected and certified in a single *"repository"* and then it was *distributed and shared*, in a series of successive waves, by all business players, from those who were closely involved in the processes to those who were related to them more indirectly.

Snaidero's objective was to pursue a specific model of extended enterprise which would go beyond the traditional concept: this model has been identified the *knowledge-based* extended enterprise, where the sharing of logistics, of technical information (and not only) and practice knowledge in general are added to the main concept of the extended enterprise.

From an external observer's point of view, the knowledge-based extended enterprise should appear as a single company, that, from a perspective of material and non material operation flows, has undistinguishable single components.

The use of Internet technology, combined with the Management Intelligence tool, was the core in developing this specific concept of *extended enterprise.*

- The company's Intranet and the DSA were the vehicles for the diffusion of information internally, predominantly with an eye on Knowledge and Human Resource Management,
- Internet has been the vehicle for the distribution of the company's values to the public and clientele primarily to diffuse and consolidate the brand,
- The Extranet system, due to the complexity of its predefined goals, was developed in different timeframes, initially integrating the activities of the sales force and distributors, and then constructing the basis for the suppliers e-marketplace through the components of certification, evaluation and e-procurement.

Fig 10.6   Resellers' Extranet: Sales Analysis by product (Source: Italian
Snaidero Portal screenshot)

The Distributors' Extranet

The creation of the Distributors' Extranet, in addition to representing an important component of the extended enterprise, has been an excellent example of "remote collaborative working". It has allowed the effective collaboration of several professional entities, for both a long time and over significant physical distances. Moreover, everything was made possible by using the same basic technologies adopted in the project.

The contribution of SDG in the development of the distributor's portal consisted, apart from the technical implementation of the portal component, in the integration and optimization of the information from the DSA to the system that was being developed.

With the progressive importance acquired by the extended enterprise model, the previous tools of information diffusion have been changed: first, via their integration with the DSA, and afterwards, with the numerous modules of the Extranet.

The greatest development effort were focused on adapting the Management Intelligence models and the specificity of the media where the information would have been conveyed. At the same time, an adequate level of navigability and information use have been maintained.

The Management Intelligence component of the Distributors' Extranet combines diverse areas of analysis for the use of distributors and sales force. Not only can they consult, but they can also analyze with a remote Intelligence tool, the information of their area of responsibility regarding:

- sales analysis (trend, geographical comparisons, segmentations, etc.),
- campaign analysis,
- credit management,
- specific KPI's (i.e. errors in orders).

Fig 10.7   Resellers' Extranet: Sales Analysis by district (Source: Italian
Snaidero Portal screenshot)

This has allowed the sales force and each final distributor to access, in real-time, the portions of DSA which are useful to them. As such, these portions have been exalted by the power of the technological tools (Internet, DSS, etc.) and of the supporting conceptual model (Extended Enterprise, Management Intelligence, etc.).

The Suppliers' Extranet

The ambitious objective of creating an e-marketplace for suppliers is in development phase. In addition to the on-line management of the entire in-logistics cycle, the procurement marketing component, whose first module consists of a certification system and an evaluation of suppliers, has also been planned.

The contribution of SDG to the Suppliers' Extranet has two main elements:

- the evaluation system of the internal circuit, integrated with the DSA,
- the remote components of the evaluation system, available to the suppliers and based on the web extensions of the adopted Management Intelligence tool.

In the debit cycle component, an analysis system is created for each supplier on the basis of the information coming from the DSA and from the integrated system between suppliers and production. This system estimates "ratings", "savings", "poor-quality costs", "Total Cost of Ownership (TCO)", and other evaluation parameters. The set of performance indicators re-enter in the *"tableau de bord"* of the DSA to be used by the management team and procurement department.

Most of the evaluation information will be made available, on a remote basis as well, to each supplier who will be able to view his or her rating parameters. This possibility is in line with the transparent behaviour that is typical of a partnership relationship.

The launch of the pilot program includes a test with a group of suppliers who have been selected, among those considered to be appropriate, for their dimension and business structure.

Future Developments

The two areas of future development include:

- the evolution of the extended enterprise concept, with similar modalities and the necessary "made to measure" changes, to the other companies of the Group,
- the harmonization of "Group Knowledge" – a sort of Intra-group DSA. This will be the third phase of the project that will allow management to obtain the most important information and available knowledge necessary to support the various decisional processes and

management requirements; in real time, in a difuse and homogeneous manner from the various companies.

Dedication

Luca Quagini, along with the two authors of this book and the project partners in Snaidero, would like to dedicate this chapter to the Eng. Matteo Martello, our unforgettable colleague who died in the Linate Airport disaster on October 8, 2001. Many of the concepts described above had been made possible thanks to his intuition and work.

11. The Extended Supply Chain: Enabler of Business Drives

Alvise Braga Illa[1] and Andrea Cencini[2]

11.1 Evolution Scenario of the Supply Chain

Supply Chain Management (SCM) lies at a meeting point between the evolution of business and the evolution of technology, where the support of technology to the new business models becomes a fundamental element for success and innovation of the way one conceives and realizes his business. Over the following years, the management of Supply Chain will assume ever more importance for those companies that aim at increasing their competitiveness through differentiation, improving customer service while maintaining the operational efficiency and reducing costs. In this period, processes will be extended across the company walls, so as to incorporate *collaborative* SCM processes and face *network scenarios:* sales and suppliers networks. Companies will have to re-design single partnership processes and Supply Chain structures, in order to define a strategy that allows a quick reply and collaborative interactions.

Another fact to be considered is that the customers' requirements are guiding the logistic chains towards a transformation *from a linear model to a non-linear one.* In a traditional linear Supply Chain, each participant has his own role and transfers his product and information to the following link of the chain. There is, thus, a linear flow of processes and information along the Supply Chain and every company has only a partial view on the final customer and the Supply Chain as a whole.

The emerging model of customer satisfaction is "non-linear". The determining force is the elimination of the inefficiency towards the final client when supplying a product, a service or information. In a non-linear model, the symmetric relation between the activities of the Supply Chain and the role of each operator is based upon the key-competences and upon the optimization of capital resources. The orders are gathered in different points and the supply of the product can assume different modes.

The infrastructure based upon the Web and the integration technologies assume a key-role, allowing the companies to co-ordinate the supply of the product, the service and the information between all the actors involved in the value chain. In this context, the SCM applications, if im-

---

[1] President – TXTe-solutions S.p.A. (www.txt.it)
[2] Business Unit Manager "Supply Chain" – TXTe-solutions S.p.A.

plemented contemporarily with business processes, will continue to offer a doubtless competitive advantage.

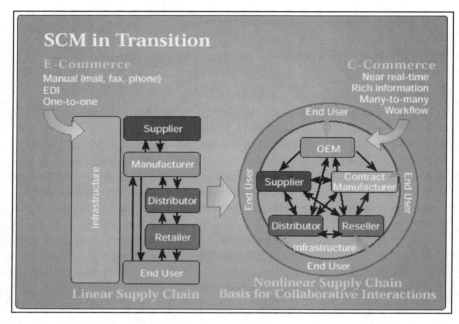

Fig 11.1 From a linear Supply Chain to a non-linear one

11.2   TXT E-Solutions

TXT e-solutions is an important Italian reality, European leader in the market of enterprise applications. Specialized in e-business applications, the company supplies information products and solutions for Supply Chain & Customer Management (TXT SC&CM) to industrial and service companies. Since 1999 TXT e-solutions also addresses the on-line content industry with the products of TXT Polymedia, its multi-channel platform of Content Management for companies of the Media sector, the main information portals and company intranet networks.

TXT e-solutions is European leader for standard and modular solutions for medium and big societies. The offer allows customization of the solution and quick implementation and integration times. The deep knowledge of the specific problems of each industry sector permitted TXT e-solutions to become one of the few companies in Italy and abroad able to offer solutions for different market segments, from food to automotive, from publishing to fashion and public administration.

Quoted at the Nuovo Mercato of the Stock Market of Milan, with headquarter in Milan and offices in Rome, Turin, Genoa, Bari, London, Paris, Barcelona and Frankfurt, TXT employs more that 350 people between managers and professionals.

The Offer TXT Supply Chain and Customer Management

The suite TXT SC&CM is composed of a series of software products that aim at supplying the company which adopts them, the best decision and operation tools for the management of the entire value chain. The solutions allow to cover not only all the planning and optimization aspects of the internal processes – from demand planning and forecast to the optimization of the activities on the production plants – but also to govern efficiently all the processes between the company and its partners (suppliers and subcontractors, distributors, resellers, agents and final customers).

The processes of the *extended* company, which extend the visibility of the value chain to the participants of this chain, can thus be fully governed through the solutions of the TXT suite. In particular, special attention is paid to the *collaborative aspects between the different actors involved in the processes – from visibility on key-information up to targets sharing during negotiation with suppliers* – where TXT has acquired an experience which certainly puts it in the lead.

Customers gain added value thanks to TXT's choice to create specialized versions (verticals) of its suite for particular industrial or market segments. The main feature of these verticals is the presence of modules focused on typical problems of the sector – like for example the management of the collections for the fashion industry or the sequencing on the assembling lines for the manufacturing or automotive sectors – and the possibility to use predefined configurations and process workflows. The advantage for the companies is not only in the fact that they can recognize themselves immediately in a typical context of their sector (best practice), but above all in the possibility to capitalize this basis in order to create quickly customizations able to give true value to the peculiarities and winning features of the company within its own market.

Verticalizations of the suite have thus been created for the industries of fashion, apparel and accessories (Fashion), vehicles (Automotive & Heavy Equipment), Discrete Manufacturing (Manufacturing), Food (Food & Beverage), distribution and management of retail networks (Retail), services (Utilities & Services).

The solutions based upon the suite TXT SC&CM are highly scalable and modular. This means that the company which adopts them, can focus every time on the business processes where the major benefice can be obtained in short time and, capitalizing on these processes, enlarge the scope and the focus in order to obtain ever major benefices, in a "virtuous" sequence.

The *suite* TXT SC&MC is composed of the following modules:

- Demand Planning (allows to analyze and realize sales forecast in quantity and in value, per market and per channel, variants and purchase components),
- Web Suppliers Management (allows to co-ordinate subcontractors and suppliers optimizing the replenishment cycle),
- Production & Procurement Planning (this is an interactive Supply Chain Planning tool which allows to balance a multi-site production, included subcontractors. It allows a simultaneous planning of demand, capacity and material on different hierarchical levels),
- Operation Planning & Scheduling (allows to generate feasible and efficient production plans, combining priorities and commercial emergencies with production constraints and optimizations),
- Web Order Management (it supports the product configuration, dating and feasibility online in order to verify, generate a proposal and satisfy the customer),
- Product Process Price Configuration (this is an interactive tool for the configuration of products with features specified by the customer).

The products are easily integrated with the existing company information system, with the major ERP-systems and with systems created within the company itself.

11.3   The Supply Chain in the Extended Enterprise

The different company functions – Sales and Marketing, Product Engineering, Production and/or Logistics – are guided by different targets, which can however be related one with the other. For example, the Sales function could gain benefit from a frequent update of the product range, in order to maintain or increase the interest of the market, while the Production can improve efficiency thanks to scale economies or long lifecycle productions.

The success of a company is largely determined by the capacity to balance targets and constraints of the different functions. Help the different functions to work in the best and most coordinated way will ensure that the single targets are always aligned with the general scopes of the company, while not neglecting the constraints of the other functions, in order to facilitate the action. The efficient balancing of targets and constraints has to be supported by an internal process which:

- allows a global vision, in order not to loose sight of the overall and priority targets of the company,
- enhances collaboration between functions, facilitating the capacity to work together on a common target,
- allows a clear sharing of constraints and targets as direct element of collaboration,
- works quickly; the speed of convergence between the actions of the different functions co-determinates the efficiency and, sometimes, the feasibility of the choices.

The continuous changes of the market scenario and the research of successful differentiators with respect to the competitors, push companies to extend the sharing and the pursuit of these targets across the company walls, towards the sales and the suppliers network. The target to which strive the collaborative actions between actors of the value chain is to improve quality of production and distribution processes, in order to increase the competitiveness of the company. In the past, the focus point was to reduce costs; nowadays optimization of resources remains a priority target, but companies have now clearly understood that it is not sufficient to simply spend less. To perceive in real time the requirements of the market, to react timely to the contingent variables, to plan efficiently production times and modes now represent the key-factors of success and can be pursued only through the integration of the different company realities and the synergic management of the activities with partners – suppliers, subcontractors, distributors and resellers.

This route foresees a series of fundamental moments. *First of all,* it is necessary to make some order, *through exchange of information and integration between different company functions,* thinking by processes and abandoning the traditional logic of sequence. From a technological point of view, this means to make available solutions to manage and exploit information in real time, so that each variation is reflected immediately in all the aspects of the business process. *Secondly,* it is necessary to *cross the company borders* and *build collaborative relationships* with suppliers, subcontractors, distributors and resellers, in order to share data and increase mutual visibility on process. The *third* phase sees the *synchronization of the processes*, where the relationship between the different actors is ever tighter and guided by logics of team-working, with a collaboration extended to numerous processes and several links of the chain.

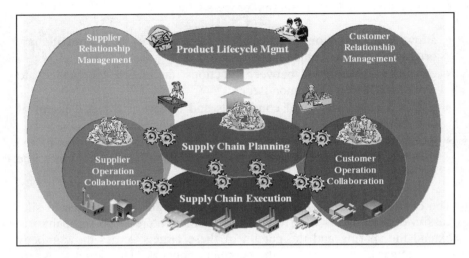

Fig 11.2   Processes of the *extended* Supply Chain

The integrated Supply Chain Planning is the best supporting tool for this evolution, as it is an ideal "hinge" between the *Demand side* and the *Supply side* of the entire logistic chain.

In the Supply Chain Planning cycle, in fact, tactical decisions are taken on the medium-long term. The basic idea is to anticipate and analyze possible situations and opportunities that can be taken advantage of, trying to find a solution already during the planning phase. The advantage of this approach is obvious: when thinking on a medium-long term it is possible to seize degrees of freedom which might not be available anymore on the short term. To work on a time-horizon of medium-long term, anyway, implies an ineluctable aspect of insecurity: the turbulence of the markets, actions of competitors, economical circumstances can change the forecasted demand profile. Generally, the uncertainty and the possible forecast error increase the more the analyses are distant in time. This means that managers, when working on a prospective of medium-long term, have to do with ever less reliable data and higher risk levels, but on the other side they have major freedom. The more time is lost before deciding, when the medium-long term turns to a short term, the more the available degrees of freedom are exhausted and, consequently, the advantages and opportunities the company could seize; for example, the possibility to use overwork or to move the production towards another plant could not be possible anymore in the short term scenario.

In this context, it is fundamental for the manager that he can count on the right tools to help him in taking decisions. Those tools supporting the Supply Chain Planning are thus characterized as Decision Support Systems (DSS).

The process of Supply Chain Planning can be efficiently supported by decision supporting tools for the management. Which are the features such a system is supposed to have?

- It has to be *integrated*, i.e. it has to include the sales vision (sales & marketing) as well as the logistic and production aspects. All the involved decision-takers must dispose of the same data, which everyone will analyze according to his own prospective,
- It has to be *simulating*, i.e. allow a "what-if" mode. In order to work in a context of medium-long term, offering numerous degrees of freedom, although with uncertain data, the most useful tool is the one able to evaluate and confront quickly – even with a certain degree of approximation ("rough-cut") – different hypotheses, rather than a tool characterized by sophisticated optimizing algorithms,
- It has to be *collaborative*, i.e. lead to and enforce a collaborative behavior in the managers responsible for the various functions. Sales, marketing, production (internal and external), purchase and replenishment of direct material and, although maybe less frequently, product engineering, need to find in this tool the support for moments of joined solution of problems and critical points – a kind of "war room" where the elements are shared in order to take the required decision in a coordinated way.

The positive effects a decision supporting tool for the Supply Chain Planning are manifest in all the production sectors, but in some of them they can become more immediate: for example, in the food or in the customer industries. In these sectors, in fact, it is mandatory to co-ordinate tightly on one side the demand management which is strongly dependant on promotions and with ever more reduced profit margins, and on the other side the production management, with a strong need to saturate as much as possible and in the most uniform way different plants that have been realized thanks to important investments.

11.4   The Extended Supply Chain of Snaidero

The model and the business strategies of Snaidero show two contrasting features and targets:

- a market strategy striving at a high quality product and the satisfaction of all the requirements of the customer, actually a custom-made kitchen,
- a production which, due to operational policies and volumes, is an industrial production of a Group acting at world-level.

To combine the requirements resulting from these two targets, while maintaining the operational efficiency of the organization and reducing industrial costs, required an important re-organization by processes and the adoption of suitable supporting tools. The relationships and the sharing of knowledge in this kind of context, impose in fact a timely and suitable transmission of all the information data to all the actors involved in a certain process. For example (Figure 11.3), the order issued by the point of sales contains detailed information, like the drawing of the marble hob, which has to be known by the responsible managers of the internal company functions as well as by the artisan who produces these elements of the kitchen for Snaidero.

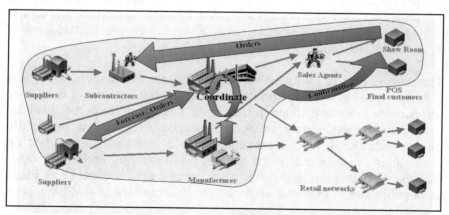

Fig 11.3   The extended Supply Chain of Snaidero

The project guided by TXT e-solutions was divided in different areas, according to a complex design in synergy with the company targets, but realized in several sub-projects, each of which allowed to support in a suitable way and to consolidate the systems of part of the entire Supply Chain.

Following this strategy, the first step was related to the systems supporting the operational planning activities of the different production areas of Snaidero, which have allowed, within the Extranet Project, to integrate and extend the applications for the management of the sales network and the management of the suppliers network.

In this presentation, we will focus on the two areas placed at the "opposed extremes" of the extended Supply Chain:

- The *sales network*, as far as concerns all the issues related to the management of the orders of kitchen and accessories,
- The *suppliers,* as far as concerns the need for operational collaboration and the importance of their role for the target of increasing the quality of the service towards the final customer.

The Supply Chain applications for Snaidero's production dimension, which had been designed and realized previously during the Nineties, allowed to integrated easily the new Extranet applications and to extend the supporting systems also towards the external relationships and processes.

The Resellers' Order Management in Snaidero

In the above described business context of the Group Snaidero, the management of the orders from resellers is certainly one of the most articulated and complex company processes, with immediate effects on the quality of the service offered to the customer as well as on the efficiency of the operational processes.

These issues are empathized by the international dimension of the Group, with a tight sales network in 50 countries (through 3000 points of sales, coordinated by about one hundred agents) and with a fidelity degree that varies very much from country to country. On top of that, the type of the "core business" product of Snaidero: the kitchen models are featured by a very high number of variants and the composition of the kitchen has to obey to extremely precise design rules. This reality is classified in the methodology of the Supply Chain systems as a highly configurable product requiring suitable management policies.

The realization process of a strong integration of the sales network, from a point of view of the order management, with the company's operational processes was started in Snaidero at the beginning of the Nineties. This activity lead to the definition and the realization of a supporting tool for the point of sales, as far as concerns the kitchen engineering activities, which is strongly integrated with the Supply Chain systems. The solution, realized in collaboration between Multigraphics and TXT e-solutions, foresees a local component in the point of sales for the graphic engineering and the order redaction, and a central component for the gathering and the technical/commercial confirmation of the orders.

Each point of sales disposes of a graphic 3D kitchen designing system (nowadays version "Projet 2000"), in which Snaidero loads and updates regularly the complete catalogues of the products with all their technical features. The reseller is provided with a mode to design and compose the kitchen, which facilitates considerably his task, and validates immediately the engineering constraints and the automatic calculation of some components (for example, the length of linear parts like hobs and sockets of the kitchen).

This tool represents a fundamental supporting element from two different points of view:

- towards the customer: the graphical 3D functions, reproducing the design of the kitchen viewed from different angles and inserted in its environment, supply a valid marketing and sales instrument, which sets off the specific features of the product and offers the customer a precise perception of the proposed solution,
- towards Snaidero: the use of the system in the points of sales minimizes interpretation errors, as all data are received electronically and are constructed directly from the catalogue. The graphical visualization of the kitchen project, through a tool acting like a "common language" on the entire sales network, facilitates central controls and activities and makes them more efficient.

Furthermore, the orders, which are received and controlled electronically, are transferred directly as input in the Supply Chain Planning tools, which now dispose of all the required information for the definition and optimization of the production plans.

This integrating infrastructure between the sales process and the logistic/production ones, was the fundamental starting point for the realization of the components for the order management of the Resellers' Extranet.

The business process for order management, obviously, does not finish with the receipt of the order and its transmission to the production department. In the period between the redaction of the order and the final delivery, there are a variety of relationships, that can be structured or not, between sales people, agent, reseller and final customer. These relationships can concern formal standard steps (like the order confirmation), but also different communications concerning variations, clarifications, order integrations, additional custom-made parts. Each customer orders contained all the data related to these relationships and communications in specific "paper folders", that integrated the entire history of the order. Considering the number of different actors involved in the process, their different interactions and geographical locations, it was not always easy to update and share all these data in a congruent way.

One of the targets of the Resellers' Extranet was to support these *collaborative processes for order management with one shared (electronic) tool*, that allowed to dispose at any time of a precise history, updated in real time, for all the actors involved in the process: the order folder.

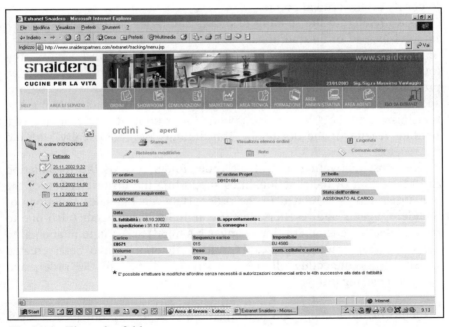

Fig 11.4   The order folder

This section of the Resellers' Extranet contains all the orders and details, organized by market-agent-resellers, related to open orders that still have to be delivered, and to the history of orders that have recently been delivered.

The order folder supports the life cycle of the order in all its phases. Initially, it structures and gathers the information exchanges between reseller and agent, relieving the latter from all the most practical and repeating activities at low added value, leaving him more time to concentrate on his role of resellers' consultant. This phases sees the redaction of the most adapted solution for the customer, the most conform one for his requirements, through the predisposition and development of various proposals.

Afterwards, the order folder gathers and structures all the data related to the order confirmation: this document is created by the central order receipt systems, which reassume and detail the single elements of the order in terms of technical features and prices. Considering the formal aspect of the order confirmation and the need to clarify quickly eventual issues in order to respect production constraints and delivery terms, the use of a single shared electronic file permits to minimize time and especially to clarify all the critical points.

Issues related to the sending of orders and order confirmation through Internet instead of by traditional fax also lead to an important case study on the effects of the new communication technologies in business contexts. While from an organizational point of view, there have been no problems, because the procedures were anyway already in use before, special attention had to be paid to the functionalities completing the transmission of the different documents: for example the introduction of a sending receipt of the document, substituting "psychologically" the old fax receipt.

The most innovating part of the order folder regards the formulation and realization of the functionalities supporting the historicization of the non-structured data related to the order. Between the sales functions of Snaidero, agents and resellers, many communications occur (also due to the fact that the customer often changes his mind) and it is fundamental to keep a shared trace of these. Therefore, functions have been created which allow connecting all the non-structured data to the order, and namely those regarding:

- memo of the content and agreements of telephone conversations between Snaidero, agents and resellers,
- requests of possible order variations and responses to these requests by Snaidero sales people,

- variation of the economic agreements after order variations,
- link to possible related orders (for example each integrating order is linked to the main order for an easy retrieval and consultation of the entire history, also transversely to different orders),
- eventual specification drawings of non-standard elements,
- eventual faxes related to the order.

The order folder finally supplies a detailed *order tracking* with daily update of all the information about the production status, delivery date and place and all the transport information.

The adoption of the order folder in electronic format significantly facilitated the collaborative processes for order management, increasing the efficiency and comprehension in the communication between the different involved actors, and contributing to improve the relationship with the sales network and also one of the main targets of each company on the market: the quality of the customer service.

The Suppliers' Order Management in Snaidero

Within the Suppliers Extranet project, which realizes a new approach of the entire issue of the relationship between supplier and company, the component of the operational management of the orders has been implemented by TXT with the module of its suite TXT Web Suppliers Management (TXT WSM).

The Group Snaidero produces about one hundred kitchens per day, and all the semi-finished products and varnishing for these kitchens are made in the production departments of the company. Snaidero relies on over 140 suppliers for the accessories, which – this needs to be highlighted – can include also small components (like handles), as well as definitely bigger and more expensive products (like white goods). It is obvious that the more the production of the kitchen is synchronized with the delivery of the accessories, the lower are the costs for the storage of the involved material. Another important feature of the supply chain of the Group Snaidero is the heterogeneity of its suppliers: from the artisan-type of company like those who work the marble, up to industrial companies producing tables and chairs, and national and international colossi like the producers of white goods.

In the world of Snaidero, which is common to different industrial companies, the management of suppliers' orders is divided in three categories:

- on simple order basis, i.e. tailor-made components. In this case it is necessary to communicate to the supplier also the detailed drawing of the component, in order to exclude interpretation misunderstandings,
- standard components, which are purchased only in function of the needs of the order. In this case, there is no storage of the material. The components have to be delivered by the supplier at the moment in which they are assembled,
- on an inventory basis, i.e. those accessories that require a communication towards the supplier indicating a punctual forecasted quantity for each product code.

Within the Suppliers Extranet, therefore, a common denominator has been specified for the communication and order management process, integrating the suppliers directly with the production plants of Snaidero. The scope is the realization of an efficient integration of the suppliers in the logistic chain of Snaidero, with a quick diffusion of the sales priorities and emergencies of the market, with an immediate and coordinated reaction and a quick interception of constraints generated outside the internal production chain.

Through the Suppliers Extranet and thanks to the communication potentialities offered by the new technologies of Internet, substituting the traditional fax, the suppliers receive daily information concerning the operational orders and information forecasting quantities and types of components for the medium period (two-six months). A special environment is made available to the suppliers through which they can easily communicate with Snaidero and confirm delivery terms and modes, as well as communicate possible exceptions.

The scope is, on one side, to allow the logistic function of Snaidero to dispose of timely information regarding the entire replenishment cycle at any time; from the moment in which the order is published/transmitted to the supplier up to the delivery.

A daily feedback from the supplier regarding possible production problems, in order to agree upon modifications of delivery time and quantities, allows Snaidero to know always and exactly which materials will arrive at their plants. This permits to respond quickly to these events, in order to maintain and further improve an already high quality level of customer service.

On the other side, the forecasted information allow to share with the supplier, the detailed data on how the request of Snaidero will be structured on a medium term, and allow the supplier, in turn, to create his own production and replenishment plans in order to comply with these future requirements.

The punctuality of the deliveries is the key-factor for synchronization of each Supply Chain, and in the case of Snaidero, this is amplified by the fact that the production concerns custom-made kitchens. The problem of the "missing", i.e. those elements that are not available when needed during the production cycle, represent an indicator of primary importance in the evaluation of the replenishment policies and of the service offered by the suppliers. The re-organization by processes allowed to focus on this problem in a suitable way, by measuring the efficiency through specific KPI of the Business Intelligence system made by SDG. Those KPI demonstrated a constant reduction of the number of missings and a consequent increase of the service quality.

The management of the orders through TXT WSM extended the scope of improvement of the operational replenishment systems to a contemporaneous reduction of the engagement of the resources required for that process. The availability of an integrated and real-time process for the operational management of the suppliers allows to reduce the time necessary to handle standard and special parts. In this way, it is thus possible to dedicate resources to the activities of the purchase and replenishment functions with a major added value.

The measurement of the efficiency of the processes is a fundamental element to evaluate correctly the effect of the adopted changes. This methodology, which is strongly structured and used in Snaidero, has also been extended to the network of the suppliers, using a set of KPI's covering punctuality, completeness and qualities of the deliveries. The system TXT WSM measures, for these areas, a set of values for daily events and transfers them to the module of Business Intelligence, which gathers and integrates them in a homogeneous way. In this project phase, which is now being activated, no historical data are yet available, but it is doubtless that thanks to these measurement modes, Snaidero will be able to evaluate the commercial and operational relationship with each single supplier, based upon objective events, and reward the most punctual ones and those who are ready to share the same business targets.

The implementation of the project foresaw a gradual solution, which initially interested 20% of the suppliers, and then has been extended to 70% of them. As indicated in the previous chapters, the introduction of the tool is indeed a component of a wider project aiming at re-designing the relationship between supplier and company and which lead to the definition of the entire Suppliers Extranet. A new partnership has thus to be created with these suppliers, which requires a mentality change that has to be proposed, shared and accepted by each of them. Therefore, the suppliers have been involved in the phase of definition and engineering of the Extranet, so as to create a model of relationship that reflects not only the needs of Snaidero, but also those of the suppliers themselves.

12. Infrastructures and Web-Based Business Applications for an Integrated Supply Chain

Mario Bonzano[1] and Enrico Liverani[2]

12.1 Company Profile of Oracle Corporation

With more then 40,000 employees in 145 countries, Oracle Corporation was the first company in the world of software for enterprises to develop and market complete and global 100% Internet-based enterprise solutions for E-Business: technological and applications solutions that are offered to the market together with consultation, training and support services. The Oracle offer is organised on *two macro areas*, the *Oracle10g technological platform* made up of the complex information management elements, *database application server* and *development tools*; the *E-Business Suite*, an integrated application suite, designed to adapt all company processes to the new models of E-Business, in ERP environments, human resources management, Internet Procurement, Supply Chain and Customer Relationship Management.

As far back as 1995, Oracle proved its leadership identifying a strong innovative impulse in Internet technologies and correlated business models that led the company to redesign its entire offer (with regard to both technology and business solutions) with Internet in mind. Oracle's offer is aimed at large and medium-sized enterprises that operate in vertical sectors, for example discrete production, process production, banking, insurance, telecommunications, chemicals, pharmaceuticals as well as in central and local public administration.

Acknowledging the enormous potential benefits offered by E-Business, in particular those correlated to cost control and increased profit margins, in May '99 the Chairman and CEO of Oracle Corporation, Larry Ellison himself, launched a strategy aimed at adopting and disseminating the E-Business model within Oracle with the goal of cutting global operating costs by 1 billion dollars. The company began to rethink its business at a world level and the initial results confirm the benefits of converting to an E-Business organisation: the goal was reached and exceeded and the first real advantages have been seen in the areas of marketing, support and

---

[1] Senior Vice President – Oracle South Europe (www.oracle.com)
[2] Senior Director Sales Consulting – Oracle Italia

administrative processes and have also made Oracle a real reference model for all those companies that intend to move in this direction.

12.2   From Integrated Logistics to the Supply Chain

The expression Supply Chain represents the ultimate and definitive evolution of a new approach to logistics management, which became established at the end of the 80s.

In fact, many of the principles and concepts associated with the Supply Chain are not totally new and can be considered to be broadly consolidated in wide-ranging sectors of the industrial world.

It is sufficient to recall the components section for the car and domestic appliances sectors, where the concept of information sharing between the manufacturer and his suppliers spans practically the entire industrial cycle:

- from product design, totally conditioned by the specifications of the final product,
- to the sharing of assembly plans, as input for defining production and purchase requirements.

In these contexts, the definition of *EDI* standards has played an important role. These standards have allowed companies to automate sending and handling of the principal flows of information linked to materials logistics and their commercial transactions.

Today however, the Internet technology revolution has made widespread, low-cost network connectivity available, allowing companies to evolve towards E-Business models and to achieve significant improvements in terms of the efficiency of business management. Companies therefore turn to solutions that use the new technology to create increasingly closer relations with customers, to optimise demand and their own Supply Chains and to test new business models that are in line with the emerging technologies of Web services.

All these operational, organisational and management opportunities are the result of the attentive use of people's capacity to connect and of the integration of systems and processes between companies over the Web.

In this way, models of integration put to the test in the more consolidated sectors have been able to spread into traditionally less structured sectors, even if they are organised with very complicated logistics/productive procedures.

The prime example of this evolution is given by the experiments conducted in some industrial areas which have managed to define and implement data exchange protocols strongly personalised to their own needs.

The predominant characteristic of these experiments however, remains the automation of the process of sending and interpreting "structured data"; that is to say codified data within company information systems (ERP) formatted to the conventions adopted.

But, are the use of Internet and the widespread diffusion of broadly consolidated concepts enough to meet the new market challenges? What is the "extra" within a modern concept of Supply Chain? And above all, what is Oracle's vision and the contribution it makes to the market with its architectures and products?

There are several elements that characterise a modern concept of Supply Chain and which consequently guide the development of Oracle solutions in this field. Namely:

1) the *unity of the information* within the "extended" company system,
2) the integration of business *processes* and the applications solutions, which aid implementation of the extended company,
3) the useability and accessibility of the information and the applications, potentially "total", thanks to *web-based architecture;* that is to say the new E-Business technologies.

Observing Oracle's strategy over recent years, we can see how efforts have been effectively concentrated on offering a suite of truly complete and integrated products (infrastructural and applications software), that:

- support company processes, not only for automating transactions,
- create global and extended Information Systems, exploiting Web-based technology,
- simplify the process of implementing and maintaining the systems, reducing the total cost of ownership. The following paragraphs will comment on the three aspects just mentioned: the unity of the information; orientation to the processes; the evolution of technologies for the extended company.

12.3   Unity of the Information

The characterising element of the Oracle approach certainly lies in the central role of information. In some way this element is part of Oracle's DNA, due to its undisputed leadership as builder of databases.

Regarding this theme, there are two aspects that must be explored more deeply: the theme of unity itself and the different meanings that the term information can take on. Unity is clearly understood as the capacity to represent the information just once, making it useable to all those operators (internal and external) that can benefit from it within the "extended company system".

Theoretically, the principle is flawless, since it is hard to argue for an advantage deriving from a solution that favours the duplication of information. *In practice, however, there are not many solutions that implement it.*

A classic example of this is shown by companies with close integration between the estimates phase and the subsequent sales phase on one side and the production/assembly phase on the other.

The problem these companies have is enabling their agents and resellers to develop estimates in a rapid and controlled manner, so as to streamline subsequent processing of the order.

To do this the commercial officer must have the same information base available to him, which will subsequently serve to manage the order, plan the production, to purchase and lastly, to realise the product the customer has ordered.

In other words, the different operators involved in the various phases of the process, but also in different processes, even if they are connected, have to be able to share information such as: product details, the rules for configuration, pricing, customer details, etc.

It is precisely this sharing that can occur in two ways: either by representing the data once or by duplicating the information on more than one database, realigned with a varying degree of frequency and automation.

The first solution leads to the concept of *Suite*, that is to say integration based on centralised information management, embraced by Oracle as a basic element of its own product strategy in the logistics/manufacturing sector (Supply Chain).

The second solution leads to the concept of the so-called Best-of-Breed, which as a result requires the development of "ad hoc" integration projects, which are often expensive both in the realisation phase, but also and above all in the subsequent maintenance and evolution phase.

Regarding the example given, we can say that the concept of Suite implemented by Oracle cancels out the distinction between the application environment commonly labelled as *CRM* (estimates phase) and the application environment commonly labelled as *ERP* (order management and production phases) through the unified design of the data model.

The second aspect that will be discussed below is the meaning of the term *information*.

In most cases when we speak of Supply Chain, we inevitably tend to speak of structured information; in other words of *data* that is of practical use to the execution of codified transactions.

This is largely justified by the history and evolution of information systems in integrated logistics management in the past.

There is however, a large quantity of information, accompanying the structured data, which is just as useful to the realisation of a model of extended company.

While the concept of data fits in with the world of ERP solutions, the concept of information definitely fits in better with the world of the information portal and when all is said and done with the concept of Knowledge Management itself.

In this vision there must be a single access point, which can be personalised according to each authorised operator's profile, allowing *access to both the world of the management applications (ERP/CRM) and the world of the applications for spreading knowledge (KM).*

In the extended company, authorised operators can be internal or external and the quantity and quality of the services available is determined according to specific jobs and roles.

In Oracle's vision then, a complete Information System must not only be able to manage operativeness, but must also be able to support the achievement of business objectives, through the use of concepts, processes and tools that favour the increase and sharing of knowledge in the extended organisation.

Fundamental elements of this vision are:

- *Knowledge Management* is not an extra, but a distinguishing competitive element, since it contributes to the excellence of the organisation,
- activities targeted at Knowledge Management are not optional extras, but part of normal (natural) business processes,
- the sharing and "proprietorship" (ownership) of the contents must be widespread, but the system is tightly controlled from the centre.

These elements form the basis of the experiment conducted within Oracle's own organisation. The fundamental components of the Oracle Suite are the Portal itself and the Collaboration Tools. In the implementation carried out at Oracle these two components were developed in an extended mode. In particular, the Portal:

- represents the "Single Point-of-Contact",
- allows personalised access to all the company applications,
- allows personalised access to internal information sources:
    - Knowledge Areas: qualified information on Products, Markets, Competition, Partners, Customers, Analysts, etc.,
    - Organisational Areas: information concerning business processes and organisational entities,
    - Community Areas: internal collaboration areas dedicated to professional or interest groups (Communities),
- allows personalised access to external sources.

To give a practical example of how the concept of *extended knowledge* has been applied in Oracle, suffice to consider the support service, dispensed to fixing the technical problems pointed out by the customers.

The service was restructured during 2001, by opening the information system that manages requests for support to customers. The system allows requests to be entered in self-service mode and to trace their progress at every step, but it also allows users to consult answers and solutions that Oracle has already given for similar or identical cases. The result produced by the introduction of this new service has been doubly positive: with end customers being more satisfied thanks to the transparency and efficiency of the service and with a drastic reduction in the number of requests for support, thanks to all the duplicated cases being eliminated.

12.4   Orientation to the Processes

The second element that characterises a modern concept of Supply Chain is represented by the *way in which information is treated and circulated* between the various "players" in the extended company organisation.

As previously seen, the "natural" characteristics of the *extended company* are the high number and above all, the differences between the "players" at work within it.

In such a complex context, it becomes even more essential to adopt an *organisational approach orientated to the processes*: an approach that aims to target each action to a precise business objective, whether it is the design of a new product, rather than the launch of a promotional campaign through the sales network.

In this sense, an organisation orientated to the processes *overcomes both internal barriers (between company ranks) and external barriers (between the company and its partners)*, asking each "player" to perform a useful role for the prescribed objective.

The evolution of organisational models in this direction over recent years has naturally had an important impact on the world of company information systems. Indeed, to be able to operate effectively, each "player":

- must have at his disposal up-to-date, selected information, that is consistent with and pertinent to his role,
- must only perform the activities within his scope,
- must collaborate with the other "players" involved in the process, alerting them and bringing them into play in a timely and precise manner.

In other words the information must be handled and circulated in a predetermined and controlled manner and be consistent with the flow of the business process. From the point of view of information system architecture, the answer to this type of requirement is represented by *Workflow Systems*.

In brief, Workflow Systems allow three things to be done:

- model the *process* (i.e. define which steps it is composed of and associate activities and expected players to each step),
- execute the *process* (i.e. control the execution of the individual steps, keeping watch over the launch mechanisms of the individual notification/activation activities of the players involved automatically),
- monitor the *process* (i.e. display its progress state in real time).

Fig. 12.1 represents a generalised model of an "approval cycle" that can be applied in various contexts: from the approval of a price list to the approval of a request for purchase.

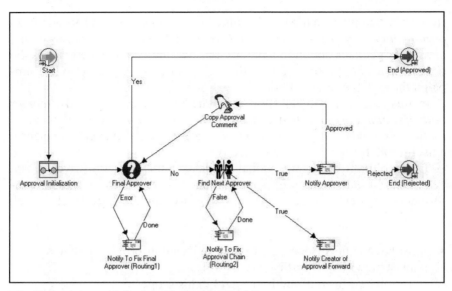

Fig 12.1   Approval Cycle with Oracle Workflow

The Workflow engine is a fundamental part of the Oracle platform, which has been chosen by Snaidero in the creation of its own information system.

Workflow allows internal company processes as well as processes that involve companies and people from outside the company to be modelled and managed, using standard, low-cost tools such as electronic mail and web browsers.

In addition, it is also an efficient tool for integrating applications procedures, since it is able to manage synchronisation between stand alone and different software systems, whether they are in or outside the company.

Workflow constitutes an integral part of Oracle's iAS (internet Application Server) solution, whose strongpoint lies in native interaction with the database.

As well as containing the Workflow engine, the iAS platform integrates the actual server, the portal, Business Intelligence, application integration tools, the wireless application and lastly the system's administrative services in a single environment.

Coming, more specifically, to the Snaidero project, the application of the concept of extended company consisted – in an initial phase – in creating and implementing a collaboration model with the company's distribution chain. The business objectives of the project were and are:

- to connect Snaidero directly and rapidly with the other partners in the value chain,
- to improve the quantity and quality of shared information,
- to reduce the times and costs of creating and using information,
- to disseminate new techniques and new tools for getting to know markets and customers (Business Intelligence),
- to improve automation when processing customer purchases and dispatching orders,
- to gain the confidence of the trade,
- to offer, for good, a greater level of service to the end customer.

The pursuit of these objectives had an important impact on the number of processes and bodies involved and consequently also required thorough innovation of the information systems. The innovation mainly concerned the following aspects:

- the creation of a Content Management system with the Oracle database as its central element; a repository for all the information for "publication",
- the use of the Workflow engine to manage the creation, approval and information publication phases in a controlled manner,
- the implementation of a Portal, as a unified access point for all the company applications, which can be personalised according to the user profiles of the different enabled players,
- the company's Extranet, which constitutes the enabling infrastructure for communications between the company and the network of resellers,
- integration of the new environment with the back-office management information system (which Snaidero has not modified for the moment).

A relatively complex example that illustrates the operation of the system regards managing new customers/resellers.

In this case the agents that are authorised for this type of activity access the system through the portal and use the application to store the information required.

However, the addition of a new customer/reseller requires a process of evaluation and approval by Sales Management and Administration.

The notice regarding the request for approval is automatically sent through the Workflow system mechanisms to the Administration and Management.

At the end of a complex cycle of approval, the customer is enabled (/refused) and all the information regarding him (economic and geographical classification, financial position, etc.) is stored in the Snaidero's customers archive and made available to the authorised user, always through the portal.

Of course, storage in the customers archive entails integration between the Snaidero company information system (back-office) and the repository of information available on the network (front-office).

In addition to automatic interaction with the database, the solution's other strongpoint is the great flexibility and ease in modelling the process flows.

This aspect acquires greater importance the greater the dynamism of the system, or rather, the greater the company's need to grow, to change and accordingly revise its internal operating processes; a typical condition of a strongly evolving company like Snaidero.

This is in line with Oracle's vision of the design and development of its Supply Chain applications solutions.

In particular, in the Oracle vision, the processes that implement the model of the extended company refer to five main areas (which will be commented on below):

- product development,
- planning,
- purchase,
- production,
- sales.

Where *product development* is concerned, company business objectives are the capacity to grasp market needs, reduction in the time required to design and launch of new products and, if possible, a limitation on budgetary expenditure.

In this area the Oracle solution supports the processes of:

- gathering and processing input coming from the market,
- the definition of the development projects,
- technical management of the projects, in particular co-engineering with strategic partners (especially suppliers of components and/or tooling),
- administrative management of the projects,
- integration with the productive process.

Where *planning* is concerned, the business objective is to improve "quality", through closer collaboration between the different sales channels (direct and indirect), marketing, production and purchases.

In this area the Oracle solution supports the following processes:

- gathering forecasts from internal and external sources (analysts),
- consolidating the forecasts and managing the "consensus" process,
- modelling the extended logistics chain (internal and external resources),
- acquiring and consolidating the operational data (stock positions, productive capacities, commitments, etc.),
- developing the sales/production/procurement plans.

Where *purchases* are concerned, on the one hand companies' objectives are to expand the base of suppliers and the reduce costs and on the other to reduce time and costs in the procurement process for on-going supplies (open-end contracts).

In this area Oracle solutions support two main process categories:

- negotiation processes via auctions, RFI (Request for Information), RFP (Request for Proposal), RFQ (Request for Quotation),
- procurement processes via self-service purchasing and sharing information on the suppliers' portals.

Where *production* is concerned, companies' objectives are to increase flexibility, both in terms of adapting rapidly to variations in demand and in terms of the capacity to personalise the product to the customer's requirements.

In this area Oracle solutions support the processes of:

- integrating with customers for the acquisition of delivery plans (applicable for repetitive-type open-end contracts),
- sharing programmes with labour suppliers,
- configuring the products,
- production management, also hybrid management (discrete, process, flow, assemble-to-order).

Lastly, where *sales* are concerned, the objective of companies' is to consolidate relations with the customer, in an extended cycle that goes from marketing to after-sales service.

In this area Oracle solutions support processes of:

- campaigns management,
- distribution network management,
- multi-channel sales management (telesales, Internet store, direct, channel, etc.),
- service,
- business intelligence.

In Oracle's vision *the extended company model therefore corresponds to a system of processes that create extended forms of collaboration between companies and people.*

This system can also be very complex, depending on the industry sector and the size and characteristics of the individual company.

For this reason choosing Workflow as a configuration system for the applications supporting the processes ensures a very high level of flexibility, since it allows different solutions to be constructed through the personalised assembly of standard procedures and functions.

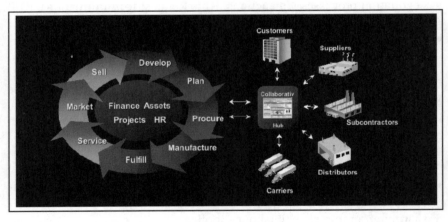

Fig 12.2 Supply Chain Management solutions

12.5   Technological Prospects for the Extended Enterprise

We have already spoken of the advantages introduced by Internet technology and of how the concept of the extended company itself is by now closely tied to an architectural model of information systems, based on the Web and network services. In addition to allowing collaboration with the outside, this model favours the process of consolidating systems and databases within the company. In fact, it becomes possible to rationalise the systems distributed in the company's different operational centres into a single (or a few) data centres. In the case of complex organisations this consolidation process permits considerable economies of scale in systems management, as has been the case at Oracle itself, which restructured its systems for relating with customers and suppliers by creating a *single* system (on a worldwide scale) of applications, that can be used through the network.

A second aspect we would like to highlight in relation to systems architecture, concerns the growing need to extend services to new *devices*, in particular *wireless devices*. Looking at extended companies, this technology is rapidly spreading, above all in the area of sales and after-sales service to the customer. Where sales are concerned, the processes are tied to, sales negotiation management, from tracing activities carried out by salesmen/agents to drawing up economic proposals (quotation, product configuration/service, etc.). Where after-sales service is concerned on the other hand, the processes involved are those of on-site service, from planning to budgeting the interventions carried out on the customer's premises.

The final aspect concerns the evolution towards *Web-services*, which are becoming established as the standard for creating network interoperability between different applications. The objective in this case is to *automate* and structure the exchange of information between resident processes on *different systems*, both in *synchronous* mode (by one system requesting service from another corresponding system) and *asynchronous* mode (by event).

From what has been said above on Workflow, it can be understood how the *integration between the two components of Workflow and Web-service* allows the company to automatically configure and control processes that are also very complex and complicated, partly carried out within the company itself and partly outside.

Oracle's choice to integrate all these components in a single software platform designated *i*AS ("Internet Application Server") expresses its vision of an architectural model that is increasingly orientated to supporting extended organisations, formulated with cooperation and interoperability in mind. For this reason too, Snaidero has chosen Oracle.

Bibliography and Web Sites

Chapter 1

Armistead C., Rowland P., *Managing Business Processes: BPR and Beyond*, John Wiley & Sons, Chichester, UK, 1996

Biazzo S., «A Critical Examination of the Business Process Re-engineering Phenomenon», *International Journal of Operations & Production Management*, vol. 18, n° 9/10, pg. 1000-1016, 1998

Cagliano R., Spina G., Verganti R., Zotteri G., «Designing BPR Support Services for Small Firms», *International Journal of Operations & Production Management*, vol. 18, n° 9/10, pg. 865-885, 1998

Chapple E. D., Sayles L. R., *The Measure of Management*, Macmillan, New York, 1961

Childe S. J., Maull R. S., Bennett J., «Frameworks for Understanding Business Process Re-engineering», *International Journal of Operations & Production Management*, vol. 14, n° 12, pg. 22-34, 1994

Davenport T. H., Short J. E., «The New Industrial Engineering: Information Technology and Business Process Redesign», *Sloan Management Review*, pg. 11-27, summer 1990

Davenport T. H., *Process Innovation: Reengineering Work through Information Technology*, Harvard Business School Press, Boston, MA, 1993

Drucker P. F., *The Practice of Management*, Harper & Bros., New York, 1954

Dutta S., Manzoni J.-F., *Process Re-engineering, Organizational Change and Performance Improvement*, McGraw-Hill, New York, 1998

Evered R. D., Selman J. C., «Coaching and the Art of Management», *Organizational Dynamics*, vol. 18, n° 2, pg. 16-32, 1989

Ghoshal S., Bartlett C. A., «Changing the Role of Top Management: Beyond Structure to Processes», *Harvard Business Review*, pg. 86-96, jan./feb. 1995

Grover V., Malhotra M. K, «Business Process Reengineering: A Tutorial on the Concept, Evolution, Method, Technology and Application», *Journal of Operations Management*, vol. 15, pg. 193-213, 1997

Hall G., Rosenthal J., Wade J., «How to Make Reengineering Really Work», *Harvard Business Review*, pg. 119-131, nov./dec. 1993

Hammer M., «Reengineering Work: Don't Automate! Obliterate», *Harvard Business Review*, pg. 104-112, july/august 1990

Hammer M., Champy J., *Reengineering the Corporation: A Manifesto for Business Revolution*, Nicholas Brealey Publ., London, 1993

Hammer M., Stanton S., «How Process Enterprises Really Work», *Harvard Business Review*, pg. 108-116, nov./dec. 1999

Harrington H. J., *Business Process Improvement: The Breakthrough Strategy for Total Quality, Productivity and Competitiveness*, McGraw-Hill, New York, 1991

Hronec S. M., *Vital Signs: Using Quality, Time and Cost Performance Measurement to Chart Your Company's Future*, AMACOM, American Management Association, New York, 1993

Johansson H. J., McHugh P., Pendlebury A. J., Wheeler W. A., *Business Process Reengineering*, John Wiley & Sons, Chichester, UK, 1993

Johnson H. T., «Performance Measurement for Competitive Excellence», in Kaplan R. S. (ed.), *Measures for Manufacturing Excellence*, Harvard Business School Press, Boston, MA, 1990

Kaplan R. S., Murdock L., «Rethinking the Corporation: Core Process Redesign», *The McKinsey Quarterly*, n° 2, pg. 27-43, 1991

Keen P. G. W., *Process Edge: Creating Value Where It Counts*, Harvard Business School Press, Boston, MA, 1997

King W., Sethi V., *Organizational Transformation Through Business Process Reengineering*, Prentice-Hall, Englewood Cliffs, New Jersey, 1998

Odiorne G. S., *Management by Objectives*, Pitman Publishing, New York, 1965

Ostroff F., *The Horizontal Organization*, Oxford University Press, New York, 1999

Rohleder T. R., Silver E. A., «A Tutorial on Business Process Improvement», *Journal of Operations Management*, vol. 15, pg. 139-154, 1999

Rummler G., Brache A., *Improving Performance: How to Manage the White Space on the Organizational Chart*, Jossey-Bass Publ., San Francisco, 1990

Tonchia S., «Lean Organization, Management-by-Process and Performance Measurement», *International Journal of Operations & Production Management*, vol. 16, n° 2, pg. 221-236, 1996 (with De Toni A.)

Tonchia S., «Manufacturing Flexibility: A Literature Review», *International Journal of Production Research*, vol. 36, n° 6, pg. 1587-1617, 1998 (with De Toni A.)

Turney P. B. B., «What an Activity-Based Cost Model Looks Like», *Journal of Cost Management*, vol. 6, n° 1, pg. 54-60, 1999

UNI EN ISO 9000:2000 («Quality Management Systems – Fundamentals and vocabulary»), UNI EN ISO 9001:2000 («Quality Management Systems – Requirements»), UNI EN ISO 9004:2000 («Quality Management Systems – Guidelines for performance improvements»), December 2000

Youkl G. A., *Leadership in Organizations*, Prentice-Hall, Englewood Cliffs, New Jersey, 1981

Zeleny M., «What Is Integrated Process Management», *Human Systems Management*, n° 7, pg. 265-267, 1988

Chapter 2

Bartezzaghi E., Spina G., Verganti R., *Nuovi modelli d'impresa e tecnologie d'integrazione*, Franco Angeli, Milano, 1994 (in italian)

Bhatt G. D., «An Empirical Examination of the Effects of Information Systems Integration on Business Process Improvement», *International Journal of Operations & Production Management*, vol. 20, n° 11, pg. 1331-1359, 2000

Davenport T. H., Short J. E., «The New Industrial Engineering: Information Technology and Business Process Redesign», *Sloan Management Review*, pg. 11-27, summer 1990

Davenport T. H., *Process Innovation: Reengineering Work through Information Technology*, Harvard Business School Press, Boston, MA, 1993

Earl M., Khan B., «How New Is Business Process Redesign», *European Management Journal*, vol. 12, n° 1, pg. 20-30, march 1994

Gilbreath R. D., *Winning at Project Management*, John Wiley & Sons, New York, 1986

Hammer M., Stanton S., «How Process Enterprises Really Work», *Harvard Business Review*, pg. 108-116, nov./dec. 1999

IBM, *Business Systems Planning*, guide GE 20-0527-1, 1975

Koestler A., *The Ghost in the Machine*, Hutchinson & Co., London, 1967

Malone T. W. and other 11 authors, «Tools for Inventing Organizations: Toward a Handbook of Organizational Processes», *Management Science*, vol. 45, n° 3, pg. 425-443, march 1999

Mandelbrot B. B., *The Fractal Geometry of Nature*, W. H. Freeman, San Francisco, 1982

Marchand D. A., Kettinger W J., Rollins J. D., «Information Orientation: People, Technology and the Bottom Line», *Sloan Management Review*, pg. 69-80, summer 2000

Ould M., *Business Processes*, John Wiley & Sons, Chichester, UK, 1995

Porter M. E., *Competitive Advantage: Creating and Substaining Superior Performance*, The Free Press, New York, 1985

Ross D. T., «Structured Analysis: A Language for Communicating Ideas», *IEEE Transactions on Software Engineering*, vol. 15, n° 1, 1977

Rummler G., Brache A., *Improving Performance: How to Manage the White Space on the Organizational Chart*, Jossey-Bass Publ., San Francisco, 1990

Scheer A. W., Abolhassan F., Jost W., Kirchmer M. (eds.), *Business Process Change Management: ARIS in Practice*, Springer & Verlag, Berlin, 2003

Scott-Morton M. S. (ed.), *The Corporation of 1990s*, Oxford University Press, New York, 1991

Chapter 3

Afuah A., «How Much Do Your Co-Opetitors' Capabilities Matter in the Face of Technological Uncertainty?», *Strategic Management Journal*, vol. 21, pg. 387-404, 2000

Alavi M., Leidner D. E., «Knowledge Management and Knowledge Management Systems: Conceptual Foundations and Research Issues», *MIS Quarterly*, vol. 25, pg. 107-136, 2001

Amit R., Zott C., «Value Creation in e-Business», *Strategic Management Journal*, vol. 22, pg. 493-520, 2001

Aoki M., *The Cooperative Game Theory of the Firm*, Oxford University Press, Oxford (UK), 1984

Armstrong A., Hagel J. III, «The Real Value of On-line Communities», *Harvard Business Review*, pg. 134-141, may/june 1996

Bacon F., *The Advancement of Learning*, London, 1605

Bartezzaghi E., Ronchi S., «The Role of the Internet in Customer-Supplier Relationships», in Christiansen J., Boer H. (eds.), *Operations Management and the New Economy*, 9th EurOma International Conference, Copenaghen, 2002

Bartlett C. A., Ghoshal S., «Building Competitive Advantage Through People», *Sloan Management Review*, pg. 34-41, winter 2002

Becker M., «Managing Dispersed Knowledge», *Journal of Management Studies*, vol. 38, n° 7, pg. 1037-1051, 2001

Benjamin R., Wigand R., «Electronic Markets and Virtual Value Chains on the Information Superhighways», *Sloan Management Review*, pg. 62-72, winter 1995

Boisot M. H., *Knowledge Assets: Securing Competitive Advantage in the Information Economy*, Oxford University Press, Oxford (UK), 1999

Bolisani E., Scarso E., «Information Technology Management: A Knowledge-based Perspective», *Technovation*, vol. 19, n° 4, pg. 209-217, 1999

Boyson S., Dresner M. E., Harrington L., Corsi T. M., Rabinovich E., *Logistics and the Extended Enterprise: Benchmarks and Best Practices for the Manufacturing Professional*, John Wiley & Sons, New York, 1999

Buchel A., Schonsleben P. (eds.), *Organizing the Extended Enterprise*, IFIP - International Federation of Informational Processing, Kluwer Academic Publisher, London, 1998

Burn J., Marshall P., Barnett M., *E-Business Strategies for Virtual Organizations*, Digital Press, Oxford (UK), 2001

Camarinha-Matos L. M., Asarmanesh H. (eds.), *Infrastructures for Virtual Enterprises*, Kluwer Academic Publisher, Boston, MA, 1999

Cohen W. M., Levinthal D. A., «Absorptive Capacity: A New Perspective on Learning and Innovation», *Administrative Science Quarterly*, vol. 35, pg. 128-152, 1990

Combs J. G., Ketchen D. J. jr, «Explaining Interfirm Cooperation and Performance: Toward a Reconciliation of Predictions from the Resource-Based View and Organizational Economics», *Strategic Management Journal*, vol. 20, pg. 867-888, 1999

Conner K. R., Prahalad C. K., «A Resource-Based Theory of the Firm: Knowledge Versus Opportunism», *Organization Science*, vol. 7, n° 5, pg. 447-501, 1996

Cross R., Baird L., «Technology Is Not Enough: Improving Performance by Building Organizational Memory», *Sloan Management Review*, pg. 69-78, spring 2000

D'Aveni R. A., *Hypercompetition: Managing the Dynamics of Strategic Maneuvering*, The Free Press, New York, 1994

Davenport T. H., Prusak L., *Working Knowledge: How Organizations Manage What They Know*, Harvard Business School Press, Boston, MA, 1997

den Hertog J. F., Huizenga E., *The Knowledge Enterprise: Implementation of Intelligent Business Strategies*, Imperial College Press, 2000

Duguay C. R., Landry S., Pasin F, «From Mass Production to Flexible/Agile Production», *International Journal of Operations & Production Management*, vol. 17, n° 12, pg. 1183-1195, 1997

Dyer J. H., «Effective Interfirm Collaboration: How Firms Minimize Transaction Costs and Maximize Transaction Value», *Strategic Management Journal*, vol. 18, pg. 535-556, 1997

Dyer J. H., *Collaborative Advantage: Winning Through Extended Enterprise Supplier Networks*, Oxford University Press, New York, 2000

Dyer J. H., Singh H., «The Relational View: Cooperative Strategy and Sources of Interorganizational Competitive Advantage», *Academy of Management Review*, vol. 23, n° 4, pg. 660-679, 1998

Edvinsson L., «Developing Intellectual Capital at Skandia», *Long Range Planning*, vol. 30, pg. 366-373, 1997

Eisenhardt K. M., Martin J. A., «Dynamic Capabilities: What Are They?», *Strategic Management Journal*, vol. 21, pg. 1105-1121, 2000

Fisher L., *Excellence in Practice Vol. III: Innovation & Excellence in Workflow Process and Knowledge Management*, Future Strategies Inc., Lighthouse Point, Florida, 2000

Goranson H. T., *The Agile Virtual Enterprise: Cases, Metrics, Tools*, Quorum Books, Westport, CT, 1999

Grandori A., *Organization and Economic Behavior*, Routledge, London, 2001

Grandori A., *Interfirm Networks*, eBooks, www.ebookmall.com, 2003

Grant R. M., «Toward a Knowledge-Based Theory of the Firm», *Strategic Management Journal*, vol. 17, pg. 109-122, 1996

Grover V., Davenport T. H., «General Perspectives on Knowledge Management: Fostering a Research Agenda», *Journal of Management Information Systems*, vol. 18, n° 1, pg. 5-21, 2001

Gulati R., Nohria N., Zaheer A., «Strategic Networks», *Strategic Management Journal*, vol. 21, pg. 203-215, 2000

Hagel J. III, Rayport J. F., «The New Infomediaries», *The McKinsey Quarterly*, n° 4, 1997

Hansen M. T., Nohria N., Tierney T., «What's Your Strategy for Managing Knowledge?», *Harvard Business Review*, pg. 106-116, march/april 1999

Hansen M. T., von Oetinger B., «Introducing T-Shaped Managers: Knowledge Management's Next Generation», *Harvard Business Review*, pg. 107-116, march/april 2001

Hedlund G., «The Hypermodern MNC: A Heterarchy? », *Human Resource Management*, vol. 25, n° 1, 1986

Hite J. M., Hesterly W. S., «The Evolution of Firm Networks: From Emergence to Early Growth of the Firm», *Strategic Management Journal*, vol. 22, pg. 275-286, 2001

Hitt M. A., Ireland R. D., Camp S. M., Sexton D. L., «Guest Editors' Introduction to the Special Issue Strategic Entrepreneurship: Entrepreneurial Strategies for Wealth Creation», *Strategic Management Journal*, vol. 22, pg. 479-491, 2001

Inkpen A. C., «Creating Knowledge Through Collaboration», *California Management Review*, pg. 123-140, fall 1996

Jones C., Hesterly W. S., Borgatti S. P., «A General Theory of Network Governance: Exchange Conditions and Social Mechanisms», *Academy of Management Review*, vol. 22, n° 4, pg. 911-945, 1997

Kalakota R., Robinson M., *E-business: Roadmap for Sucess*, Addison-Wesley Longman, Don Mills, Ontario, 1999

Kanter R. M., *Rosabeth Moss Kanter on the Frontiers of Management*, Harvard Business School Press, Boston, MA, 1997

Kanter R. M., *Change Is Everyone's Job: Managing the Extended Enterprise in a Globally-Connected World*, e-book, Goodmeasure Inc., Cambridge, MA, 2000

Kanter R. M., *Evolve! Succeeding in the Digital Culture of Tomorrow*, Harvard Business School Press, Boston, MA, 2001

Kaplan R. S., Norton D. P., «The Balanced Scorecard: Measures That Drive Performance», *Harvard Business Review*, pg. 71-79, jan./feb. 1992

Kim W. C., Mauborgne R., «Fair Process: Managing in the Knowledge Economy», *Harvard Business Review*, pg. 65-75, july/august 1997

Kogut B., Zander U., «What Firms Do? Coordination, Identity and Learning», *Organization Science*, vol. 7, n° 5, pg. 502-518, 1996

Lee C., K. Lee, Pennings J. M., «Internal Capabilities, External Networks, and Performance: A Study on Technology-Based Ventures», *Strategic Management Journal*, vol. 22, pg. 615-640, 2001

Lengnick-Hall C. A., Wolff J. A., «Similarities and Contradictions in the Core Logic of Three Strategy Research Streams», *Strategic Management Journal*, vol. 20, pg. 1109-1132, 1999

Leonard-Barton D., *Wellsprings of Knowledge*, Harvard Business School Press, Boston, MA, 1995

Lorenzoni G., Lipparini A., «The Leveraging of Interfirm Relationships as a Distinctive Organizational Capability: A Longitudinal Study», *Strategic Management Journal*, vol. 20, pg. 317-338, 1999

Makadok R., «Toward a Synthesis of the Resource-Based and Dynamic-Capability Views of Rent Creation», *Strategic Management Journal*, vol. 22, pg. 387-401, 2001

McDermott R., «Why Information Technology Inspired But Cannot Deliver Knowledge Management», *California Management Review*, pg. 103-117, summer 1999

Nahapiet J., Ghoshal S., «Social Capital, Intellectual Capital, and the Organizational Advantage», *Academy of Management Review*, vol. 23, n° 2, pg. 242-266, 1998

Nassimbeni G., «Network structures and coordination mechanisms: a taxonomy», *International Journal of Operations & Production Management*, vol. 18, n° 6, pg. 538-554, 1998

Nohria N., Eccles R. (eds.), *Networks and Organizations*, Harvard Business School Press, Boston, MA, 1992

Nonaka I., «The Knowledge Creating Company», *Harvard Business Review*, pg. 96-104, nov./dec. 1991

Nonaka I., Konno N., «The Concept of "Ba": Building a Foundation for Knowledge Creation», *California Management Review*, pg. 40-54, spring 1998

Nonaka I., Takeuchi H., *The Knowledge Creating Company*, Oxford University Press, New York, 1995

Normann R., Ramirez R., «From Value Chain to Value Constellation: Designing Interactive Strategy», *Harvard Business Review*, pg. 65-78, july/august 1993

O'Dell C., Grayson C. J., *If Only We Knew What We Know: The Transfer of Internal Knowledge and Best Practice*,

Penrose E. T., *The Theory of Growth of the Firm*, Basil Blackwell, London, 1959

Piore M., Sabel C., *The Second Industrial Divide: Possibilities for Prosperity*, Basic Books, New York, 1984

Polanyi M., *The Tacit Dimension*, Routledge & Kegan Paul, London, 1967

Porter M. E., *Competitive Advantage: Creating and Substaining Superior Performance*, The Free Press, New York, 1985

Porter M. E., «Strategy and the Internet», *Harvard Business Review*, pg. 63-78, march/april 2001

Prahalad C. K., Hamel G., «The Core Competence of the Corporation», *Harvard Business Review*, pg. 79-91, may/june 1990

Presley A. R., Liles D. H., «A Holon-based Process Modeling Methodology», *International Journal of Operations & Production Management*, vol. 21, n° 5-6, pg. 565-581, 2001

Quintas P., Lefrere P., Jones G., «Knowledge Management: A Strategic Agenda», *Long Range Planning*, vol. 30, pg. 385-391, 1997

Rayport J. F., Sviokla J. J., «Exploiting the Virtual Value Chain», *Harvard Business Review*, pg. 75-85, nov./dec. 1995

Rullani E., «Tecnologie che generano valore: divisione del lavoro cognitivo e rivoluzione digitale», *Economia e Politica Industriale*, pg. 141-168, n° 93, 1997 (in italian)

Savage C., *5th Generation Management: Co-Creating through Virtual Enterprising, Dynamic Teaming and Knowledge Networking*, Butterworth Heinemann, Oxford (UK), 1996

Sawhney M., Prandelli E., «Communities of Creation: Managing Distributed Innovation in Turbulent Markets», *California Management Review*, pg. 24-54, summer 2000

Schiuma G., Marr B., «Measuring and Managing Intellectual Capital and Knowledge Assets in New Economy Organisations», in Bourne M. (ed.), *Performance Measurement Handbook*, GEE Publishing, London, 2001

Schumpeter J. A., *The Theory of Economic Development*, Harvard University Press, Boston, MA, 1934

Senge P. M., «The Leader's New Work: Building Learning Organizations», *Sloan Management Review*, pg. 7-23, summer 1990

Shapiro C., Varian H. R., *Information Rules: A Strategic Guide to the Network Economy*, Harvard Business School Press, Boston, MA, 1998

Spencer L. M., Spencer S., *Competence at Work: Models for Superior Performance*, John Wiley & Sons, New York, 1993

Spender J.-C., «Making Knowledge the Basis of a Dynamic Theory of the Firm», *Strategic Management Journal*, vol. 17, pg. 45-62, 1996

Stacey R. D., «The Science of Complexity: An Alternative Perspective for Strategic Change Processes», *Strategic Management Journal*, vol. 16, pg. 477-495, 1996

Stalk G., Evans P., Shulman L. E., «Competing on Capabilities: The New Rules of Corporate Strategy», *Harvard Business Review*, pg. 57-69, march/april 1992

Tapscott D., *Digital Capital*, Nicholas Brealey Publishing, London, 2000

Teece D. J., «Strategies for Managing Knowledge Assets: The Role of Firm Structure and Industrial Context», *Long Range Planning*, vol. 33, pg. 35-54, 2000

Teece D. J., Pisano G., Shuen A., «Dynamic Capabilities and Strategic Management», *Strategic Management Journal*, vol. 18, pg. 509-533, 1997

Tiwana A., *The Knowledge Management Toolkit*, Prentice-Hall, Upper Saddle River, New Jersey, 2000

Tonchia S., «Editorial», Guest Editor of the special issue on "E-Business Strategic Planning & Development", *International Journal of Business Performance Management*, vol. 4, n° 4, pg. 129-135, 2002

Tsoukas H, «The Firm as a Distributed Knowledge Management System», *Strategic Management Journal*, vol. 17, pg. 11-25, 1996

Upton D. M., McAfee A., «The Real Virtual Factory», *Harvard Business Review*, pg. 123-133, july/august 1996

Venkatraman N., Henderson J. C., «Real Strategies for Virtual Organizing», *Sloan Management Review*, pg. 33-48, fall 1998

Von Krogh G., «Care in Knowledge Creation», *California Management Review*, pg. 133-153, spring 1998

Watson R. T., Berthon P., Pitt L. F., Zinkhan G. M., *Electronic Commerce*, The Dryden Press, New York, 2000

Webber A. M., «What's so new about the new economy? », *Harvard Business Review*, pg. 24-42, jan./feb. 1993

Wenger E., Snyder W., «Communities of Practice: The Organisational Frontier», *Harvard Business Review*, pg. 139-145, jan./feb. 2000

Williamson O. E., *Markets and Hierarchies: Analysis and Antitrust Implications*, The Free Press, New York, 1975

Yli-Renko H., Autio E., Sapienza H. J., «Social Capital, Knowledge Acquisition, and Knowledge Exploitation in Young Technology-Based Firms», *Strategic Management Journal*, vol. 22, pg. 587-613, 2001

Zack M. H., «Managing Codified Knowledge», *Sloan Management Review*, pg. 45-59, summer 1999

Chapter 5

Clark K. B., Fujimoto T., *Product Development Performance: Strategy, Organization and Management in the World Auto Industry*, Harvard Business School Press, Boston, MA, 1991

Cusumano M. A., Nobeoka K., *Thinking Beyond Lean: How Multi-Project Management Is Transforming Product Development at Toyota and Other Companies*, The Free Press, New York, 1998

Garvin D. A., *Managing Quality: The Strategic and Competitive Edge*, The Free Press, New York, 1988

Lambin J.-J., *Marketing strategico e operativo*, McGraw-Hill Libri Italia, Milano, 2000

Mc Carthy E. J., *Basic Marketing: A Managerial Approach*, Irwin, Homewood, IL, 1960

Tonchia S., *Il Project Management: Come gestire il cambiamento e l'innovazione*, Il Sole 24 ORE Libri, Milano, 2001 (in italian)

Womack J. P., Jones D. T., Roos D., *The Machine That Changed the World*, Rawson Associates - Macmillan, New York, 1990

Chapter 6

Abernathy W. J., Utterback J. M., «Patterns of Industrial Innovation», *Technology Review*, pg. 40-47, june/july 1978

Ansari A., Modarress B., *Just-In-Time Purchasing*, The Free Press, New York, 1990

Bonazzi G., *Il tubo di cristallo: Modello giapponese e fabbrica integrata alla Fiat Auto*, Il Mulino, Bologna, 1993

Bowersox D. J., Closs D. J., Helferich O. K., *Logistical Management*, 3th edition, Macmillan, New York, 1986

Cusumano M. A., Takeishi A., «Supplier Relation and Management: a Survey of Japanese-Transplant, and U.S. Auto Plants», *Strategic Management Journal*, vol. 12, pg. 563-588, 1991

Flynn B. B., Schroeder R. G., Sakakibara S., «A Framework for Quality Management Research and an Associated Measurement Instrument», *Journal of Operations Management*, vol. 11, n° 4, pg. 339-366, 1994

Garvin D. A., *Managing Quality: The Strategic and Competitive Edge*, The Free Press, New York, 1988

Hartley J. L., Meredith J. R., McCutcheon D., Kamath R. R., «Suppliers' Contribution to Product Development: An Exploratory Study», *IEEE Transactions on Engineering Management*, vol. 44, n° 3, pg. 258-267, 1997

Kraljic P., «From Purchasing to Supply Management», *The McKinsey Quartely*, pg. 2-17, spring 1983

Porter M. E., *Competitive Advantage: Creating and Substaining Superior Performance*, The Free Press, New York, 1985

Ragatz G. L., Handfield R. B., and Scannell T. V., «Success factors for integrating suppliers into new product development», *Journal of Product Innovation Management* , vol. 14, n° 3, pg. 190-202, 1997

Schmenner R. W., *Production/Operations Management: Concepts and Situations*, Science Research, Chicago, 1984

Schonberger R. J., *Bulding a Chain of Customers*, The Free Press, New York, 1990

Schonberger R. J., Knod E. M. jr, *Operations Management: Customer-Focused Principles*, 6th edition, McGraw-Hill, New York, 1997

Slack N., Chambers S., Harland C., Harrison A., Johnston R., *Operations Management*, 2nd edition, Pitman Publishing, London, 1998

Tonchia S., «New Trends in the Supply Environment», *Logistics Information Management*, vol. 7, n° 4, 1994 (with De Toni A. and Nassimbeni G.)

Tonchia S., «Service Dimensions in the Buyer-Supplier Relationship», *International Journal of Physical Distribution & Logistics Management*, vol. 24, n° 8, pg. 4-14, 1994 (with De Toni A. and Nassimbeni G.)

Tonchia S., «Small Local Firms inside the Supply Chain: Challenges and Perspectives», *Small Business Economics*, vol. 7, n° 3, pg. 241-249, 1995 (with De Toni A. and Nassimbeni G.)

Tonchia S., «An Instrument for Quality Performance Measurement», *International Journal of Production Economics*, vol. 38, pg. 199-207, march 1995 (with De Toni A. and Nassimbeni G.)

Tonchia S., «An Artificial Intelligence-based Production Scheduler», *Integrated Manufacturing Systems - The International Journal of Manufacturing Technology Management*, vol. 7, n° 3, pg. 17-25, 1996 (with De Toni A. and Nassimbeni G.)

Tonchia S., «New Production Models: A Strategic View», *International Journal of Production Research*, vol. 40, n° 18, pg. 4721-4741, 2002 (with De Toni A.)

Tonchia S., «Measuring and Managing the After-Sales Service: Aprilia's Experience», *International Journal of Services Technology & Management*, vol. 5, n° 3, pg. 1-10, 2004 (with De Toni A.)

Vollmann T. E., Berry W. L., Whybark D. C., *Manufacturing Planning and Control Systems*, 3rd edition, Business One Irwin, Homewood, IL, 1992

von Hippel E., *The Sources of Innovation*, Oxford University Press, New York, 1988

Zeithaml V. A., Parasuraman A., Berry L. L., *Delivering Quality Service*, The Free Press, New York, 1990

Chapter 7

Anthony R. N., *A Review of Essentials of Accounting*, 6th edition, Addison-Wesley Publ., Reading, MA, 1997

Anthony R. N., Hawkins D. F., Merchant K. A., *Accounting: Text and Cases*, 6th edition, McGraw-Hill, New York, 1999

Becker B. E., Huselid M. A., Ulrich D., *The HR Scorecard: Linking People, Strategy, and Performance*, Harvard Business School Press, Boston, MA, 2001

Collis D. J., Montgomery C. A., *Corporate Strategy: Resources and the Scope of the Firm*, McGraw-Hill, New York, 1997

Cooper R., Kaplan R.S., *The Design of Cost Management Systems: Text, Cases and Readings*, Prentice-Hall, Englewood Cliffs, New Jersey, 1991

Corbett C., Van Wassenhove L., «Trade-Offs? What Trade-Offs? Competence and Competitiveness in Manufacturing Strategy», *California Management Review*, pg. 107-122, summer 1993

Ferdows K., De Meyer A., «Lasting Improvements in Manufacturing Performance», *Journal of Operations Management*, vol. 9, n° 2, pg. 168-184, 1990

Filippini R., Forza C., Vinelli A., «Trade-off and Compatibility Between Performance: Definitions and Empirical Evidence», *International Journal of Production Research*, vol. 36, n° 12, pg. 3379-3406, 1998

Grant R. M., *Contemporary Strategy Analysis*, Blackwell Publishing, 1997

Hill T., *Manufacturing Strategy: Text and Cases*, Irwin, Homewood, IL, 1989

Hunsaker P. L., Cook C. W., *Managing Organizational Behavior*, Addison Wesley, New York, 1986

Kaplan R. S., Norton D. P., «The Balanced Scorecard: Measures That Drive Performance», *Harvard Business Review*, pg. 71-79, jan./feb. 1992

Miller J.G., Vollmann T.E., «The Hidden Factory», *Harvard Business Review*, pg. 142-150, sept./oct. 1985

Morrow M., *Activity-based Management: New Approaches to Measuring Performance and Managing Costs*, Woodhead-Faulkner, Hemel Hempsted, UK, 1992

Porter M. E., *Competitive Strategy: Techniques for Analyzing Industries and Competitors*, The Free Press, New York, 1980

Porter M. E., «What Is Strategy?», *Harvard Business Review*, pg. 61-78, nov./dec. 1996

Tonchia S., «Linking Performance Measurement System to Strategic and Organisational Choices», *International Journal of Business Performance Management*, vol. 2, n° 1, pg. 15-29, 2000

Tonchia S., «Performance Measurement Systems: Models, Characteristics and Measures», *International Journal of Operations & Production Management*, vol. 21, n° 1-2, pg. 46-70, 2001 (with De Toni A.)

Tonchia S., «Strategic Planning and Firm's Competencies: Traditional Approaches and New Perspectives», *International Journal of Operations & Production Management*, vol. 23, n° 9, pg. 947-976, 2003 (with De Toni A.)

Wheelwright S. C., «Manufacturing Strategy: Defining the Missing Link», *Strategic Management Journal*, vol. 16, pg. 77-91, 1984

Web Sites

Journals

Business Process Management Journal (www.mcb.co.uk/bpmj.htm)
International Journal of Process Management and Benchmarking (www.inderscience.com)
Journal of Knowledge Management (www.emeraldinsight.com/jkm.htm)
International Journal of Knowledge-Based Intelligent Engineering Systems (www.bton.ac.uk/kes/journal)
International Journal of Networking and Virtual Organisations (www.inderscience.com)

On Process Management

http://ccs.mit.edu/ph
www.phios.com
www.brint.com/BPR.htm
www.bpmi.org
www.waria.com
www.prosci.com
www.intelligentbpm.com
www.reengineering.net
www.reengineering.com/articles
www.c3i.osd.mil/org/bpr.html
www.compinfo-center.com/entsys/bpr.htm
www.infogoal.com/dmc/dmcprc.htm

On Knowledge Management

www.balancescorecard.org
www.cherrytreeco.com
www.dmreview.com
www.kmmagazine.com
www.km.gov
www.knowledgeboard.com
www.kmresource.com
www.kmnetwork.com
www.eknowledgecenter.com
www.kmci.org

www.km-vision.org
http://businessintelligence.ittoolbox.com
www.sap.com/solutions/bi

Process Management Software

www.ids-scheer.com
www.sciforma.com
www.qpr.com
www.igrafx.com
www-3.ibm.com/software/integration/holosofx
www.proformacorp.com
www.wizdom.com
www.c3i.osd.mil/bpr/bprcd

Enterprise Resource Planning (ERP) Systems

www.sap.com/solutions/r3-enterprise
www.oracle.com/lang/it/features/ebs
www.jdedwards.com
www.baan.com/solutions
http://ca.com/products